Decorating
CAKES

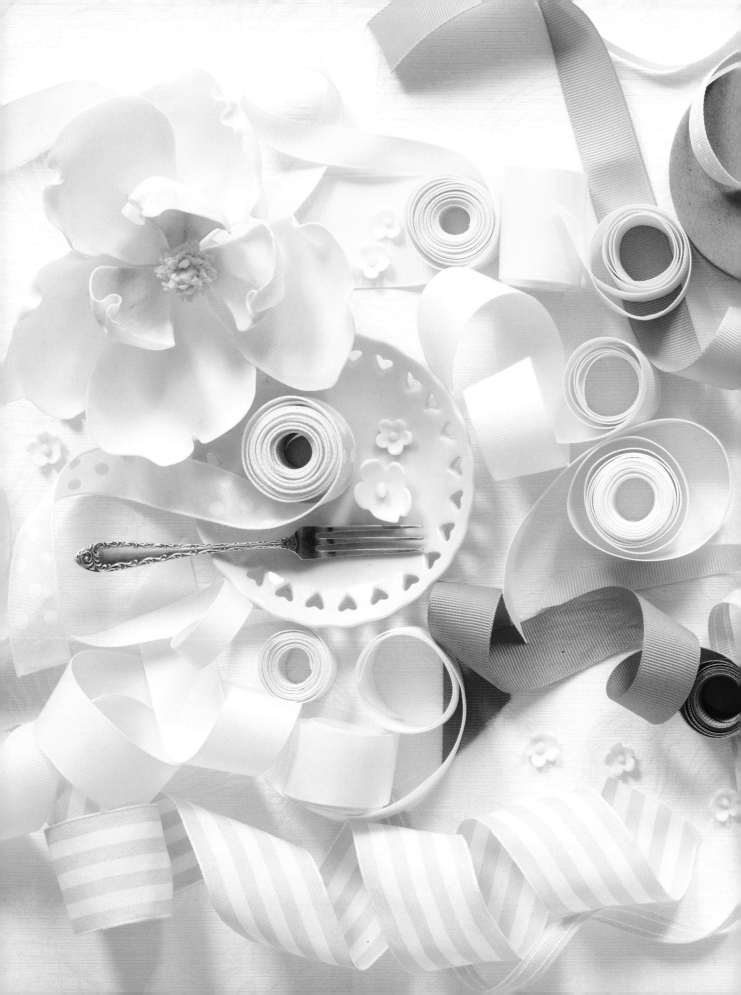

THE AUSTRALIAN
Women's Weekly

Decorating
CAKES

BAUER

CONTENTS

Welcome

TO OUR WORLD OF

wonderfully decorated cakes.

WE'VE DIVIDED THIS BOOK

INTO THREE CHAPTERS:

An easy chapter,

WHERE LITTLE OR NO CAKE DECORATING

EXPERIENCE IS NECESSARY;

A mid-range chapter

WHERE SOME SKILLS ARE

REQUIRED; AND FINALLY

A more difficult chapter

WHERE SOME SKILLS ARE EITHER

A MUST-HAVE OR HAVE TO BE

PRACTISED *and* LEARNED.

You'll find the ideas in the easy chapter are charming, easy to follow and the results will be worth the little effort involved. It's a great place to start to build and improve your decorating skills. There is one cake that is covered with ready-made icing, just so you get to practise rolling it out and covering a cake with it.

Macaroons are more popular than ever, so we've used them to decorate two lovely cakes. As well, we have a few cakes that could double as glamorous desserts, plus cupcakes and cookies that can be used for many occasions.

We've developed the medium-range chapter for the newly-experienced cake decorator. Most of the cakes in this chapter are covered with ready-made icing so, if you're a first-timer using this icing, it's worthwhile buying a packet from the supermarket to get the feel of it. Practise rolling out the icing and covering a cake pan with it, take the icing off, re-knead and re-roll it and cover the pan again, do this a few times until you feel confident about covering a real cake.

Using smoothing tools on the icing, once it's been smoothed with your hands, makes a big difference to the finished look of the icing. When it comes to using ready-made icing to make shapes, such as numbers and flowers, think of the icing as play dough – it's very user-friendly.

While the last chapter is for experts, many of the cakes are really not that hard – especially if you've had a little experience in cake decorating from the previous chapters. They may be a bit fiddly, but practise and it'll soon become easier. In this chapter we teach you how to do some basic piping, how to make a few different flowers out of modelling paste, and even how to make an awesome croquembouche.

You should read the final chapter in this book (*The Mechanics*, page 188) before even thinking about making and decorating any of these cakes. We assume when you make these cakes that you have read it, as not all the information is repeated in each recipe, so refer to these pages often. There is so much to know and many tips and shortcuts that will help. There are lists of cake pans, equipment, information about cake boards, how to make tiered cakes, the different types of cake coverings and frostings, and many useful techniques. There are eight charts of excellent cake recipes – all with the quantity of ingredients worked out for you, so whichever cake you choose, the quantity of mixture you'll need to fill the chosen pans is in the chart. It's also a must that you read each recipe through before starting, as most cakes require 3 days to complete – some up to a week. Make as many of the decorations as you can in advance, so you're not doing them at the last minute.

Changing the colour of the icing can change the look of the cake, and the occasion for which it can be used. This can be done with all the cakes throughout this book – adjust the colour to suit the theme of your celebration.

This is not just a book of wedding cakes. A lot of the cakes can be used for many different celebrations – Mother's day, Valentine's day, christenings, anniversaries, birthdays, as well as weddings and, of course, the many wedding-related occasions often held before the big day.

Pamela Clark

Pamela Clark

Decorations

BEAUTIFUL EMBELLISHMENTS WILL ADD A
PROFESSIONAL TOUCH TO YOUR MASTERPIECE

PIPING

PIPING IS NOT THAT HARD – A LITTLE PRACTISE IS ALL
THAT'S REQUIRED. SEE 'PIPING TECHNIQUES' ON PAGE 224.

Piping

ALL OF THESE TECHNIQUES WERE
ACHIEVED USING JUST 3 PIPING TUBES

Decorating cakes of all shapes
and sizes is rewarding and fun.
This chapter is a good place to start
to build your skills and confidence.
We minimised the use of piping and
using ready-made icing to cover cakes,
simply because most people think that
these skills are beyond them - however,
trust us - they're not.

CHAPTER ONE
EASY

QUILTED WEDDING
Cake Cookies

THESE PRETTY COOKIES COULD BE USED AT A KITCHEN TEA, A HENS' NIGHT, AS A BONBONNIERE, OR TAGGED AND USED AS PLACE NAMES AT A WEDDING.

EQUIPMENT
oven trays
10cm x 10.5cm (4-inch x 4¼-inch) wedding cake cutter
pastry brush
small patchwork cutter trellis
fine artist's paint brush
tweezers
COOKIES
125g (4 ounces) butter
2 eggs
1 teaspoon vanilla extract
⅔ cup (150g) caster (superfine) sugar
1⅓ cups (200g) self-raising flour
1 cup (150g) plain (all-purpose) flour
DECORATIONS
500g (1 pound) ready-made white icing
cornflour (cornstarch)
1 egg white, beaten lightly
2 tablespoons tiny silver cachous

1 Have the butter and eggs at room temperature for the cookies.
2 Beat butter, extract and sugar in small bowl with electric mixer only until combined. Beat in eggs, one at a time; beat only until combined.
3 Transfer mixture to large bowl. Stir in sifted flours, in two batches; mix to a soft dough. Knead dough on floured surface until smooth, cover; refrigerate 30 minutes.
4 Preheat oven to 180°C/375°F. Grease oven trays; line trays with baking paper.
5 Roll dough, in batches, between sheets of baking paper until 5mm (¼-inch) thick. Using wedding cake cutter, cut 18 shapes from dough, re-rolling dough as necessary. Place shapes, about 3cm (1¼ inches) apart, on trays. Bake about 10 minutes or until cookies are browned lightly.
6 Stand cookies on trays 5 minutes; lift onto wire racks to cool.

7 Knead ready-made icing on surface dusted with a little cornflour until icing loses its stickiness. Roll icing on cornfloured surface into a 3mm (⅛-inch) thickness. Using wedding cake cutter, cut 18 shapes from icing; re-roll icing as necessary. Cover icing shapes with plastic wrap.
8 Working with one cookie at a time, brush the top of the cookie with egg white. Lift icing shapes onto cookie. Using patchwork cutter, press onto icing to make a quilted pattern.
9 Dip paint brush into water, wipe brush almost dry, dab onto one join in the quilted pattern; use tweezers to position cachous on join. Repeat with remaining cachous. Stand until set.

makes 18
tip Completed cookies can be made up to 4 weeks ahead; store at room temperature in an airtight container.

Roll out dough between sheets of baking paper until 5mm thick. Using the wedding cake cutter, cut 18 shapes from the dough.

Brush cookies with egg white, top with icing shapes. Press patchwork cutter firmly onto the icing to make a quilted pattern.

Dip paint brush into water, wipe brush until almost dry. Lightly dab one join at a time with brush then position cachous on join.

SUGAR CONFETTI
Cupcakes

THESE PERFECTLY SIMPLE CAKES ARE IDEAL FOR ANYTHING TO DO WITH WEDDINGS, HENS' NIGHTS, KITCHEN TEAS AND ENGAGEMENT PARTIES.

EQUIPMENT
12 plain white paper cases
large piping bag
1cm (½-inch) plain piping tube
CAKE
1 quantity cupcake mixture of choice (page 190)
jam of choice
DECORATIONS
12 plain decorative cupcake wrappers
1½ quantities white chocolate ganache, whipped (page 210)
2 tablespoons sugar confetti

1 Divide cupcake mixture into paper cases; bake cupcakes according to recipe. Stand cakes in pan 5 minutes; turn top-side up onto wire rack to cool.
2 Cut a small cavity in the top of each cake; fill with a little jam. Place cakes into cupcake wrappers.
3 Fit piping bag with tube; half-fill bag with ganache. Pipe swirls of ganache on top of each cake. Sprinkle ganache with confetti.

makes 12
tips Cupcakes stale quickly, so it's best to use a fruit or mud cake for the best keeping qualities. The cakes can be made and frozen for about 3 months. Choose the cake you like, then a type of jam, or a thick fruit puree, to match the cake. For example, any berry jam or puree goes well with a chocolate cake. To make a puree: Push fresh or thawed frozen berries through a sieve; sweeten to taste with a little sifted icing sugar, and add a little liqueur, if you like. Make sure you cover the tops of the cakes with the ganache to keep the cakes as fresh as possible. The ganache will keep them sealed and fresh for a day or two. Completed cakes should be stored in a cool or air-conditioned room. Sprinkle confetti over ganache up to half a day before they're served.

Cut a small cavity in the cake top using a small pointed vegetable knife. Fill cavity with jam; use a flavour that will complement the cake.

Whip the white chocolate ganache in a small bowl with an electric mixer until the ganache is smooth and thick enough to pipe.

Half-fill the piping bag with ganache. Start piping from the centre of the cake, covering the top of each cake to make a large swirl.

CHOCOLATE *Box*

WHO WOULDN'T LOVE TO RECEIVE A GIFT AS WONDERFUL, AND AS DELICIOUS,
AS THIS CHOCOLATE BOX? IT'S THE PERFECT PRESENT FOR ANY OCCASION.

EQUIPMENT
20cm (8-inch) square wooden
  cake board (page 208)
medium metal spatula
craft glue
cheese slicer
CAKE
deep 15cm (6-inch) square cake
  of choice (page 190)
DECORATIONS
1 quantity white chocolate
  ganache (page 210)
250g (8 ounces) white chocolate
  Melts
golden yellow food colouring
1.5m (1½ yards) wide ribbon
3 x 180g (5½-ounce) blocks
  white eating chocolate

1 Trim cake (page 209); secure cake to board (page 209). Spread cake all over with ganache.

2 Cut baking paper into four strips measuring 10cm x 16cm (4-inches x 6½-inches). Melt chocolate Melts in medium heatproof bowl over medium saucepan of simmering water (don't let water touch base of bowl). Remove from heat; tint chocolate with a little yellow colouring.

3 Using spatula, spread chocolate evenly over the baking-paper strips. Leave chocolate to set for a few minutes, then carefully pick up paper and move to another sheet of baking paper (this neatens the edges). Stand about 5 minutes or until chocolate sets.

4 Peel baking paper away from chocolate panels; press panels onto sides of cake. Wrap ribbon around panels; secure ends with glue. Make bow (page 226); secure over ribbon with glue.

5 Place one block of chocolate upside down on bench. Place your hand on the chocolate to warm it slightly. Drag a sharp cheese slicer over the chocolate to make curls. Repeat with remaining chocolate to make enough curls to cover and fill the top of the chocolate box. Fill box with chocolate curls.

tips We found that using a cheese slicer is an easy and effective way of making large chocolate curls. The box panels can be completed at least one week before they're needed; store at a cool room temperature. You can use this recipe as a guide to make the boxes smaller or larger.

Place chocolate upside down on bench. Rub your hand over chocolate to warm slightly; drag cheese slicer over chocolate for curls.

To make chocolate panels, spread melted chocolate over 4 strips of baking paper. When starting to set, lift onto clean baking paper.

Stand the chocolate at room temperature until it's set. Turn the chocolate over, peel away baking paper. Position panels around cake.

MONOGRAMMED
Cupcakes

JUST THE THING FOR A 21ST, ENGAGEMENT PARTY OR EVEN A CHRISTENING PARTY.
THESE MONOGRAMMED IMAGES ADD A PERSONAL TOUCH TO THE OCCASION.

EQUIPMENT
fine artist's paint brush
3.5cm (1½-inch) round cutter
12 plain white paper cases
large plastic disposable piping bag
CAKE
**1 quantity cupcake mixture of
    choice (page 190)**
DECORATIONS
**500g (1 pound) ready-made
    white icing**
cornflour (cornstarch)
**3cm (1¼-inch) monogrammed
    edible images**
12 fancy cupcake wrappers
**1½ quantities dark chocolate
    ganache (page 210)**

1 Knead ready-made icing on surface dusted with a little cornflour until it loses its stickiness. Roll icing out on cornfloured surface into about 3mm (⅛-inch) thickness.
2 Lift 12 monogrammed images off backing paper; brush backs of images lightly with a little water; secure to icing about 1cm (½-inch) apart.
3 Use cutter to cut neatly around each image; transfer to baking-paper-lined tray to dry overnight.
4 Divide cupcake mixture into paper cases; bake cupcakes according to recipe. Stand cakes in pan 5 minutes; turn top-side up onto wire rack to cool.
5 Secure cupcake wrappers around cakes. Half-fill piping bag with ganache. Cut the tip from the bag; the opening should be about 2cm (¾-inch) wide. Pipe a swirl of ganache on each cake; top with monogrammed rounds.

makes 12

tips The cupcakes stale quickly so it's best to use a fruit or mud cake for the best keeping qualities. The cakes can be made and frozen for 3 months. The monograms can be prepared at least a month ahead; store them in an airtight container between layers of baking paper. Position the monograms up to half a day before they're needed. Personalise the cupcakes to suit the occasion – there are lots of similar edible images available at cake decorating shops and online. Make sure you cover the tops of the cakes with the ganache to keep the cakes as fresh as possible. The ganache will keep them sealed and fresh for a day or two. Once completed, the cakes should be stored in a cool or air-conditioned room.

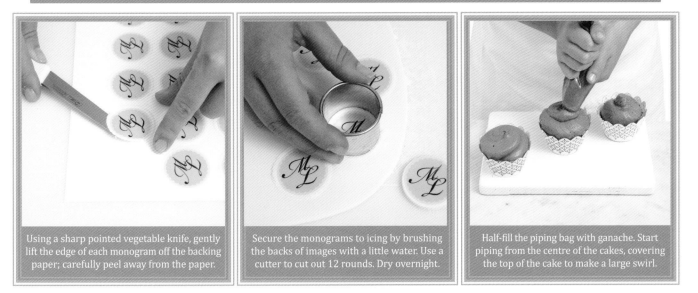

Using a sharp pointed vegetable knife, gently lift the edge of each monogram off the backing paper; carefully peel away from the paper.

Secure the monograms to icing by brushing the backs of images with a little water. Use a cutter to cut out 12 rounds. Dry overnight.

Half-fill the piping bag with ganache. Start piping from the centre of the cakes, covering the top of the cake to make a large swirl.

BROWNIE & BLONDIE
Mini Wedding Cakes

THESE MINIATURE WEDDING CAKES WOULD MAKE A LOVELY GIFT TO HAND AROUND TO FRIENDS AT A BRIDAL SHOWER OR ENGAGEMENT PARTY.

EQUIPMENT
2 x 24cm x 32cm (9½-inch x 13-inch) swiss roll pans
5cm (2-inch) round cutter
3.5cm (1½-inch) round cutter
2.5cm (1-inch) round cutter
paper piping bag (page 221)

DARK CHOCOLATE BROWNIE
300g (9½ ounces) dark eating (semi-sweet) chocolate
185g (6 ounces) butter
¼ cup (25g) cocoa powder
1 cup (220g) firmly packed light brown sugar
¾ cup (165g) caster (superfine) sugar
2 teaspoons vanilla extract
4 eggs
1½ cups (225g) plain (all-purpose) flour

WHITE CHOCOLATE BLONDIE
300g (9½ ounces) white eating chocolate
185g (6 ounces) butter
1 cup (220g) caster (superfine) sugar
3 eggs
1¼ cups (185g) plain (all-purpose) flour
⅔ cup (110g) self-raising flour

DECORATIONS
½ quantity dark chocolate ganache (page 210)
2 tablespoons icing (confectioners') sugar
½ teaspoon edible silver glitter

1 Preheat oven to 150°C/300°F. Grease swiss roll pans; line base and long sides with baking paper.
2 Make dark chocolate brownie and white chocolate blondie.
3 Turn blondie and brownie onto board, trim all sides of both cakes.
4 Using all of the cutters, cut out 12 rounds of each size from both the brownie and the blondie.
5 Make three-tier stacks, alternating rounds of brownies and blondies; securing each tier with ganache.
6 Dust stacks with combined sifted icing sugar and glitter before serving.

dark chocolate brownie Break chocolate into medium saucepan, add chopped butter and sifted cocoa; stir over low heat until smooth. Cool until just warmed; whisk in sugars, extract, eggs and sifted flour. Spread mixture into one swiss roll pan. Bake about 35 minutes. Cool in pan.

white chocolate blondie Break chocolate into medium saucepan, add chopped butter; stir over low heat until smooth. Cool until just warmed; whisk in sugar, eggs and sifted flours. Spread mixture into second swiss roll pan. Bake about 35 minutes. Cool in pan.

makes 24
tips The completed cakes will keep for about 3 days in an airtight container at a cool room temperature, or keep them in the fridge if the weather is hot. The cakes can also be frozen for a month. Dust the cakes with sifted icing sugar and glitter just before serving.

Turn brownie onto a cutting board. Using a long, sharp serrated knife, trim all sides of brownie. Repeat step with the blondie.

Using all 3 of the different-sized round cutters, cut out 12 rounds of each size from both the brownie and the blondie.

Make three-tier stacks, alternating rounds of brownie and blondie. Pipe a dab of chocolate ganache onto tiers to secure.

We decided to use packet cake mixes just for fun – the cake will keep and cut well and has a fine texture. If you want to make your own cake from scratch, we suggest the deep 25cm round butter cake recipe on page 190. One quantity of this recipe will be equivalent in volume to one packet of cake mix.

POLKA DOTS
and Stripes

WHAT A FUN CAKE THIS IS TO HAVE AT A PARTY – A RIOT OF COLOUR ON THE INSIDE AND POLKA DOTS ON THE OUTSIDE. THE DOTS WILL ALSO HIDE ANY IMPERFECTIONS ON THE ICING, SO IT'S A GREAT FIRST-TIME CAKE.

EQUIPMENT
25cm (10-inch) round cake pans
35cm (14-inch) round wooden cake board (page 208)
smoothing tools
2cm (¾-inch), 1.5cm (¾-inch) and 1cm (½-inch) round cutters
fine artist's paint brush
CAKE
4 x 470g (15-ounce) packets butter cake mix
golden yellow, rose pink, mauve and leaf green food colourings
DECORATIONS
4 quantities white chocolate ganache (page 210)
800g (1½ pounds) ready-made white icing
cornflour (cornstarch)

1 Preheat oven to 180°C/360°F. Grease cake pans; line base with baking paper.
2 Make one cake mix according to packet directions. Tint mixture with yellow colouring, spread into pan, bake cake about 30 minutes. Stand cake in pan 5 minutes; turn top-side up onto wire rack to cool. Repeat with remaining cake mixes and pink, mauve and green colouring. Trim cakes level (page 209), if necessary.
3 Secure one cake to board with a little ganache; top with remaining cakes using about ½ cup of the ganache between each layer. Spread cake evenly all over with remaining ganache (page 210).
4 Knead 600g (1¼ pounds) ready-made icing on surface dusted with a little cornflour until icing loses its stickiness. Roll icing on cornfloured

surface until large enough to cover cake. Using rolling pin, lift the icing onto cake; smooth with hands then smoothing tools. Trim icing neatly around base of cake.
5 Knead remaining icing on surface dusted with cornflour until smooth. Divide into 4 equal portions; colour pale pink, green, mauve and yellow. Keep each enclosed in plastic wrap while not using. Roll one colour out to 1mm (¹/₃₂-inch) thick. Using cutters, cut rounds from icing, re-rolling icing as necessary. Repeat with remaining icings. Brush backs of dots sparingly with water; position dots on cake. Cut some dots in half to decorate around bottom of cake. Dry cake overnight.

tips We used the end of a 1cm piping tube to cut out the smallest dots.

Using all 3 cutters, cut out rounds from all 4 colours of icing. Keep the icings you're not using airtight by wrapping in plastic wrap.	Brush backs of dots lightly with water and randomly position on cake. Don't use too much water or the dots will slip and slide off.	Position half-dots around base of the cake. Position the dots before they dry so they will more readily take on the contour of the cake.

TOWER OF
Golden Macaroons

THIS CONTEMPORARY TOWER CAKE WOULD MAKE A STYLISH WEDDING OR ENGAGEMENT CAKE – AND THE GOLD LEAF ADDS A TOUCH OF ELEGANCE.

EQUIPMENT
oven trays
large piping bag
1.5cm (¾-inch) plain piping tube
25cm (10-inch) deep croquembouche mould (diameter 18cm/7¼-inch)
medium-sized ice-cream scoop
25cm (10-inch) round wooden cake board (page 208)
wooden skewer
MACAROONS
6 egg whites
½ cup (110g) caster (superfine) sugar
2½ cups (480g) pure icing (confectioners') sugar
¼ cup (25g) ground almonds
2½ cups (200g) desiccated coconut
CAKE
deep 30cm (12-inch) square coconut cake (page 196)
DECORATIONS
2 quantities white chocolate ganache (page 210), whipped
gold leaf

1 Grease oven trays; line with baking paper.

2 To make macaroons, beat egg whites and caster sugar in medium bowl with electric mixer until soft peaks form and sugar is dissolved.

3 Meanwhile, blend or process icing sugar, ground almonds and coconut until fine and powdery. Sift through fine strainer; discard solids in strainer.

4 Transfer egg white mixture into large bowl. Fold in almond mixture in two batches.

5 Fit large piping bag with tube. Half-fill bag with macaroon mixture. Pipe 50 x 2cm (¾-inch) rounds about 2cm (¾-inch) apart onto trays. Pipe 50 x 3.5cm (1½-inch) rounds about 2cm (¾-inch) apart onto trays. Pipe 50 x 4.5cm (1¾-inch) rounds about 2cm (¾-inch) apart onto trays. Refill bag with macaroon mixture as needed. Tap trays on bench so macaroons spread slightly. Stand macaroons for about 1 hour or until they feel dry to touch.

6 Preheat oven to 120°C/250°F.

7 Bake small macaroons, in batches, about 15 minutes. Cool on trays. Bake remaining macaroons, in batches, about 20 minutes. Cool on trays.

8 Line inside the croquembouche mould with plastic wrap.

9 Cut a 5cm (2-inch) and a 17cm (6¾-inch) round from the coconut cake. Place the small round of cake inside croquembouche mould. Use the ice-cream scoop to scoop rounds of cake; chop remaining cake coarsely.

10 Using half the ganache, pack the mould with a random mix of cake and dollops of ganache. Top with the large round of cake; press down firmly. Refrigerate tower for 3 hours or overnight until firm.

11 Secure cake tower to board with a little ganache (page 210); remove the croquembouche mould. Remove plastic wrap; spread tower all over with remaining ganache.

12 Using skewer, gently push small pieces of gold leaf onto macaroons. Gently press large macaroons around bottom of the cake, followed by the medium macaroons, then the small macaroons at the top.

tips If you prefer, make the macaroons in 2 or 3 batches – base the proportions on 2 or 3 egg whites (either a third or half of the recipe ingredients) and use a small bowl for beating the egg whites and sugar mixture. Ovens are often inaccurate at low temperatures, so reduce the oven temperature if the macaroons are browning. The tower of cake can be made at least a week ahead, and frozen or refrigerated. The ganache coating and macaroons should be positioned on the day of serving. Gold leaf is delicate and fiddly to handle, but worth the effort. The coconut cake can be kept at room temperature in an airtight container for a week or frozen for up to 2 months. Choose the best macaroons for the tower. Leftovers will keep in an airtight container at room temperature for at least a week, or can be frozen for about 6 weeks.

ALTHOUGH THIS TOWER OF MACAROONS IS EASY TO MAKE – IT IS TIME CONSUMING. HOWEVER, THE CAKE AND MACAROONS CAN BE MADE WELL AHEAD OF WHEN THE TOWER IS NEEDED. MAKE SURE YOU HAVE ROOM IN THE FRIDGE FOR THE CAKE TO SET. YOU NEED TO MAKE ABOUT 150 MACAROONS (WE MADE EXTRA IN CASE OF BREAKAGES), SO IT IS PROBABLY EASIER TO MAKE THEM IN 2-3 BATCHES – MAKE SURE YOU HAVE PLENTY OF OVEN TRAYS. DRAW CIRCLES THE SIZE OF THE MACAROONS ONTO THE BACK OF THE BAKING PAPER TO USE AS A GUIDE WHEN PIPING THE ROUNDS.

Pipe macaroons on baking-paper-lined oven trays. Tap trays firmly several times on bench so macaroons spread a little.

Macaroons must feel dry and develop a "skin" before baking; this takes up to an hour depending on the temperature and humidity.

Cut a 5cm and 17cm round from the coconut cake. Push a cake pan or plate firmly into the cake to leave a mark to use as a guide.

Scoop out rounds from some of the leftover coconut cake using the ice-cream scoop. Coarsely chop the remaining cake scraps.

Remove mould; secure tower to board with a little ganache. Remove plastic wrap; spread tower all over with remaining ganache.

Gently transfer small pieces of gold leaf onto macaroons. Avoid over-handling the gold leaf as it will stick to your fingers.

BRIGHT LITTLE *Jelly Bean Cakes*

THESE QUIRKY LITTLE CAKES ARE SO EASY TO MAKE, AND ARE IDEAL FOR KIDS' PARTIES AND BABY SHOWERS. MIX AND MATCH THE COLOURS AND FLAVOURS OF THE JELLY BEANS AND THE BUTTER CREAM TO SUIT THE OCCASION.

EQUIPMENT

2 x 10cm (4-inch) round cardboard cake boards (page 208)
10cm (4-inch) round wooden cake board (page 208)
2 x 12cm (4¾-inch) round wooden cake boards (page 208)
6 wooden skewers

CAKE

3 x deep 10cm (4-inch) round cakes of choice (page 190)
2 x deep 12cm (5-inch) round cakes of choice (page 190)

DECORATIONS

2 quantities butter cream (page 218)
rose pink, leaf green and yellow food colouring
200g (6½ ounces) jelly beans, approximately, in colours to match butter cream

1 Divide butter cream evenly into three medium bowls; tint pink, green and yellow.

2 Trim cakes (page 209). Secure two 10cm cakes to the 10cm cardboards with a little butter cream (page 209). Secure the remaining 10cm cake to the 10cm wooden board. Secure the two 12cm cakes to the 12cm boards.

3 Push 3 trimmed skewers into both 12cm cakes to support the top tiers (page 212).

4 Secure the two 10cm cakes on the cardboards to the 12cm cakes (page 212). You will have 2 x two-tiered cakes and 1 x one-tier cake.

5 Spread cakes all over with butter cream. Using picture as a guide, decorate cakes with jelly beans to match the colours of the butter cream.

tip Use ganache instead of butter cream, if you prefer. Once the cakes are covered in butter cream or ganache, they will keep for about a week at a cool room temperature. The jelly beans can be placed on the cakes as soon as the butter cream has been applied.

Secure two 10cm cakes to 10cm cardboards with a little butter cream. Secure remaining 10cm cake to the 10cm wooden board.

Using a sharp serrated knife, trim skewers to the height of the cake. Push skewers into the largest cakes to support the top tiers.

Once all cakes are on boards, secure two of the smaller cakes onto the larger cakes with a little of the butter cream.

EMBOSSED
Lace Cupcakes

DISPLAY THESE ELEGANT LITTLE CAKES ON A CAKE STAND TO SHOW THEM OFF.
WE USED PATTERNED CUPCAKE WRAPPERS TO HIDE THE PLAIN PAPER CASES.

EQUIPMENT
12 plain white paper cases
texture-embossing mat
7cm (2¾-inch) round cutter
new large soft-bristled brush
CAKE
**1 quantity cupcake mixture of
choice (page 190)**
DECORATIONS
**1 quantity white chocolate
ganache (page 210)**
**500g (1 pound) ready-made
white icing**
cornflour (cornstarch)
12 fancy cupcake wrappers
food-grade white shimmer

1 Divide cupcake mixture into paper cases; bake cupcakes according to recipe. Stand cakes in pan 5 minutes; turn top-side up onto wire rack to cool.
2 Spread tops of cakes evenly all over with ganache.
3 Knead ready-made icing on surface dusted with a little cornflour until icing loses its stickiness. Roll icing on cornfloured surface until about 5mm (¼-inch) thick.
4 Place textured mat on top of the icing, using a rolling pin, firmly press and roll pattern onto icing. Carefully remove mat. Using cutter, cut out 12 rounds from icing; carefully place rounds on cakes without touching the embossed pattern. Knead and re-roll the icing and cut out more rounds as needed.

5 Carefully place cakes into cupcake wrappers. Dip brush into shimmer; brush lightly over embossed pattern.

makes 12
tips Ensure you have enough cakes for all the guests. If you like, choose a few different cake recipes, so you get a variety of cakes. The ganache and ready-made icing covering will keep the cakes fresh for a few days in a cool or air-conditioned room. Apply the shimmer to the icing a few hours before serving; a soft-bristled make-up brush is ideal for doing this.

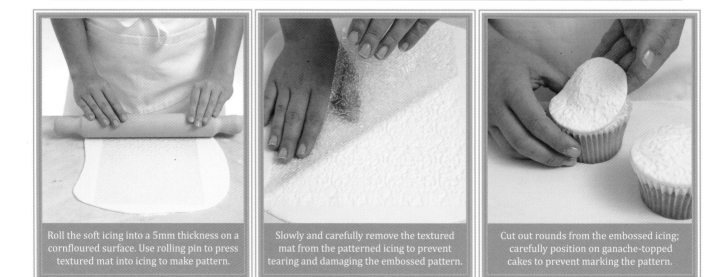

Roll the soft icing into a 5mm thickness on a cornfloured surface. Use rolling pin to press textured mat into icing to make pattern.

Slowly and carefully remove the textured mat from the patterned icing to prevent tearing and damaging the embossed pattern.

Cut out rounds from the embossed icing; carefully position on ganache-topped cakes to prevent marking the pattern.

PINK VELVET
Macaroon Cake

PINK VELVET
Macaroon Cake

YOU CAN MAKE YOUR OWN, BUT THESE STORE-BOUGHT MACAROONS ARE JUST LIKE HOMEMADE, SO NO-ONE WILL SUSPECT YOU DIDN'T MAKE THEM YOURSELF. NONE OF THE HARD WORK, YET ALL OF THE COMPLIMENTS – IT'S A REAL WINNER.

EQUIPMENT
deep 22cm (9-inch) round cake pan
deep 15cm (6-inch) round cake pan
30cm (12-inch) round wooden cake board (page 208)
15cm (6-inch) round wooden cake board (page 208)
medium offset metal spatula
3 wooden skewers

CAKE
250g (8 ounces) butter
4 eggs
2 teaspoons vanilla extract
3 cups (660g) caster (superfine) sugar
3 cups (450g) plain (all-purpose) flour
⅓ cup (50g) cornflour (cornstarch)
⅓ cup (35g) cocoa powder
2 cups (500ml) buttermilk
2 tablespoons rose pink food colouring
2 teaspoons white vinegar
2 teaspoons bicarbonate of soda (baking soda)

CREAM CHEESE FROSTING
185g (6 ounces) butter
500g (1 pound) cream cheese
2 tablespoons strained lemon juice
9 cups (1.4kg) icing (confectioners') sugar

DECORATIONS
3 x 114g (3½ ounce) packets small french macaroons

1 Have butter and eggs at room temperature for cake.

2 Preheat oven to 180°C/350°F. Grease and line cake pans (page 206).

3 To make cake, beat butter, eggs, extract and sugar in small bowl with electric mixer until mixture is light and fluffy. Transfer mixture to large bowl; stir in sifted flour, cornflour and cocoa, and combined buttermilk and colouring in two batches.

4 Combine vinegar and soda in small bowl; allow to fizz, then fold into cake mixture. Divide mixture between pans. Bake large cake about 1 hour 20 minutes and small cake about 1 hour.

5 Stand cakes in pans 10 minutes; turn top-side up onto wire racks to cool. Wrap cooled cakes in plastic wrap, freeze about 40 minutes or until cakes are firm.

6 Make cream cheese frosting.

7 Trim cakes (page 209). Split large cake into three even layers. Secure one layer to largest board with a little frosting. Top with remaining layers using about ¼ cup of the frosting between each layer.

8 Split smaller cake into three even layers. Secure one layer to small board with a little frosting. Top with the remaining layers using about ¼ cup of the frosting between each layer. Use spatula to spread remaining frosting over top and sides of both cakes.

9 Push trimmed skewers into large cake to support the top tier (page 212). Position small cake on large cake. Smooth frosting with spatula.

10 Gently twist each macaroon to separate into two halves (or carefully cut with a small sharp knife if they're firmly stuck); press the macaroon halves around the sides of both cakes before the frosting sets.

cream cheese frosting Have butter and cream cheese at room temperature. Beat butter, cream cheese and juice in large bowl with electric mixer until light and fluffy. Gradually beat in sifted icing sugar until frosting is smooth.

tips We bought packaged macaroons from a supermarket (they are available from the refrigerated section), but you can make your own (see page 30, *Tower of Golden Macaroons* and halve the recipe); you need about 70 single macaroons. Homemade macaroons will keep well in the freezer for about 2 months. This cake freezes well, filled or unfilled. It's at its best assembled on the day of serving.

THE COMBINATION OF THIS LUSCIOUS CAKE WITH THE LIGHT SWEET CRUNCH OF THE
MACAROONS IS A REAL WINNER. USE THE CAKE FOR A SPECIAL OCCASION DESSERT
– A BIRTHDAY, OR WHEREVER GLAMOUR AND FLAVOUR ARE REQUIRED TO IMPRESS.

To make frosting, have the cream cheese and butter at room temperature. Beat butter, cream cheese and lemon juice until combined.

Gradually beat in the sifted icing sugar until the frosting is smooth. Scrape down the sides of the bowl to incorporate all the icing sugar.

Wrap the cakes in plastic wrap and freeze for about 40 minutes or until the cakes are firm. Split each cake into three even layers.

Using a spatula, spread the frosting evenly all over the top and sides of cakes. Smooth frosting after positioning the smaller cake.

Gently twist macaroons to separate into two halves or, if they're firmly stuck, carefully cut through the centre with a small sharp knife.

Gently press the macaroon halves around the sides of both cakes. Arrange the macaroons in any colour combination you like.

LEMON
Meringue Cupcakes

WHILE IMPRESSIVE AT ANY CELEBRATION, THESE CUTE LITTLE CAKES WOULD LOOK STRIKING AT A BABY SHOWER. THEY LOOK SPECTACULAR ON A CUPCAKE STAND.

EQUIPMENT
12 straight-sided fancy paper cases
oven tray
large piping bag
2cm (¾-inch) plain piping tube
craft glue
CAKE
1 quantity cupcake mixture of
   choice (page 190)
MERINGUES
2 egg whites
½ cup (110g) caster (superfine)
   sugar
lemon yellow food colouring
DECORATIONS
1 cup (320g) lemon curd
3m (3 yards) narrow ribbon

1 Divide cupcake mixture into paper cases; bake cupcakes according to recipe. Stand cakes in pan 5 minutes; turn top-side up onto wire rack to cool.
2 Reduce oven temperature to 100°C/210°F. Grease and line oven tray with baking paper (see tips).
3 To make meringues, beat egg whites and sugar in small bowl with electric mixer until sugar is dissolved and mixture is thick and glossy. Tint meringue pale yellow.
4 Fit piping bag with tube, half-fill bag with meringue; pipe 12 meringues, with bases 5cm (2 inches) wide, onto oven tray, about 5cm apart, refilling bag as necessary. Bake meringues about 45 minutes or until dry to touch. Cool in oven with door ajar.
5 Trim tops from cakes so the tops are flat and 1cm (½ inch) below the top of the paper cases. Spread one tablespoon of curd over each cake to completely cover the surface of the cake. Top cakes with meringues.
6 Position a length of ribbon around each cake; secure ends with glue. Use ribbon to make bows (page 226); secure over joins with glue.

makes 12

tips Use a 5cm round cutter to draw circles on baking paper about 5cm apart. Turn the paper over and use circles as a guide to pipe the meringues. Cakes can be frozen for up to 3 months. Meringues can be made a week ahead and stored in an airtight container at a cool room temperature. Assemble the cakes up to a day before needed.

Pipe meringues onto tray. If you like, draw 5cm circles, 5cm apart, on the baking paper as a guide; turn paper over before piping.

Trim tops from the cakes so they are about 1cm below the top of the paper cases to make room for the curd and meringue.

Using craft glue, secure a length of ribbon around the cakes. Cover the ribbon ends with small bows secured with glue.

MANGO ROSE
Cheesecakes

EVERYBODY LOVES THEIR OWN INDIVIDUAL DESSERT – HERE, THE TROPICAL FLAVOURS BLEND HAPPILY WITH THE CREAMY CHEESECAKE FILLING. THE MANGO ROSE PATTERN IS SIMPLE TO ACHIEVE, BUT LOOKS IMPRESSIVE ON THE CHEESECAKES.

EQUIPMENT
4 x 10cm (4-inch) (closed) springform pans
CHEESECAKE
250g (8 ounces) cream cheese
1 x 450g (14½ ounce) unfilled store-bought sponge slab (13cm x 18cm) (5¼-inch x 7¼-inch)
1 teaspoon powdered gelatine
2 tablespoons lime juice
2 teaspoons finely grated lime rind
¼ cup (55g) caster (superfine) sugar
1 cup (250ml) pouring cream
DECORATION
2 medium firm ripe mangoes (860g)

1 Have cream cheese at room temperature.
2 Split sponge cake into two even layers. Using base of one springform pan as a guide, cut out four rounds of sponge. Use scraps of sponge to patch and complete rounds, as necessary.
3 Line base and sides of springform pans with baking paper. Place sponge rounds into pans.
4 To make cheesecake: Sprinkle gelatine over juice in small heatproof jug. Stand 5 minutes then place jug in small saucepan of simmering water, stir until gelatine is dissolved. Cool 5 minutes.
5 Beat cream cheese, rind and sugar in small bowl with electric mixer until smooth; beat in cream. Stir in gelatine mixture.

6 Divide cream cheese mixture evenly between pans; level tops. Refrigerate overnight.
7 Remove cheesecakes from pans, place on serving plates. Slice mango into 3mm (⅛-inch) thick slices. Starting from the centre of each cheesecake, and using small pieces of mango first, arrange slices into a rose shape.

makes 4
tips We used a plain store-bought sponge for this recipe; you can make your own, if you like. Grate the rind from the lime before juicing it. The cheesecakes are at their best made one day ahead; keep refrigerated.

Using base of the springform pan, cut out two sponge rounds close to the edge. Use scraps to complete second sponge round.

You need mangoes that are ripe, but firm enough to slice thinly. Peel mangoes, remove cheeks from seed, and then slice the cheeks.

Starting from the centre of the cheesecake, and using small slices of mango for the bud, arrange mango slices into a rose shape.

COCONUT DREAM
Cream Cake

THIS IS AN EASY CAKE TO MAKE AND DECORATE – USE ANY CAKE YOU LIKE – WE PREFER A WHITE CHOCOLATE MUD OR COCONUT CAKE. WHICHEVER TYPE YOU CHOOSE, THE CAKE WILL BE HEAVY TO MOVE AND LIFT, SO GET SOMEONE TO HELP.

EQUIPMENT
45cm (18-inch) round wooden cake board (page 208)
25cm (10-inch) round wooden cake board (page 208)
20cm (8-inch) round wooden cake board (page 208)
15cm (6-inch) round wooden cake board (page 208)
10cm (4-inch) round wooden cake board (page 208)
12 wooden skewers
small offset metal spatula
CAKE
deep 30cm (12-inch) round cake of choice (page 190)
deep 25cm (10-inch) round cake of choice (page 190)
deep 20cm (8-inch) round cake of choice (page 190)

deep 15cm (6-inch) round cake of choice (page 190)
deep 10cm (4-inch) round cake of choice (page 190)
DECORATIONS
3 quantities white chocolate ganache (page 210)
white food colouring
1.8kg (3½ pounds) ball-shaped coconut chocolates

1 Trim cakes (page 209). Secure largest cake to the largest board (page 209). Secure the remaining cakes to the same-sized boards.
2 Push 3 trimmed skewers into centre of each cake except the smallest cake to support the next tier (page 212).

3 Assemble cakes, securing each tier to the tier below (page 212).
4 Beat ganache in large bowl with electric mixer. Beat in enough white colouring to match the colour of the ganache to the coconut chocolates. Spread cake all over with ganache.
5 Cut chocolates in half, press cut-sides around each cake, starting at the bottom of the largest cake.

tips The cake can be completed a day ahead. It will be fine kept in a cool or air-conditioned room. Instead of making the ganache, you could buy 3 x 453g (16-ounce) tubs of vanilla frosting to cover this cake.

Beat ganache in large bowl with electric mixer. Use white colouring to match the colour of the ganache to the chocolates.

Secure and stack cakes together. Using a small metal spatula, spread ganache evenly all over the cake to make the cake airtight.

Using a sharp knife, cut coconut chocolates in half. Starting from the bottom of the cake, push cut sides of chocolates onto ganache.

COCONUT
Ruffle Cake

'SIMPLY STUNNING' BEST DESCRIBES THIS DREAMY CAKE. THE COCONUT
RESEMBLES THE FRILL, OR FLOUNCE, FOUND ON TRADITIONAL WEDDING GOWNS.

EQUIPMENT
**40cm (16-inch) round wooden
cake board (page 208)**
**30cm (12-inch) round wooden
cake board (page 208)**
**25cm (10-inch) round wooden
cake board (page 208)**
**20cm (8-inch) round wooden
cake board (page 208)**
**15cm (6-inch) round wooden
cake board (page 208)**
12 wooden skewers
medium offset metal spatula
CAKE
**deep 35cm (14-inch) round cake
of choice (page 190)**
**deep 30cm (12-inch) round cake
of choice (page 190)**
**deep 25cm (10-inch) round cake
of choice (page 190)**
**deep 20cm (8-inch) round cake
of choice (page 190)**
**deep 15cm (6-inch) round cake
of choice (page 190)**

DECORATIONS
**5 quantities white chocolate
ganache (page 210)**
white food colouring
1kg (2 pounds) flaked coconut

1   Trim cakes (page 209). Secure
largest cake to largest board with a
little ganache (page 209). Secure the
remaining cakes to same-sized boards.
2   Push 3 trimmed skewers into
centres of all cakes except the
smallest cake to support the next
tier (page 212).
3   Assemble cake, securing each
tier to the tier below (page 212).
4   Place half the ganache in a large
bowl; whisk in at least 1 tablespoon
of white colouring until the ganache
is as white as possible. Beat ganache
with an electric mixer until light and
fluffy. Repeat with remaining ganache.

5   Spread cake all over with ganache.
Gently press handfuls of the flaked
coconut all over the cake.

tips We used flaked coconut labelled
"coconut chipped" found in health
food stores. Instead of making the
ganache you could buy 5 x 453g
(16-ounce) tubs of vanilla frosting
to cover this cake. This cake can be
assembled completely a week before
it's required; It will be fine kept in a
cool or air-conditioned room. Use any
cake recipe you like – our favourite is
the coconut cake (page 196). This five
tier cake is very heavy to move and
lift, so get someone to help you.

Place half the ganache in a large bowl. Whisk
at least 1 tablespoon of food colouring into
the ganache to whiten it as much as possible.

Beat half the ganache at a time in large bowl
with electric mixer until light and fluffy,
scrape down side of bowl during beating.

Once the cake is covered with the ganache,
firmly press handfuls of coconut all over
the cake. Choose long flakes for the top tier.

HEARTS AND
Bows Forever

HEARTS AND BOWS ARE PERFECT TOGETHER. THIS CAKE COULD BE USED FOR A BIRTHDAY, WEDDING OR, FOR A SENTIMENTAL OPTION, VALENTINE'S DAY – THINK WHITE CAKE, RED HEARTS AND RED RIBBON – SO ROMANTIC.

EQUIPMENT
3cm (1¼-inch) heart cutter
22cm (9-inch) round wooden cake board (page 208)
small offset metal spatula
CAKE
2 x deep 18cm (7-inch) round cakes of choice (page 190)
DECORATIONS
150g (4½ ounces) ready-made white icing
cornflour (cornstarch)
lemon yellow food colouring
1½ quantities white chocolate ganache (page 210)
1m (1 yard) wide ribbon

1 Knead ready-made icing on surface dusted with a little cornflour until icing loses its stickiness. Tint icing yellow with colouring. Roll icing out on cornfloured surface into 3mm (⅛-inch) thickness.

2 Using cutter, cut out about 70 heart shapes from icing, re-rolling scraps as necessary. Place hearts on baking-paper-lined tray for about 3 hours, or until hearts are firm, but not dried out or hard.

3 Trim cakes (page 209). Secure one cake to board (page 209); top with remaining cake, joining cakes with a little ganache (page 212).

4 Beat remaining ganache in small bowl with electric mixer until light and fluffy.

5 Using spatula, spread ganache all over cake.

6 Starting from the bottom of the cake, press heart shapes onto ganache in rows before the ganache sets.

7 Just before serving, decorate the top of the cake with a bow made from the ribbon (page 226).

tips If you prefer, use butter cream instead of ganache; both will keep the cake airtight and fresh for at least a week in a cool or air-conditioned room.

Cut out 70 heart shapes from the ready-made icing; place on a baking-paper-lined tray until firm, but not dried out or hard.

Secure one cake to board; join remaining cake to bottom cake with ganache. Spread cake evenly all over with remaining ganache.

Starting from the bottom of the cake, gently press the heart shapes in rows around the cake. Do this before the ganache sets.

WHITE CHOCOLATE
Rose-Print Cake

INSTEAD OF ONE LARGE CAKE, PLACE SMALLER CAKES RANDOMLY ON THE TABLE; DISPLAY THEM ON STEMMED GLASS CAKE PLATES FOR A CHARMING EFFECT.

EQUIPMENT
3 x 10cm (4-inch) round cardboard cake boards (page 208)
small offset metal spatula
tape measure
plastic ruler
4.5cm (1¾-inch) fluted round cutter
3.5cm (1½-inch) fluted round cutter
CAKE
3 x 10cm (4-inch) round cakes of choice (page 190)
DECORATIONS
1½ quantities white chocolate ganache (page 210)
2 x 25cm x 40cm (10-inch x 16-inch) chocolate transfer sheets
750g (1½ pounds) white chocolate Melts
2m (2 yards) wide ribbon

1   Trim cakes (page 209). Secure cakes to boards (page 209). Using spatula, spread cakes all over using two-thirds of the ganache (page 210).

2   Using tape measure, measure the circumference and height of the cakes and add 1cm (½ inch) to each measurement. Using sharp knife and ruler, cut 3 rectangles from the transfer sheets using these measurements. Reserve any leftover transfer sheet.

3   Melt chocolate in medium bowl over medium saucepan of simmering water (don't allow water to touch base of bowl). Place one cut transfer sheet, print-side up, on a clean surface. Using spatula, spread sheet with one-third of the melted chocolate. Chocolate should be 3mm (⅛-inch) thick to make it easy to handle. Leave chocolate to set for a few minutes, then carefully pick up transfer sheet and move to a sheet of baking paper (this neatens the edges). While the chocolate is still wet to the touch, and before the edges have begun to set, carefully pick up the top two corners and wrap the transfer sheet around one

cake, chocolate-side in. Repeat with the remaining transfer sheets, chocolate and cakes. Stand 20 minutes then remove the backing paper. (To remove the backing paper, start from one top corner and carefully peel paper away.)

4   Spread remaining chocolate over any leftover pieces of transfer sheet; leave to set completely before removing the backing paper. Using both fluted cutters, cut out rounds from sheet. Top cakes with remaining ganache, then chocolate rounds. Tie ribbon around cake, finish with a bow (page 226).

makes 3
tips Cakes can be completed at least a week before required. Store in a cool or air-conditioned room. Position the fluted chocolate rounds on top of the cake on the day of serving.

Using a ruler and sharp knife, cut transfer sheets into 3 rectangles large enough to cover the cake. Reserve any transfer scraps.

Cover cake with chocolate-covered transfer sheet; stand 20 minutes, then carefully and gently peel backing paper away from transfer.

Coat transfer sheet with chocolate; remove backing paper when dry, then use both the fluted cutters to cut rounds from transfers.

You can buy the sponge cakes for this recipe – preferably jam and cream filled. You could also buy a large meringue as well, to break up and use to fill and decorate the cake. In this case, you'll need half the meringue ingredients only, to make the meringue sticks. Meringue sticks can be made a month ahead; store in an airtight container at a cool room temperature. Make the large meringue the day before.

MERINGUE
Cloud Cake

ALMOST EVERYONE LOVES THE COMBINATION OF SPONGE CAKE, MERINGUE, CREAM AND BERRIES, AND THIS SPECTACULAR DESSERT HAS THEM ALL.

EQUIPMENT
oven trays
medium offset metal spatula
large piping bag
7.5mm (¼-inch) plain piping tube
30cm (12-inch) round wooden cake board (page 208)
15cm (6-inch) round wooden cake board (page 208)
3 wooden skewers
craft glue
MERINGUE
8 egg whites
2 cups (440g) caster (superfine) sugar
2 tablespoons cornflour (cornstarch)
2 teaspoons white vinegar
CAKE
deep 20cm (8-inch) round cake of choice (page 190)
deep 15cm (6-inch) round cake of choice (page 190)
DECORATIONS
300ml (½ pint) thickened (heavy) cream
125g (4 ounces) fresh raspberries
50cm (20 inches) wide ribbon

1 Preheat oven to 120°C/250°F. Line oven trays with baking paper. Mark an 18cm (7¼-inch) circle on one tray; turn paper over. Mark 9cm (3¾-inch) straight lines (you need about 100) on remaining trays; turn paper over.
2 To make meringue: Beat egg whites in large bowl with electric mixer until soft peaks form; gradually add sugar, beat until dissolved between additions. Beat in sifted cornflour, and vinegar. Using spatula, spread half the mixture inside circle on tray. Shape sides up and in towards the centre.
3 Fit piping bag with tube. Half-fill bag with meringue; pipe about 100 x 9cm finger-width meringue sticks, about 2cm (¾ inch) apart, on remaining oven trays. Refill bag as necessary. Bake large meringue about 1 hour and the sticks about 30 minutes, or until dry to touch. Remove from oven; cool on trays.
4 Beat cream in small bowl with electric mixer until firm peaks form; cover, refrigerate until ready to use.

5 Trim cakes (page 209). Secure large cake to largest board; secure small cake to small board (page 209). Push trimmed skewers into large cake to support top tier (page 212). Secure small cake on top of large cake. Spread cakes all over with cream.
6 Position meringue sticks around sides of both cakes. Scoop out large spoonfuls of meringue; place between the tiers and on the top of small cake.
7 Sprinkle cake with raspberries. Wrap ribbon around large cake, secure ends with glue.

tips If short on oven space, halve the meringue recipe and make the large meringue and the sticks separately. The cake can be assembled and covered with cream one day ahead; store in the refrigerator. Arrange the meringue sticks and spoonfuls of meringue as close to serving as possible. The meringues will soften in about 1 hour.

Mark an 18cm circle on baking paper, invert onto an oven tray. Spread meringue inside the circle, and shape inwards and upwards.

Fit the piping bag with the tube. Pipe finger lengths of meringue, using markings as a guide, onto the baking-paper-covered trays.

Avoiding browned or caramelised meringue, scoop out large tablespoons of soft meringue onto top of cake and around top of large cake.

CHOCOLATE BOX
of Hearts

CHOCOLATE BOX
of Hearts

JUST THE THING FOR A ROMANTIC VALENTINE'S DAY OR ENGAGEMENT PARTY, OR THE PERFECT WAY TO SAY 'I LOVE YOU' TO A WONDERFUL MUM ON MOTHER'S DAY.

EQUIPMENT
22cm (9-inch) round or heart-shaped wooden cake board (page 208)
small offset metal spatula
straight-sided metal scraper
paper piping bag (page 221)
cheese slicer
CAKE
1 heart-shaped cake of choice (page 190)
DECORATIONS
1 quantity white chocolate ganache (page 210) (see step 1)
1 tablespoon instant coffee granules
370g (12 ounces) white chocolate Melts
1 x 180g (5½-ounce) block white eating chocolate
15 heart-shaped chocolates, approximately
2m (2 yards) wide ribbon

1 Make the white chocolate ganache, add coffee granules to the cream while heating; stir until smooth.
2 Trim cake (page 209). Secure cake to board with a little ganache.
3 Use spatula to spread cake all over with ganache until it is about 1cm (½-inch) thick. Stand cake about 20 minutes or until ganache becomes slightly firmer. Using metal scraper, scrape excess ganache from top and side of cake. Reserve ganache scrapings in a small bowl; cover with plastic wrap.
4 Using a small knife, cut a 2cm (¾-inch) deep line right around the cake, 1cm (½ inch) in from edge of cake. Refrigerate cake 3 hours or overnight.
5 Scoop out cake (with ganache) inside the cut line to make a recess in the cake about 2cm deep; discard scrapings. Warm reserved ganache over a small saucepan of simmering water; spread ganache evenly inside the recess (don't fill the recess with the ganache, just use it to cover the base and sides).
6 Trace around base of heart-shaped cake pan onto baking paper to make a template for the chocolate box lid. Turn paper over onto a flat tray.
7 Melt chocolate Melts in a small heatproof bowl over small saucepan of simmering water (don't let water touch base of bowl). Three-quarters fill piping bag with chocolate, snip end from bag; pipe a thick band of chocolate inside the heart outline. Spread more chocolate in the centre of the heart; stand about 10 minutes, or until chocolate is set. Repeat this process using remaining chocolate to make a thick lid; re-melt chocolate as necessary (page 222).
8 Turn the block of white chocolate upside down; rub your hand over the chocolate to soften slightly. Drag the blade of the cheese slicer over the flat surface of the chocolate to make curls. Position chocolates in box; sprinkle curls between chocolates.
9 Peel paper from back of chocolate lid; tie ribbon around lid, finish with a bow (page 226). Place on top of cake.

tips Ganache will keep the cake airtight for at least a week if stored in a cool or air-conditioned room. A cheese slicer makes curls about 2.5cm (1-inch) long; if you don't have one, use a vegetable peeler – it will make smaller curls.

WE USED A WHITE CHOCOLATE MUD CAKE IN THIS RECIPE, AND MADE A
COFFEE-FLAVOURED GANACHE TO COMPLEMENT IT AND THE CHOCOLATES,
HOWEVER, A DARK CHOCOLATE HEART CAKE WOULD ALSO LOOK WONDERFUL
FILLED WITH HEART-SHAPED CHOCOLATES IN RED WRAPPERS.

Use a straight-sided metal scraper to smooth the side and top of the heart. Reserve all the ganache scrapings in a small bowl.

Using a small sharp knife, cut a 2cm deep line around the cake leaving a 1cm border. Refrigerate the cake 3 hours or overnight.

Using a large spoon, scoop out the cake and ganache to make a recess in the cake; discard the cake and ganache scraps.

Warm reserved ganache over simmering water until spreadable. Spread ganache evenly over the base and side of the recess.

Pipe melted chocolate around heart outline; evenly spread more melted chocolate in the centre of the heart. Repeat to make a thick lid.

Allow chocolate to set at room temperature. Lift the heart from the paper; decorate with a ribbon and bow, place on top of cake.

LAST-MINUTE CAKE
with Fresh Flowers

THIS IS THE EASIEST OF THE TIERED CAKES IN THIS BOOK, BUT THE SIMPLICITY OF
THE SNOW-WHITE FROSTING AND BEAUTIFUL FLOWERS MAKE IT AN ELEGANT CAKE.

EQUIPMENT
30cm (12-inch) round wooden
cake board (page 208)
20cm (8-inch) round wooden
cake board (page 208)
15cm (6-inch) round wooden
cake board (page 208)
6 wooden skewers
small offset metal spatula
CAKE
deep 25cm (10-inch) round cake
of choice (page 190)
deep 20cm (8-inch) round cake
of choice (page 190)
deep 15cm (6-inch) round cake
of choice (page 190)
DECORATIONS
2 quantities fluffy frosting
(page 219) (see tips)
fresh organic flowers
white florist's tape

1 Trim cakes (page 209). Secure
large cake to largest board; secure
remaining cakes to same-sized
boards (page 209).
2 Push 3 trimmed skewers into
centre of large and medium cakes
to support the top tiers (page 212).
Secure medium cake on top of large
cake; secure small cake on top of
medium cake (page 212).
3 Make fluffy frosting.
4 Working quickly, spread frosting
all over cake.
5 Trim then wrap flower stems
in florist's tape. Position flowers
on top of cake.

tips Make the frosting after you have
stacked and secured the cakes; you
need to work quickly once the frosting
is ready as it sets quickly. This frosting
colours beautifully if you want a
pastel-coloured cake to fit in with the
colour theme of your event. The cakes
can be frosted one day ahead, however,
the frosting loses its sheen once it has
set. The flowers should be prepared
and placed on the day of serving.

Beat the fluffy frosting in a small bowl with
an electric mixer until it is thick, spreadable
and almost cooled to room temperature.

Make sure you're ready to spread the frosting
onto the cake as soon as it's ready; you need
to work quickly before the frosting sets.

On the day of serving, trim flower stems to
lie neatly on top of the cake. Wrap stems in
florist's tape; position flowers on top of cake.

Now that you've mastered the Easy chapter, it's time to move on and conquer the fear of rolling out ready-made icing, and of piping. Only a little practise is required to make your efforts look really great. You will be amazed at how quickly you will become proficient in these crafts.

CHAPTER TWO

EXPERIENCED

HEAVENLY HYDRANGEA
Cupcakes

EQUIPMENT
12 plain white paper cases
1.5cm (¾-inch) 4-petal blossom cutter
vinyl mat
flower mat
small ball tool
4 paper piping bags (page 221)
fine artist's paint brush
5.5cm (2¼-inch) round cutter
CAKE
1 quantity cupcake mixture of choice (page 190)
DECORATIONS
1.5kg (3 pounds) ready-made white icing
cornflour (cornstarch)
pink, violet and blue food colourings
1 quantity royal icing (page 220)
pink, green and violet petal dust
1 quantity ganache of choice (page 210)
12 fancy white paper wrappers

1 Divide cupcake mixture into paper cases; bake cupcakes according to recipe. Stand cakes in pan 5 minutes; turn top-side up onto wire rack to cool.
2 Knead ready-made icing on surface dusted with a little cornflour until icing loses its stickiness.

3 Divide icing into 4 portions. Tint 3 portions shades of blues, pinks and mauves; leave remaining portion white. Enclose each in plastic wrap. (Each portion is enough to make 3 cupcakes; you need to make about 14 blossoms for each cupcake.)
4 To make blossoms: Working with one colour icing at a time, roll small portions of icing on cornfloured surface into 3mm (⅛-inch) thickness. Using blossom cutter, cut 5 blossoms at a time; cover remaining icing with vinyl mat.
5 Place blossoms on flower mat; using small end of ball tool, roll tool in centre of each petal to round and thin the petals. Stand overnight on baking paper to dry. Repeat with remaining icings. Re-roll scraps with remaining icing of same colour; reserve, covered with plastic wrap.
6 Divide royal icing into 4 small bowls. Colour 3 portions to match colours of blossoms; leave remaining portion white. Cover surface with plastic wrap to keep airtight.
7 Half-fill each piping bag with one coloured icing, pipe same-coloured

dots into centres of blossoms; allow to dry overnight. Reserve all royal icing; cover surface to keep airtight.
8 Mix equal amounts of petal dusts and cornflour to complement colours of blossoms. Brush dust lightly into centres of blossoms.
9 Spread ganache over cupcakes. Roll out one of the reserved colours of ready-made icing on cornfloured surface into 3mm thickness. Use round cutter to cut out 3 rounds of icing, position over ganache. Place cakes in fancy wrappers. Repeat with the remaining colours.
10 Secure blossoms to same-coloured icing rounds on cupcakes to resemble hydrangeas using leftover royal icing.

makes 12

tips · The blossoms can be completed months ahead. Keep in an airtight container at room temperature. Assemble cakes up to a day before. Use a fruit or mud cake for maximum keeping qualities.

Cut out several blossoms at a time; place on flower mat. Use ball tool to shape and thin the petals of each blossom; dry overnight.

Pipe centres into blossoms with royal icing; leave to dry. Brush combined petal dust and cornflour over the centres of the blossoms.

Spread tops of cupcakes with ganache. Top cupcakes with rounds of ready-made icing to seal the cakes as much as possible.

AUTUMN
Leaves

THE AUTUMNAL COLOURS OF THIS CAKE AND ITS LEAVES ARE SO SYMBOLIC OF THE SEASON. WE USED LEAVES FROM A JAPANESE MAPLE TREE BECAUSE OF THEIR WONDERFUL SHAPES AND COLOURS, AND THEIR LACK OF TOXIC CHEMICALS.

EQUIPMENT
35cm (14-inch) round wooden cake board (page 208)
20cm (8-inch) round wooden cake board (page 208)
15cm (6-inch) round wooden cake board (page 208)
smoothing tools
6 wooden skewers
paper piping bag (page 221)
CAKE
deep 25cm (10-inch) round cake of choice (page 190)
deep 20cm (8-inch) round cake of choice (page 190)
deep 15cm (6-inch) round cake of choice (page 190)
DECORATIONS
1.4kg (2¾ pounds) ready-made white icing
cornflour (cornstarch)
orange and brown food colourings
1 quantity royal icing (page 220)
freshly picked organic leaves (see tips)
2m (2 yards) narrow ribbon

1 Trim cakes (page 209). Secure large cake to largest board; secure remaining cakes to the same-sized boards (page 209). Prepare cakes for covering with ready-made icing (page 209).

2 Knead ready-made icing on surface dusted with a little cornflour until icing loses its stickiness. Divide icing into three portions: 300g (9½ ounces), 500g (1 pound) and 600g (1¼ pounds).

3 Use both colourings to tint all the icings three different autumnal shades. Colour the largest portion the darkest, the middle portion the palest and the smallest portion a medium shade.

4 Roll the largest portion of icing on cornfloured surface until large enough to cover largest cake. Using rolling pin, lift icing onto cake; smooth with hands then smoothing tools. Trim icing neatly around base of cake. Use medium portion of icing to cover medium cake in the same way as the large cake. Use remaining icing to cover small cake in the same way. Dry cakes overnight.

5 Push 3 trimmed skewers into centres of large and medium cakes to support the next tier (page 212).

6 Assemble cakes, securing each tier to the tier below (page 212).

7 Divide royal icing into 3 bowls; tint with colourings to match cakes. Half-fill piping bag with icing; pipe around base of same-coloured cake. Use fingertip to blend icing into any gaps where cakes join the boards (page 212). Dry cakes overnight.

8 Wash leaves carefully in cold water; leave to dry on kitchen paper.

9 Wrap and secure ribbon around base of each tier with a dot of royal icing. Pipe dots of icing onto backs of leaves; position leaves on cake.

tips If you choose leaves other than the Japanese maple, check they're organic and free from toxins. Wash, dry and position leaves as close to serving time as possible (4 hours ahead is fine). Use small dried leaves, if you prefer.

Gently wash trimmed leaves in cold water; shake off excess water. Place the leaves on absorbent paper; leave until dry.

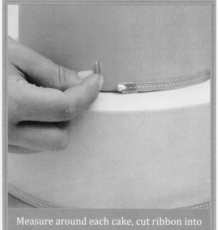

Measure around each cake, cut ribbon into corresponding lengths. Position ribbon around cakes; join ends with royal icing.

Position the leaves on the cake. Use royal icing to pipe tiny dots of icing onto the back of the leaves to secure to the cake.

CHOCOLATE &
Ivory Hearts Cake

EQUIPMENT
9cm (3¾-inch) heart cutter
20cm (8-inch) 18-gauge floral wire
wire cutters
35cm (14-inch) round wooden
  cake board (page 208)
20cm (8-inch) round wooden
  cake board (page 208)
15cm (6-inch) round wooden
  cake board (page 208)
smoothing tools
6 wooden skewers
paper piping bag (page 221)
CAKE
deep 25cm (10-inch) round cake
  of choice (page 190)
deep 20cm (8-inch) round cake
  of choice (page 190)
deep 15cm (6-inch) round cake
  of choice (page 190)
DECORATIONS
1.5kg (3 pounds) ready-made
  ivory icing
cornflour (cornstarch)
chocolate brown and ivory food
  colouring
1 quantity royal icing (page 220)
5m (5 yards) narrow ribbon

1 Colour 40g (1½ ounces) ready-made icing chocolate brown; knead on surface dusted with a little cornflour until icing loses its stickiness. Roll icing out on cornfloured surface into 3mm (⅛-inch) thickness. Using cutter, cut a heart shape from icing. Cut wire in half, push one half into the heart shape; place on baking-paper-lined tray to dry overnight. Make another heart in the same way using 40g of the ready-made ivory icing.
2 Trim cakes (page 209). Secure large cake to largest board; secure remaining cakes to same-sized boards (page 209). Prepare cakes for covering with ready-made icing (page 209).
3 Knead remaining ivory icing on surface dusted with a little cornflour until icing loses its stickiness.
4 Roll 300g (9½ ounces) of icing on cornfloured surface until large enough to cover small cake. Using rolling pin, lift icing onto cake; smooth with hands then smoothing tools. Trim icing around base of cake.
5 Use 500g (1 pound) of the icing to cover medium cake in the same way as the small cake. Use remaining icing to cover large cake in the same way. Dry cakes overnight.

6 Push 3 trimmed skewers into centres of large and medium cakes to support the next tier (page 212).
7 Assemble cakes, securing each tier to the tier below (page 212).
8 Tint royal icing ivory to match cake. Three-quarters fill piping bag with royal icing; pipe around base of each cake. Use fingertip to blend icing into any gaps where cakes join the boards (page 212). Dry cakes overnight.
9 Cut ribbon in lengths long enough to go around cakes. Secure around cakes using tiny dots of royal icing. Join ends of ribbon with royal icing.
10 Position hearts on cake by gently pushing wires into cake.

tips The hearts can be made weeks ahead; store in an airtight container. Position them on the day of serving. Positioning and securing the ribbon around these cakes can be annoying, as the ribbon can easily slip out of position. It's best to secure the ribbon after the icing has set completely, which takes about two days.

Roll some of the brown icing on surface dusted with a little cornflour. Cut out heart shape. Repeat using some of the ivory icing.

Cut the length of wire in half. Push one piece of wire about halfway into each heart shape. Dry on baking-paper-lined tray overnight.

Measure and cut ribbons to go around cakes. Secure ribbons to cakes with tiny dots of royal icing. Join the ends with royal icing.

CAKE POP
Baby Rattles

THEY MIGHT NOT BE FROM TIFFANY'S, BUT THESE CUTE CAKE POP RATTLES ARE THE HEIGHT OF FASHION – AND SO MUCH CHEAPER THAN THE REAL THING. GREAT FOR BABY SHOWERS, OR BABY'S FIRST BIRTHDAY CELEBRATION.

EQUIPMENT
18 x 30cm (12-inch) cake pop sticks
large square styrofoam block
2 paper piping bags (page 221)
CAKE POPS
4 cups (340g) firmly packed cake
    crumbs (see tips)
½ quantity butter cream,
    approximately (page 218)
DECORATION
375g (12 ounces) white chocolate
    Melts
1 quantity royal icing (page 220)
blue and pink food colouring
1.5m (1½ yards) each blue and
    pink narrow ribbon

1 Using a fork, combine the cake crumbs and enough (about ½ cup) butter cream in a medium bowl to make ingredients come together.
2 Gently roll level tablespoons of mixture into balls. Place balls on tray; freeze 1 hour or refrigerate 3 hours or overnight.

3 Stir chocolate in medium heatproof bowl over medium saucepan of simmering water until smooth (don't let water touch base of bowl). Pour into a heatproof jug.
4 Dip the end of a cake pop stick into the chocolate, then push the stick about halfway into a ball of cake. Place in freezer for 5 minutes to set.
5 Make one cake pop rattle at a time: Dip the cake pop in the chocolate, rocking back and forth to coat; don't swirl the pops, or they'll break. Allow excess chocolate to drip back into the jug. Stand cake pops upright in styrofoam to set at room temperature or in the fridge. Repeat with remaining cake pops. Re-melt the chocolate as necessary (page 222).
6 Divide royal icing into two small bowls, tint one batch pale pink, the other pale blue; cover surface of icing with plastic wrap to keep airtight.

7 Three-quarters fill one piping bag with pink royal icing; pipe spirals on top of half the cake pops, turning the cake pops in the styrofoam as you pipe. Repeat with blue royal icing and remaining cake pops. Stand in styrofoam until set.
8 Use the ribbon to tie tiny bows at the base of each cake pop (page 226).

makes 18
tips Use any firm-textured cake to make cake pops – mud, fruit, coconut or butter cakes all work well. Leftover Christmas cake or pudding are real winners as they're usually moist. Cake pop sticks (also sold as 'lollypop candy sticks') are available from cake decorating suppliers and craft shops. Store cake pops, lying down, in a single layer, in an airtight container at a cool room temperature.

Dip the end of a cake pop stick into the melted white chocolate; push the stick about halfway through into the ball of cake.

Dip each cake pop in the melted chocolate; rock them backwards and forwards to ensure that they are evenly coated.

Pipe spirals of pink and blue royal icing around the tops of the cake pops, turning the cake pops in the styrofoam as you pipe.

CHERRY BLOSSOMS
in Spring

THE CHERRY BLOSSOM IS THE SYMBOL OF JAPAN, AS WELL AS BEING THE SYMBOL
OF SPRING. THE CONTRASTING COLOURS OF THIS CAKE – THE PALE PINK OF THE
BLOSSOMS AND THE BROWN OF THE BRANCHES – GIVES IT A DRAMATIC EFFECT.

EQUIPMENT
30cm (12-inch) round wooden
  cake board (page 208)
15cm (6-inch) round wooden
  cake board (page 208)
smoothing tools
3 wooden skewers
2 paper piping bags (page 221)
5-petal plunger cutter set (small,
  medium and large)
vinyl mat
ball tool
2 fine artist's paint brushes
tweezers
CAKE
2 x deep 20cm (8-inch) round
  cakes of choice (page 190)
deep 15cm (6-inch) round cake
  of choice (page 190)
shallow 15cm (6-inch) round cake
  of choice (page 190)
jam or ganache of choice (page 210)
DECORATIONS
1.5kg (3 pounds) ready-made
  white icing
cornflour (cornstarch)
rose pink, brown and black food
  colourings
1 quantity royal icing (page 220)
100g (3 ounces) modelling paste
magenta petal dust
2 bunches small white stamens

1 Trim cakes (page 209). Secure
one 20cm cake to largest board; top
with remaining 20cm cake, joining
cakes with a little jam or ganache
(page 212). Secure deep 15cm cake to
smaller board; top with remaining
small cake, joining cakes with jam or
ganache. Prepare cakes for covering
with ready-made icing (page 209).
2 Knead ready-made icing on surface
dusted with a little cornflour until
icing loses its stickiness. Tint icing
pink with colouring.
3 Roll one-third of the icing on
cornfloured surface until large enough
to cover small cake. Using rolling pin,
lift icing onto cake; smooth with hands
then smoothing tools. Trim icing neatly
around base of cake; reserve scraps.
4 Use remaining icing to cover large
cake the same way as small cake;
reserve scraps. Dry cakes overnight.
5 Push trimmed skewers into centre
of large cake to support the top tier.
Secure small cake on top of large cake
(page 212).
6 Reserve 1 heaped tablespoon of
royal icing. Tint remaining royal icing
pink to match cakes. Three-quarters
fill piping bag with icing; pipe around
base of each cake. Use fingertip to
blend icing into any gaps where the
cakes join the boards (page 212).
Dry cakes overnight.
7 Knead modelling paste on surface
dusted with cornflour until it loses its
stickiness. Roll out a little of the paste
to 1mm (1/32-inch) thick. Cut several
blossoms from paste using all cutters.

Cover the paste with the vinyl mat to
prevent it from drying out.
8 Working quickly, place a blossom
in palm of hand dusted with a little
cornflour. Using small end of ball
tool, gently press tool into blossom
to round the petals and centre of
blossom. Place blossoms on baking-
paper-lined tray to dry overnight.
Repeat with more paste. You need
about 35 small, 35 medium and
10 large blossoms.
9 Using paint brush, dust centre of
blossoms with equal quantities of
combined cornflour and petal dust.
10 Cut stamens to about 1cm (1/2-inch)
long. Half-fill piping bag with reserved
white royal icing; pipe a small dot
of icing in centre of 6 blossoms. Use
tweezers to position a few stamens
in the icing in each blossom before
it sets; stand until dry. Repeat with
remaining blossoms.
11 Colour scraps of reserved ready-
made icing brown using a little black
and brown colouring.
12 Roll brown icing into thin strips
of random thicknesses, lengths and
shapes to resemble cherry blossom
branches; brush a little water on
backs of branches, secure to cakes
while still soft and pliable.
13 Secure blossoms to branches
with a little royal icing.

tip Flower blossoms can be made
several weeks ahead. Store at room
temperature in an airtight container.

SQUEEZE SOME OF THE ICING STRIPS FOR THE BRANCHES WITH YOUR FINGERTIPS TO MAKE THEM LOOK GNARLED AND TWISTED. SECURE THE BRANCHES TO THE CAKE BEFORE THEY DRY. POSITION ALL THE BRANCHES FIRST, FOLLOWED BY THE BLOSSOMS.

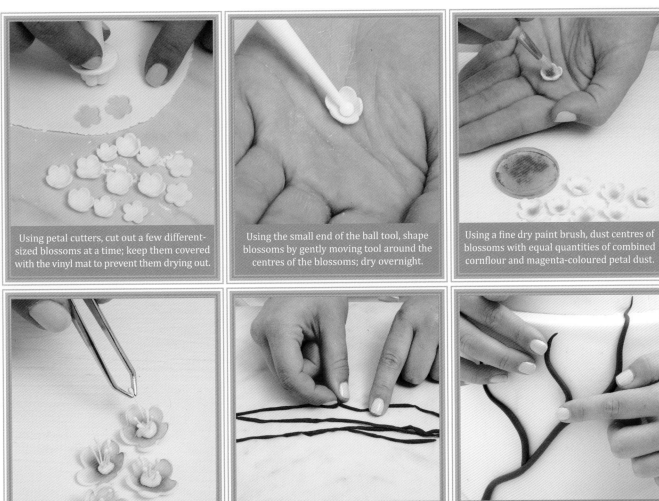

Using petal cutters, cut out a few different-sized blossoms at a time; keep them covered with the vinyl mat to prevent them drying out.

Using the small end of the ball tool, shape blossoms by gently moving tool around the centres of the blossoms; dry overnight.

Using a fine dry paint brush, dust centres of blossoms with equal quantities of combined cornflour and magenta-coloured petal dust.

Pipe small dots of white royal icing into the centres of about six blossoms. Use tweezers to position several stamens before icing sets.

Roll thin strips of brown icing into random lengths, thicknesses and shapes to make the branches for the cherry blossoms.

While icing is still soft and pliable, position branches on the cakes in a random way; brush backs of branches with a little water to secure.

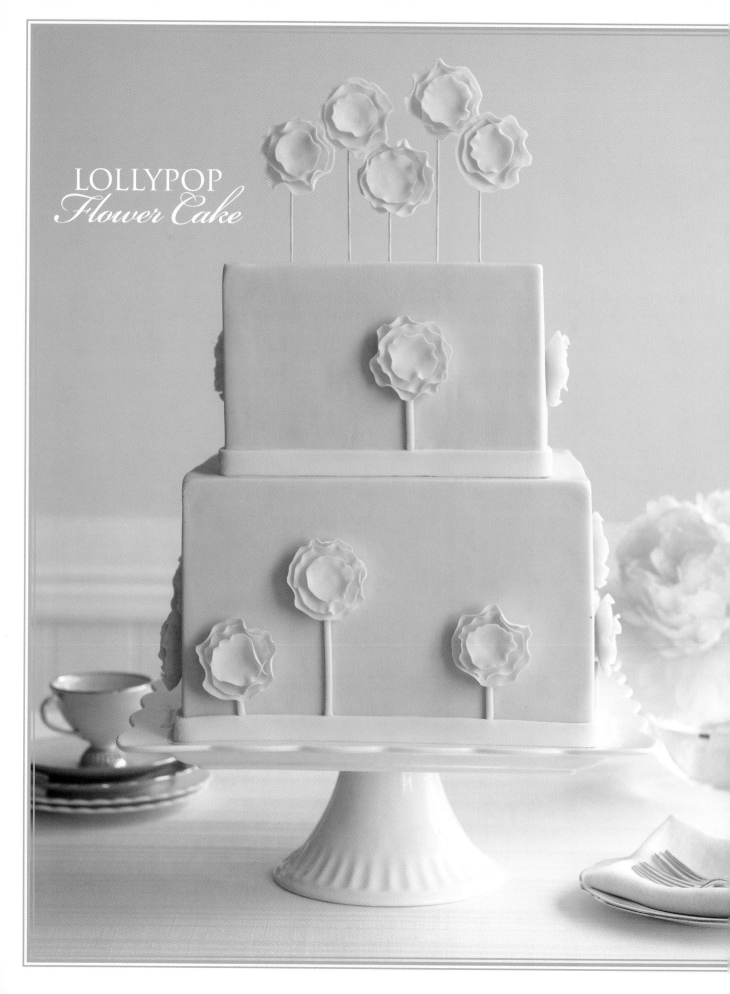

LOLLYPOP
Flower Cake

LOLLYPOP
Flower Cake

THIS CAKE IS GOOD FOR A YOUNGER CHILD'S BIRTHDAY. USE ANY COLOURS YOU LIKE.

EQUIPMENT
32cm (13-inch) square wooden
   cake board (page 208)
18cm (7-inch) square wooden
   cake board (page 208)
smoothing tools
4 wooden skewers
paper piping bag (page 221)
tape measure
plastic ruler
pizza cutter
fine artist's paint brush
5cm (2-inch) round cutter
4cm (1½-inch) round cutter
2cm (¾-inch) round cutter
vinyl mat
4 x 12-hole round-based, shallow
   (1 tablespoon/20ml) patty pans
ball tool
5 x 20cm (8-inch) 18-gauge
   floral wire
CAKE
2 x deep 22cm (9-inch) square
   cakes of choice (page 190)
deep 18cm (7-inch) square cake
   of choice (page 190)
shallow 18cm (7-inch) square cake
   of choice (page 190)
jam or ganache of choice (page 210)
DECORATIONS
2.5kg (5 pounds) ready-made
   white icing
cornflour (cornstarch)
aqua blue and lemon yellow food
   colourings
1 quantity royal icing (page 220)
tylose powder

1 Trim cakes (page 209). Secure
one 22cm cake to largest board; top
with remaining 22cm cake, joining
cakes with a little jam or ganache
(page 212). Secure deep 18cm cake
to smaller board; top with remaining
small cake, joining cakes with jam or
ganache. Prepare cakes for covering
with ready-made icing (page 209).

2 Knead ready-made icing on surface
dusted with a little cornflour until
icing loses its stickiness. Tint 2.3kg
(4½ pounds) of the icing pale aqua
blue. Tint remaining icing pale yellow;
enclose, separately, in plastic wrap.
3 Roll 1.125kg (2¼ pounds) of the
aqua icing on cornfloured surface
until large enough to cover small cake.
Using rolling pin, lift icing onto cake;
smooth with hands then smoothing
tools. Trim icing neatly around base.
4 Use icing scraps and remaining
aqua icing to cover large cake in the
same way; reserve icing scraps. Dry
cakes overnight.
5 Push trimmed skewers into centre
of large cake to support top tier. Secure
small cake to large cake (page 212).
6 Tint royal icing aqua blue to match
cakes. Three-quarters fill piping bag
with royal icing; pipe around base
of each cake. Use fingertip to blend
icing into any gaps where cakes join
the boards (page 212). Dry overnight.
7 Measure around the base of each
cake. Roll half the yellow icing on
cornfloured surface into 3mm (⅛-inch)
thickness, long enough to wrap
around cakes. Using ruler and pizza
cutter, cut a strip 1.5cm (¾-inch) wide
and long enough to wrap around the
base of the top tier. Secure strip to
cake with a little water. Repeat for
bottom tier, joining strips if necessary;
reserve icing scraps.
8 Knead a pinch of tylose powder into
150g (4½ ounces) yellow icing along
with any yellow icing scraps. Roll out
on cornfloured surface until about
1mm (¹⁄₃₂-inch) thick. Using 5cm
cutter, cut out 21 rounds; cover with
vinyl mat to prevent drying out.
9 Dust patty pan holes lightly with
cornflour. Hold one 5cm round in the

palm of a cornfloured hand, using the
large end of the ball tool, smooth the
edges of the round until it starts to
frill. Place in patty pan to dry. Repeat
with remaining rounds.
10 Using 2cm cutter, cut 21 rounds
from yellow icing (re-rolling scraps
as necessary); frill the edges in the
same way as the larger rounds. Place
rounds in patty pan (see tips). Reserve
icing scraps.
11 Knead a pinch of tylose powder
into the reserved aqua icing. Roll on
cornfloured surface until about 1mm
(¹⁄₃₂-inch) thick. Using 4cm cutter,
cut 21 rounds and frill the edges in
the same way as for the yellow
rounds. Place rounds in patty pan.
12 Join icing rounds in sets of three
with a little royal icing. Return
flowers to patty pan to dry overnight.
13 Roll scraps of yellow icing into
thin rope shapes of different lengths
on surface dusted with cornflour to
make flower stems; stand on baking-
paper-lined tray to dry overnight.
14 Cut wire into 5 different lengths,
secure to the back of 5 flowers with
a little royal icing; suspend wires
over a wooden spoon so wires dry
straight, leave to dry overnight. Push
wired flowers into the top of the cake.
15 Secure flower stems to sides of
cake with a little water (one on each
side of the top cake; three on each side
of the bottom cake). Secure flowers
into position with a little royal icing.

tips By the time you've made the
42 yellow petals they'll be firm enough
to remove from the patty pans to make
room for the aqua petals. Position the
flowers in the top of the cake on the
day of serving.

THIS IS SUCH A CUTE CAKE, HOWEVER THERE ARE A COUPLE OF TECHNIQUES
TO MASTER, SUCH AS MAKING THE FLOWERS, AND WIRING THEM TO GIVE HEIGHT
AND DIMENSION. NO REAL PIPING SKILLS ARE NEEDED TO DECORATE THIS CAKE.

Measure around base of each cake. Using a plastic ruler and pizza cutter, cut a ribbon of icing long enough to wrap around each cake.

Hold a round of icing in cornfloured hand, use the large end of a ball tool to frill the rounds. Do this to all the rounds of icing.

When set, join sets of three different-sized petals with a little royal icing. Leave to dry in patty pans dusted lightly with cornflour.

Cut wire into 5 different lengths. Secure wire to back of 5 flowers with royal icing. Suspend wire so that it dries straight; dry overnight.

To make stems of flowers, roll scraps of yellow icing on cornflour-dusted surface into thin rope shapes of different lengths.

Secure icing strips around cakes with a little water. Secure stems in the same way. Position flowers on cake using royal icing.

DIAMONDS ARE
Forever

EQUIPMENT

32cm (13-inch) square wooden
    cake board (page 208)
18cm (7-inch) square wooden
    cake board (page 208)
large plaque plunger cutter
smoothing tools
5cm x 8.5cm (2-inch x 3½-inch)
    diamond patchwork cutter
4 wooden skewers
paper piping bag (page 221)
fine pearl-headed pin
tweezers
white florist's tape

CAKE

2 x deep 22cm (9-inch) square
    cakes of choice (page 190)
deep 18cm (7-inch) square cake
    of choice (page 190)
shallow 18cm (7-inch) square cake
    of choice (page 190)
jam or ganache of choice (page 210)

DECORATIONS

1.8kg (3½ pounds) ready-made
    white icing
cornflour (cornstarch)
1 quantity royal icing (page 220)
2m (2 yards) narrow ribbon
72 x 3mm (⅛-inch) clear
    edible diamonds
fresh organic flowers

1 Trim cakes (page 209). Secure one 22cm cake to largest board; top with remaining 22cm cake, joining cakes with a little jam or ganache (page 212). Secure deep 18cm cake to smaller board; top with remaining small cake, joining cakes with jam or ganache. Prepare cakes for covering with ready-made icing (page 209).

2 Knead 200g (6½ ounces) of the ready-made icing on cornfloured surface until icing loses its stickiness. Roll icing out on cornfloured surface into 3mm (⅛-inch) thickness. Using plaque cutter, cut out 4 plaques from icing. Place plaques on baking-paper-lined tray to dry overnight.

3 Knead remaining icing with any scraps on cornfloured surface until icing loses its stickiness.

4 Roll 700g (1½ pounds) of the icing on surface dusted with a little cornflour until large enough to cover small cake. Using rolling pin, lift icing onto cake; smooth with hands then smoothing tools. Trim icing neatly around base of cake.

5 Use remaining icing and scraps to cover the large cake in the same way.

6 While the icing is still soft, press diamond patchwork cutter all around cake to make a quilted pattern. Dry cakes overnight.

7 Push trimmed skewers into centre of large cake to support top tier. Secure small cake on large cake (page 212).

8 Three-quarters fill piping bag with royal icing; pipe around base of each cake. Use fingertip to blend icing into any gaps where cakes join the boards (page 212). Dry cakes overnight.

9 Wrap ribbon around base of each cake; secure with a little royal icing.

10 Secure a plaque to the centre of the top cake with a little royal icing; repeat on all sides of cake, hold for a minute or so to make sure plaques are firmly attached.

11 Secure edible diamonds to joins in the pattern with a dab of royal icing.

12 Wrap stems of flowers with florist's tape; top cake with flowers.

tip Ask the florist to make you an appropriate arrangement for the top of the cake – they will tape the stems of the flowers for you. Prepare and place the flowers on the day of serving.

While the icing is still soft, gently press the patchwork cutter into the icing all over the bottom cake to make a diamond pattern.

Using a pin, mark the centre of the top cake on all sides. Secure the plaques to each side of the cake using a little royal icing.

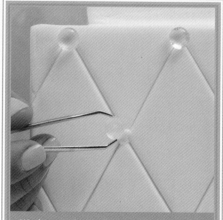

Working with one diamond at a time, pipe a dot of royal icing on the pattern, then use the tweezers to carefully position diamond.

The edible diamonds are not fragile to handle, but they do lose their sparkle quickly, so attach the diamonds to the cake as late as possible (up to 3 hours is ideal). Use tweezers or cotton gloves when handling the diamonds, as the natural oils in your fingertips can make the surface of the diamonds dull.

SHIMMERING
Wedding Crystals

SHIMMERING
Wedding Crystals

THE SHIMMER ON THE CAKE AND THE CRYSTALS ON THE STAND CAPTURE THE LIGHT, GIVING THIS STUNNING CAKE AN EYE-CATCHING SPARKLE.

EQUIPMENT

30cm (12-inch) round wooden cake board (page 208)
20cm (8-inch) round wooden cake board (page 208)
15cm (6-inch) round wooden cake board (page 208)
smoothing tools
6 wooden skewers
large new make-up brush
2 paper piping bags (page 221)
large and small stencils
fine pearl-headed pins
small offset metal spatula
straight-sided metal scraper
craft glue
16cm (6½-inch) cake stand

CAKE

deep 25cm (10-inch) round cake of choice (page 190)
shallow 25cm (10-inch) round cake of choice (page 190)
deep 20cm (8-inch) round cake of choice (page 190)
deep 15cm (6-inch) round cake of choice (page 190)
shallow 15cm (6-inch) round cake of choice (page 190)
jam or ganache of choice (page 210)

DECORATIONS

1.8kg (3½ pounds) ready-made white icing
cornflour (cornstarch)
ivory, marron brown and black food colourings
shimmer powder
1 quantity royal icing (page 220)
1.5m (1½ yards) ribbon
medium-sized crystal-style brooch
1m (1 yard) crystal trimming

1 Trim cakes (page 209). Secure deep 25cm cake on largest board (page 209); top with remaining large cake, joining cakes with a little jam or ganache (page 212). Stack and secure the two 15cm cakes to same-sized board in the same way. Secure 20cm cake to same-sized board. Prepare cakes for covering with ready-made icing (page 209).

2 Knead ready-made icing on surface dusted with a little cornflour until icing loses its stickiness. Tint 500g (1 pound) of icing ivory; enclose in plastic wrap. Tint remaining icing using brown colouring and a touch of black colouring.

3 Roll 375g (12 ounces) of the brown icing on cornfloured surface until large enough to cover 15cm cake. Using rolling pin, lift icing onto cake; smooth with hands then smoothing tools. Trim icing neatly around base.

4 Use 750g (1½ pounds) of brown icing to cover large cake in the same way as small cake. Use ivory icing to cover medium cake in the same way. Dry cakes overnight.

5 Push 3 trimmed skewers into centre of large cake to support middle tier (page 212). Push 3 trimmed skewers into centre of medium cake to support cake stand and top tier. Using the large make-up brush, brush the small and large cakes evenly with shimmer powder. Secure medium cake to larger cake (page 212).

6 Tint 1 tablespoon royal icing brown to match the cakes; tint remaining royal icing ivory to match cake. Half-fill piping bags with 1 tablespoon of royal icing to match the cakes; pipe around base of same-coloured cakes. Use fingertip to blend icing into any gaps where cakes join the boards (page 212). Dry cakes overnight. Cover the surface of the remaining royal icing with plastic wrap to prevent it drying out.

7 Secure large stencil to side of large cake with pins. Use spatula to spread royal icing over stencil, remove excess icing with scraper; return to bowl. Gently remove pins and stencil; wash and dry stencil before using again. Repeat until stencil is completed around the large cake. Stand cake about 1 hour to dry.

8 Use the smaller stencil to make a lace pattern on opposite sides of the small cake in the same way.

9 Wrap ribbon around middle cake; secure with a little royal icing. Make a bow using some of the ribbon (page 226); secure the ends with a little glue. Attach brooch to bow; attach bow to ribbon with glue.

10 Secure crystal trim to edge of cake stand with glue; wrap trim around cake stand twice, if necessary, so crystals hang close together. Secure small cake on cake stand with a little royal icing. Secure stand to middle cake with royal icing when assembling.

tips The cake stand needs to have a flat base so it can be supported by the skewers in the middle tier. If the base of the stand is not flat, cut a piece of strong white cardboard to fit the base of the stand, glue in position. It's best to position and secure the cake stand (holding the top tier) when the cake is positioned at the event.

STENCILLING IS AN EASY YET EFFECTIVE WAY TO DECORATE A CAKE, ESPECIALLY
IF THE COVERING IS NOT QUITE PERFECT. THE TRICKS TO USING THE STENCIL
ARE TO USE THE ROYAL ICING SPARINGLY AND TO REMOVE THE STENCIL GENTLY.
PRACTISE USING THE STENCIL ON A CAKE PAN BEFORE DECORATING THE CAKE.

Using a new make-up brush, dust shimmer powder all over the large and small cakes. Secure stencil to side of cake with pins.

Use spatula to spread the royal icing evenly over the stencil pattern. Use the metal scraper to scrape away the excess icing.

Remove pins from stencil. Gently remove the stencil from side of cake. Use a little coloured royal icing to hide the pin marks.

Cut a length of ribbon to fit around the middle-sized cake. Make a bow from the ribbon. Secure the ends with craft glue.

Secure a strip of ribbon over the centre of the bow with glue; allow to dry. Attach brooch to the bow with the brooch pin.

Secure crystal trim to the edge of the cake stand with glue. Wrap and glue trim around the cake stand again to thicken the layer.

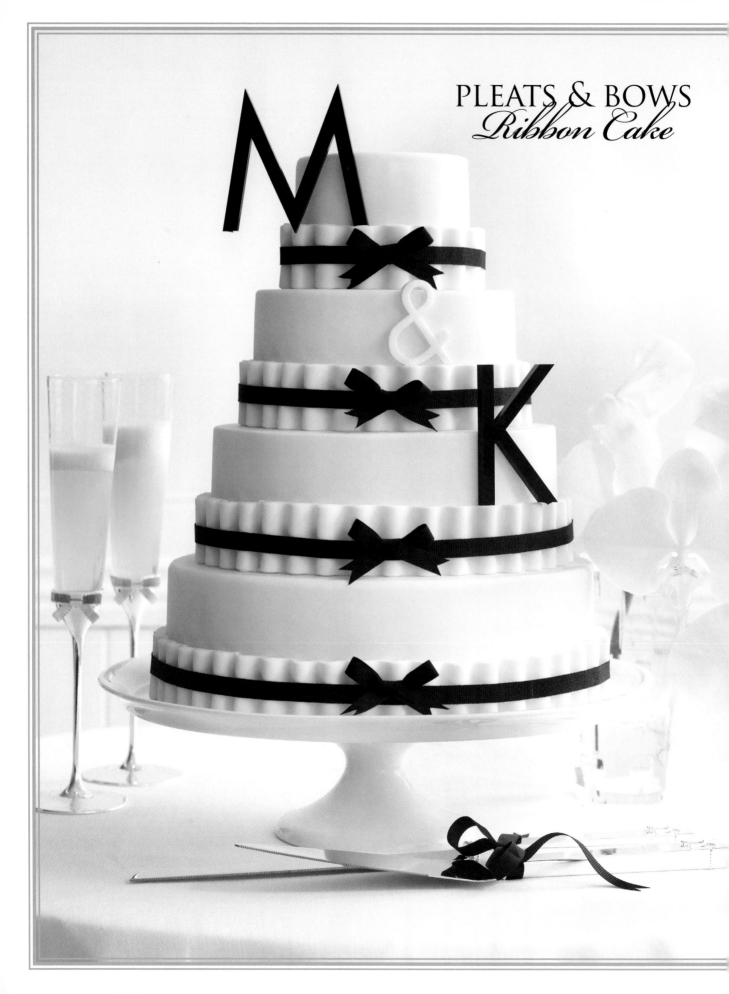

PLEATS & BOWS
Ribbon Cake

IT'S A LOVELY IDEA TO HAVE THE INITIALS OF A COUPLE ON THE TOP OF
AN ENGAGEMENT, COMMITMENT CEREMONY OR WEDDING CAKE.

EQUIPMENT
**35cm (14-inch) round wooden
   cake board (page 208)**
**20cm (8-inch) round wooden
   cake board (page 208)**
**15cm (6-inch) round wooden
   cake board (page 208)**
**10cm (4-inch) round wooden
   cake board (page 208)**
smoothing tools
19 wooden skewers
paper piping bag (page 221)
3.7cm (1½-inch) perspex measure
fine artist's paint brush
tape measure
CAKE
**deep 25cm (10-inch) round cake
   of choice (page 190)**
**deep 20cm (8-inch) round cake
   of choice (page 190)**
**deep 15cm (6-inch) round cake
   of choice (page 190)**
**deep 10cm (4-inch) round cake
   of choice (page 190)**
DECORATIONS
**3kg (6 pounds) ready-made
   white icing**
cornflour (cornstarch)
1 quantity royal icing (page 220)
4m (4 yards) narrow ribbon
perspex initials

1 Trim cakes (page 209). Secure
25cm cake to largest board; secure
remaining cakes to the same-sized
boards (page 209). Prepare cakes
for covering with ready-made icing
(page 209).

2 Knead ready-made icing on surface
dusted with a little cornflour until
icing loses its stickiness. Roll 300g
(9½ ounces) of icing on cornfloured
surface until large enough to cover
10cm cake. Using rolling pin, lift icing
onto cake; smooth with hands then
smoothing tools. Trim icing neatly
around base of cake. (Reserve and
re-use all icing scraps from each cake
for the next cake.)

3 Roll icing on surface dusted
with a little cornflour; use 400g
(12½ ounces) of icing to cover 15cm
cake; 600g (1¼ pounds) to cover
20cm cake; and 700g (1½ pounds) to
cover 25cm cake, in the same way as
the 10cm cake. Dry cakes overnight.

4 Push 3 trimmed skewers into
centres of all cakes except the
smallest cake to support the next
tier (page 212).

5 Assemble cakes, securing each
tier to the tier below (page 212).

6 Three-quarters fill piping bag with
royal icing; pipe around base of each
cake. Use fingertip to blend icing into
any gaps where cakes join the boards
(page 212). Dry cakes overnight.

7 To make pleated strips: Roll 200g
(6½ ounces) of the remaining icing at
a time on cornfloured surface into two
strips 3mm (⅛-inch) thick. Using the
perspex measure, cut strips of icing
3.7cm wide and 30cm (12 inches) long.

8 Position 5 of the wooden skewers
parallel to the edge of the bench,
about 1cm (½ inch) apart. Lift the
strips of icing over the top of the
skewers. Place 5 remaining skewers
on top of the icing, in between the first
skewers. Gently push the skewers
closer together to pleat the icing.
Carefully remove skewers, and
reposition them under and on top
of the next section of the icing strip.
Continue until the strips are pleated.

9 Use paint brush to brush bottom
3cm (1¼-inch) of cake sparingly with
water. Carefully lift pleated strip and
secure into position around cake;
cutting strip to fit cake. Continue this
process all around the base of the
cake, joining, trimming and slightly
overlapping the ends of the strips.
Repeat with remaining icing on
remaining cake tiers. Stand cake
overnight until pleats dry.

10 Measure around base of cake; trim
ribbon to fit around cake, securing to
pleats with tiny dots of royal icing.
Make small bows (page 226) to cover
joins in ribbon; secure bows with
royal icing. Secure perspex initials
to cake with a little royal icing.

tips It's important to allow time for
the icing on the assembled cakes to
dry before positioning the strips; use
the thick wooden skewers to gently
press the pleats into position on the
dampened icing.

THE PLEATED STRIPS NEED TO BE SLIGHTLY FIRM, BUT STILL PLIABLE ENOUGH TO WRAP AROUND THE CAKES WITHOUT CRACKING OR BREAKING. YOU MAY NEED TO JOIN 2 STRIPS FOR THE LARGER CAKES; OVERLAP THE NEXT PLEATED STRIP TO MAKE NEAT JOINS. WHILE WE USED PERSPEX INITIALS ON THIS CAKE, THERE ARE MANY DIFFERENT TYPES, SHAPES AND SIZES AVAILABLE. THIS IS QUITE AN EASY CAKE TO MAKE, AND LOOKS CHIC AND LOVELY ALL AT THE SAME TIME.

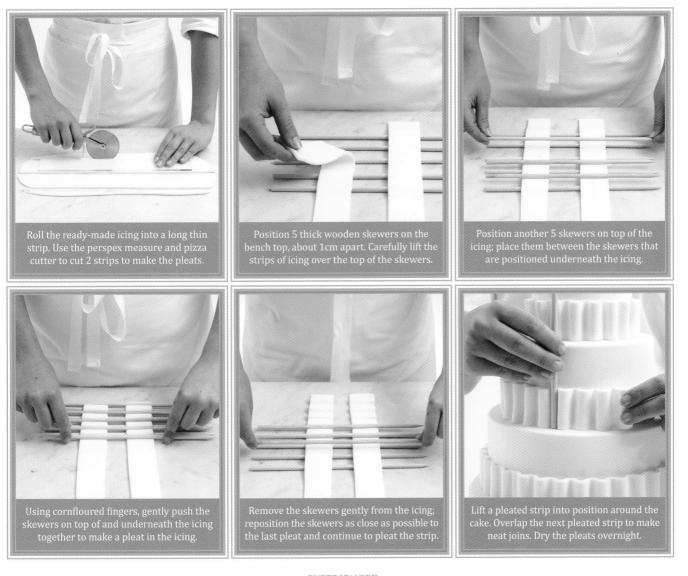

Roll the ready-made icing into a long thin strip. Use the perspex measure and pizza cutter to cut 2 strips to make the pleats.

Position 5 thick wooden skewers on the bench top, about 1cm apart. Carefully lift the strips of icing over the top of the skewers.

Position another 5 skewers on top of the icing; place them between the skewers that are positioned underneath the icing.

Using cornfloured fingers, gently push the skewers on top of and underneath the icing together to make a pleat in the icing.

Remove the skewers gently from the icing; reposition the skewers as close as possible to the last pleat and continue to pleat the strip.

Lift a pleated strip into position around the cake. Overlap the next pleated strip to make neat joins. Dry the pleats overnight.

21ST
Celebration Cake

21ST
Celebration Cake

COVERED IN PASTEL HUES, THIS VERY SIMPLE, THOUGH ELEGANT, CAKE WOULD ALSO
SUIT A BABY'S FIRST BIRTHDAY – ANOTHER VERY IMPORTANT MILESTONE OF LIFE.

EQUIPMENT
30cm (12-inch) round wooden
    cake board (page 208)
15cm (6-inch) round wooden
    cake board (page 208)
smoothing tools
4 wooden skewers
2 paper piping bags (page 221)
number 1 and 2 cutters
2 x 10cm (4-inch) pieces 18-gauge
    floral wire
fine artist's paint brush
pasta machine (see tips)
1cm (½-inch) plain piping tube
CAKE
deep 20cm (8-inch) round cake
    of choice (page 190)
deep 15cm (6-inch) round cake
    of choice (page 190)
DECORATIONS
1.5kg (3 pounds) ready-made
    white icing
cornflour (cornstarch)
pale blue, rose pink, yellow and
    orange food colourings
1 quantity royal icing (page 220)
3 teaspoons tylose powder

1 Trim cakes (page 209). Secure large cake to largest board; secure small cake to remaining board (page 209). Prepare cakes for covering with ready-made icing (page 209).
2 Knead 1kg (2 pounds) of the ready-made icing on surface dusted with a little cornflour until icing loses its stickiness. Tint with blue colouring. Roll 400g (12½ ounces) of the blue icing on cornfloured surface until large enough to cover small cake. Using rolling pin, lift icing onto cake; smooth with hands then smoothing tools. Trim icing neatly around base. Use remaining icing to cover large cake in the same way. Dry cakes overnight. Reserve icing scraps, enclose in plastic wrap.
3 Push 3 trimmed skewers into centre of large cake to support top tier. Secure small cake on top of large cake (page 212).
4 Tint royal icing blue to match cakes. Half-fill piping bag with royal icing; pipe around base of each cake. Use fingertip to blend icing into any gaps where cakes join the boards (page 212). Dry overnight. Cover the surface of the remaining royal icing with plastic wrap to prevent it drying out.
5 Knead reserved blue icing scraps with three-quarters of the remaining white icing on cornfloured surface; tint icing to a darker blue colour.
6 Knead 1 teaspoon of the tylose powder into half of the dark blue icing; roll out to 6mm (¼-inch) thickness

on surface dusted with cornflour. Use cutters to cut out numbers. Dip one end of both pieces of wire about 2cm (¾-inch) into water. Push wet end of wires into the bases of both numbers. Place numbers on baking-paper-covered trays to dry overnight.
7 Roll remaining dark blue icing into 6mm-thick rope shapes. Brush lightly around base of cakes with a little water, gently position icing ropes around cakes. Carefully join ends.
8 Divide remaining white icing into 4 portions. Tint with pink, yellow and orange colourings. Leave remaining portion white. Cover with plastic wrap.
9 To make strips: Knead ½ teaspoon tylose into one portion of icing. Roll out on cornfloured surface into 3mm (⅛-inch) thickness; roll through a pasta machine until 2mm (¹⁄₁₆-inch) thick. Cut 1cm x 10cm (½-inch x 4-inch) strips from icing. Coil strips around remaining skewer; carefully remove skewer. Use the tip of piping tube to cut dots from leftover scraps of icing. Stand strips and dots on baking-paper-lined tray for about 30 minutes or until barely firm. Repeat with remaining icings.
10 Push wired numbers into cake. Three-quarters fill piping bag with royal icing. Decorate cake with 'confetti' and 'ribbons', securing to the cake with tiny dots of royal icing.

THERE ARE NO SPECIAL CAKE DECORATING SKILLS REQUIRED FOR THIS CELEBRATORY CAKE. WHILE THE DECORATIONS CAN BE MADE BY ROLLING THE ICING OUT THINLY TO 2MM, ROLLING THE ICING THROUGH A PASTA MACHINE GIVES GREAT RESULTS. THE NUMBERS SHOULD BE POSITIONED IN THE CAKE ON THE DAY OF SERVING.

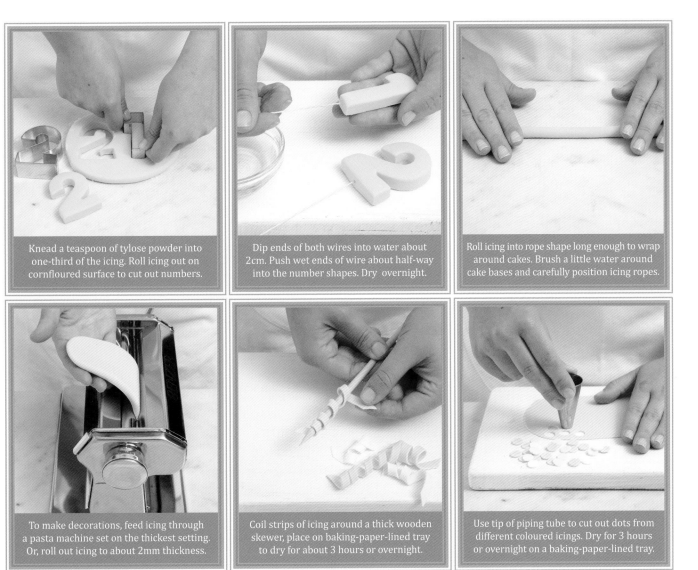

Knead a teaspoon of tylose powder into one-third of the icing. Roll icing out on cornfloured surface to cut out numbers.

Dip ends of both wires into water about 2cm. Push wet ends of wire about half-way into the number shapes. Dry overnight.

Roll icing into rope shape long enough to wrap around cakes. Brush a little water around cake bases and carefully position icing ropes.

To make decorations, feed icing through a pasta machine set on the thickest setting. Or, roll out icing to about 2mm thickness.

Coil strips of icing around a thick wooden skewer, place on baking-paper-lined tray to dry for about 3 hours or overnight.

Use tip of piping tube to cut out dots from different coloured icings. Dry for 3 hours or overnight on a baking-paper-lined tray.

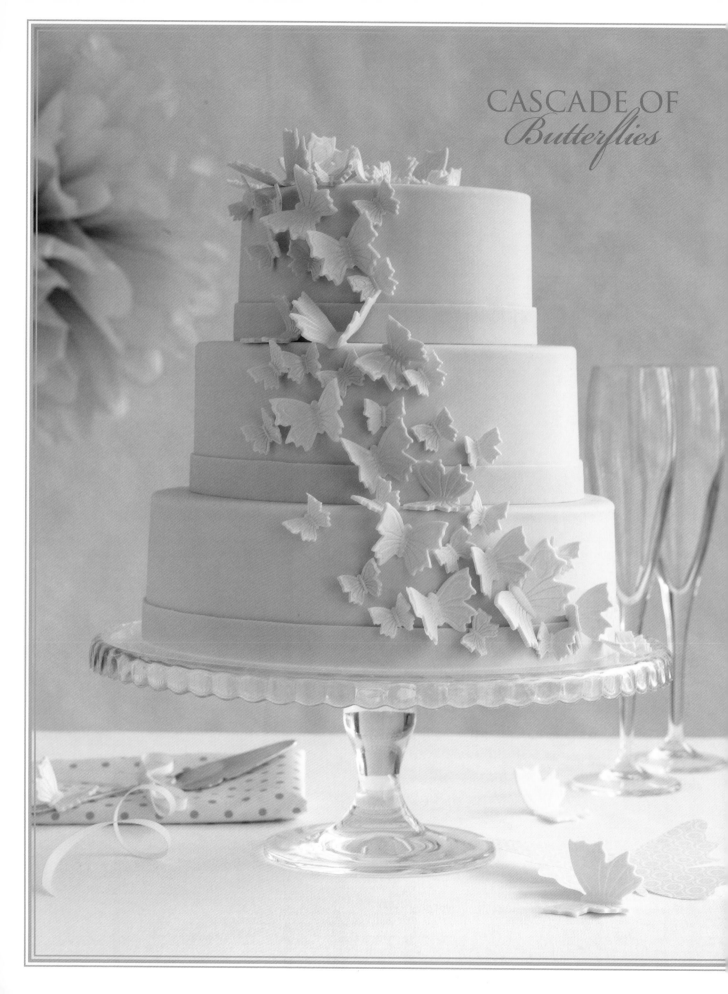

CASCADE OF *Butterflies*

EQUIPMENT
35cm (14-inch) round wooden cake board (page 208)
20cm (8-inch) round wooden cake board (page 208)
15cm (6-inch) round wooden cake board (page 208)
smoothing tools
6 wooden skewers
tape measure
2.5cm (1-inch) perspex measure
pizza cutter
fine artist's paint brush
small non-stick rolling pin
3 x 30cm (12-inch) cardboard squares
small, medium and large butterfly plunger cutter set
paper piping bag (page 221)

CAKE
deep 25cm (10-inch) round cake of choice (page 190)
deep 20cm (8-inch) round cake of choice (page 190)
deep 15cm (6-inch) round cake of choice (page 190)

DECORATIONS
2.5kg (5 pounds) ready-made white icing
cornflour (cornstarch)
sky and royal blue food colourings
tylose powder
1 quantity royal icing (page 220)

1 Trim cakes (page 209). Secure 25cm cake to largest board; secure remaining cakes to same-sized boards (page 209). Prepare cakes for covering with ready-made icing (page 209).

2 Knead ready-made icing on surface dusted with a little cornflour until icing loses its stickiness. Using both colourings, tint 200g (6½ ounces) of the icing very pale blue. Enclose in plastic wrap. Tint remaining icing pale blue.

3 Roll 300g (9½ ounces) of the pale blue icing on cornfloured surface until large enough to cover small cake. Using rolling pin, lift icing onto cake; smooth with hands then smoothing tools. Trim icing neatly around base of cake. Reserve scraps.

4 Roll 500g (1 pound) of the pale blue icing on cornfloured surface until large enough to cover medium cake in the same way as the small cake; roll 600g (1¼ pounds) icing until large enough to cover the large cake in the same way. Reserve icing scraps. Dry overnight.

5 Push 3 trimmed skewers into centre of medium and large cakes to support the next tier (page 212).

6 Assemble cakes, securing each tier to the tier below (page 212). Dry cakes overnight.

7 To make the icing ribbon: Knead the remaining pale blue icing and scraps together, divide into thirds. Reserve two-thirds for the butterflies, enclose in plastic wrap. Tint remaining third of icing a slightly darker blue than the covering on the cakes.

8 Use tape measure to measure around the bottom tier of cake. Roll out half the darker icing into a strip about 3mm (⅛-inch) thick and long enough to wrap around the cake. Use the perspex ruler and pizza cutter to cut a straight edge down one long side of the strip. Use the paint brush to brush bottom 2cm (¾-inch) of cake sparingly with water. Roll icing strip onto small rolling pin with cut edge at bottom of rolling pin; position rolling pin so that the cut edge is flush with the bottom and side of the cake. Unroll icing onto side of cake; trim ends, reserve scraps.

9 Use perspex measure and a small sharp knife to trim strip into a 2.5cm wide ribbon. Be careful not to cut through the icing underneath.

10 Use scraps and remaining icing to make and secure ribbon for the remaining two cakes in the same way; reserve scraps.

11 To make the butterflies: Knead darker blue icing scraps together with a pinch of tylose; enclose in plastic wrap. Knead a pinch of tylose into the reserved pale blue and very pale blue icing. Enclose in plastic wrap. Fold each cardboard evenly into three to make a concertina shape.

12 Roll out one portion of the reserved icing at a time on cornfloured surface into 3mm (⅛-inch) thickness. Working quickly, use all the cutters to cut out random numbers of butterflies. Place butterflies onto the folded cardboard so that the wings fold upwards; leave the butterfly shapes in the cardboard overnight to dry completely.

13 Tint royal icing the same colour as the cake. Half-fill piping bag with icing, pipe small dots of royal icing onto each butterfly; secure to cake.

tips The butterflies can be made months ahead; store in an airtight container at room temperature. Tylose powder is a hardening agent, it helps the butterflies maintain their wings in an upward position.

CASCADING BUTTERFLIES OF JUST ABOUT ANY COLOUR WILL LOOK SPLENDID
ON A TIERED CAKE LIKE THIS. KEEP THE COLOUR OF THE CAKES PALE, SO THAT
THE FLYING SWARM OF BUTTERFLIES BECOMES THE FEATURE.

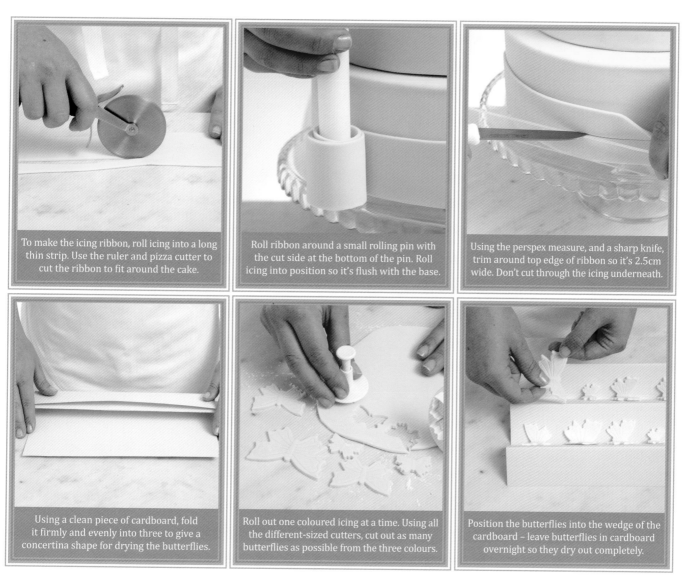

To make the icing ribbon, roll icing into a long thin strip. Use the ruler and pizza cutter to cut the ribbon to fit around the cake.

Roll ribbon around a small rolling pin with the cut side at the bottom of the pin. Roll icing into position so it's flush with the base.

Using the perspex measure, and a sharp knife, trim around top edge of ribbon so it's 2.5cm wide. Don't cut through the icing underneath.

Using a clean piece of cardboard, fold it firmly and evenly into three to give a concertina shape for drying the butterflies.

Roll out one coloured icing at a time. Using all the different-sized cutters, cut out as many butterflies as possible from the three colours.

Position the butterflies into the wedge of the cardboard – leave butterflies in cardboard overnight so they dry out completely.

BRODERIE ANGLAISE
Lace Cake

BRODERIE ANGLAISE, FRENCH FOR 'ENGLISH EMBROIDERY', IS CHARACTERISED BY CUTWORK, LACE AND SMALL EYELET PATTERNS, JUST LIKE WE'VE USED IN THIS CAKE.

EQUIPMENT
25cm (10-inch) square wooden cake board (page 208)
15cm (6-inch) square wooden cake board (page 208)
smoothing tools
4 wooden skewers
medium artist's paint brush
tape measure & plastic ruler
scalloped-edge frill cutter
set of eyelet cutters
1.5cm & 2cm (¾ inch) flower cutters
fine pearl-headed pin
small piping bag
small (number 2) plain piping tube
tweezers
22cm (8¾-inch) 20-gauge floral wire

CAKE
deep 20cm (8-inch) square cake of choice (page 190)
deep 15cm (6-inch) square cake of choice (page 190)

DECORATIONS
1.6kg (3¼ pounds) ready-made white icing
cornflour (cornstarch)
1 quantity royal icing (page 220)
pink food colouring
silver cachous

1 Trim cakes (page 209). Secure 20cm cake to largest board; secure small cake to remaining board (page 209). Prepare cakes for covering with ready-made icing (page 209).

2 Knead ready-made icing on surface dusted with a little cornflour until icing loses its stickiness. Roll 400g (12½ ounces) of icing on cornfloured surface until large enough to cover small cake. Using rolling pin, lift icing onto cake; smooth with hands then smoothing tools. Trim icing neatly around base of cake.

3 Use 550g (1 pound) of the icing to cover large cake in the same way. Dry cakes overnight.

4 Push trimmed skewers into centre of large cake to support the top tier (page 212). Secure small cake to large cake. Dry cakes overnight.

5 Use paint brush to lightly brush water around sides of cakes to cover where the pink bands of icing will be positioned.

6 Tint remaining icing pink, reserve one-third of the icing in plastic wrap.

7 Measure around large cake. Roll icing into a strip long enough to wrap around cake and wide enough to almost cover sides of cake. Using a ruler and knife, or pizza cutter, cut icing into a neat strip, almost as wide as the side of the cake. Lift into position around cake. Repeat with small cake.

8 Gently press frill cutter, at an angle, into top of pink icing to scallop edge; remove excess icing. Using eyelet and flower cutters, and picture as a guide, cut out or mark random shapes on the cakes. Use a pin to remove some of the cut pieces.

9 Tint royal icing pink. Fit piping bag with tube. Half-fill bag with icing; pipe around scallop edges and some of the cut outs.

10 Using tweezers, attach cachous to cakes with a little royal icing.

11 Re-roll scraps of pink icing, cut out several flower shapes; insert pieces of floral wire into shapes, stand on baking-paper-covered tray to dry overnight. Position wired flowers on day of serving.

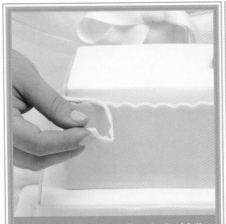

Carefully press the scalloped-edged frill cutter against the top edge of the icing strip on both cakes; gently remove excess icing.

Using a fine pin, remove some cut-out pieces of icing; leave some pieces intact. Stick some flower cut-outs to the cake with royal icing.

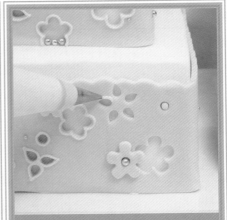

Tint royal icing pale pink. Half-fill the piping bag with icing, and pipe around the scalloped edges and some of the cut-outs.

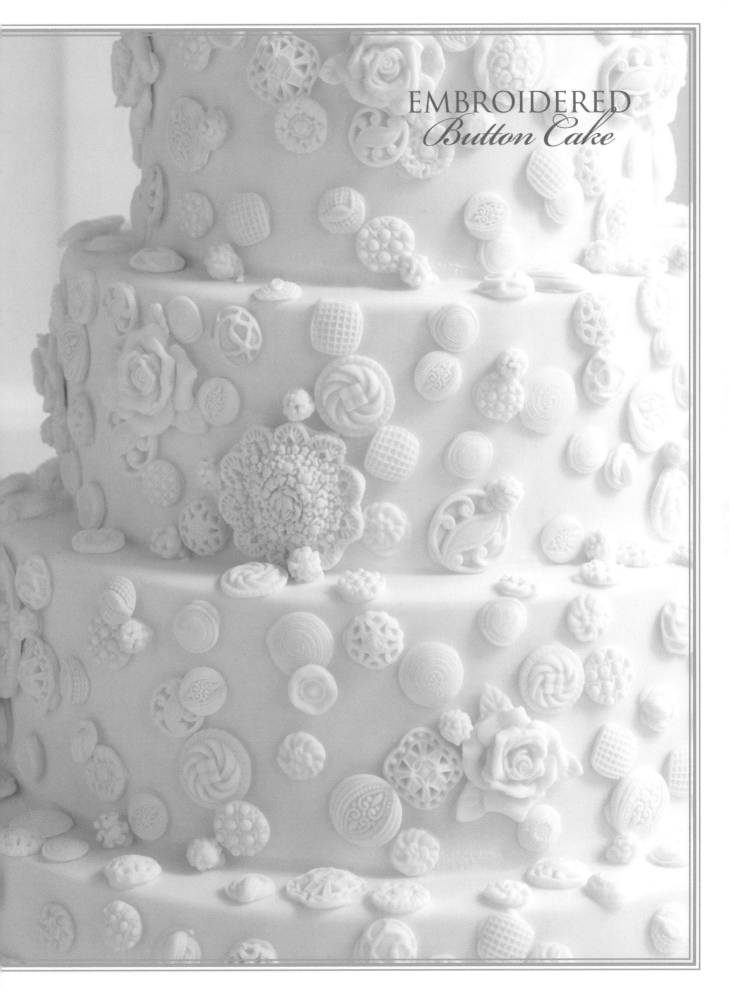

EMBROIDERED
Button Cake

THE BUTTONS ON THIS CAKE CREATE A LOOK THAT'S REMINISCENT OF
THE FLOUNCY WEDDING DRESSES OF YESTERYEAR. THE CAKE WOULD
ALSO LOOK BEAUTIFUL COVERED IN A PLAIN WHITE ICING.

EQUIPMENT
**45cm (18-inch) round wooden
cake board (page 208)**
**30cm (12-inch) round wooden
cake board (page 208)**
**25cm (10-inch) round wooden
cake board (page 208)**
**20cm (8-inch) round wooden
cake board (page 208)**
**15cm (6-inch) round wooden
cake board (page 208)**
**10cm (4-inch) round wooden
cake board (page 208)**
smoothing tools
15 wooden skewers
paper piping bag (page 221)
silicone button-shaped moulds
cooking-oil spray
small offset metal spatula
CAKE
**deep 35cm (14-inch) round cake
of choice (page 190)**
**deep 30cm (12-inch) round cake
of choice (page 190)**
**deep 25cm (10-inch) round cake
of choice (page 190)**
**deep 20cm (8-inch) round cake
of choice (page 190)**
**deep 15cm (6-inch) round cake
of choice (page 190)**
**deep 10cm (4-inch) round cake
of choice (page 190)**
DECORATIONS
**5kg (11 pounds) ready-made
ivory icing**
cornflour (cornstarch)
1 quantity royal icing (page 220)
ivory food colouring

1 Trim cakes (page 209). Secure 35cm cake to largest board; secure remaining cakes to the same-sized boards (page 209). Prepare cakes for covering with ready-made icing (page 209).

2 Working with 2kg (4 pounds) of the ready-made icing, knead on surface dusted with a little cornflour until icing loses its stickiness. Roll 250g (8 ounces) of icing on cornfloured surface until large enough to cover 10cm cake. Using rolling pin, lift icing onto cake; smooth with hands then smoothing tools. Trim icing neatly around base of cake; reserve scraps.

3 Use 350g (11 ounces) of icing to cover 15cm cake; 600g (1¼ pounds) icing to cover 20cm cake and 800g (1½ pounds) icing to cover 25cm cake in the same way as step 2; reserve icing scraps.

4 Knead another 2kg (4 pounds) icing with scraps on cornfloured surface until icing loses its stickiness. Roll 1kg (2 pounds) on cornfloured surface to cover 30cm cake; roll remaining icing to cover 35cm cake in the same way as step 2. Reserve icing scraps. Dry cakes overnight.

5 Push 3 trimmed skewers into centres of all cakes except smallest cake to support the next tier (page 212).

6 Assemble cakes, securing each tier to the tier below (page 212).

7 Tint royal icing to match cakes. Three-quarters fill piping bag with royal icing; pipe around base of each cake. Use fingertip to blend icing into any gaps where cakes join the boards (page 212). Dry cakes overnight. Reserve royal icing.

8 Knead remaining ready-made icing with scraps on cornfloured surface until icing loses its stickiness. Lightly spray moulds with cooking oil. Working with a handful of icing, push small amounts of icing firmly into moulds. Use spatula to scrape excess icing from backs of shapes so icing is flush with the mould.

9 When mould is full, bend slightly and lift out shapes; place, flat-side down, onto baking-paper-lined trays to dry out completely for 2 days.

10 Using a few buttons at a time, pipe a little royal icing onto backs of buttons; secure all over cake in a random pattern.

tips You'll need to make around 400 buttons. This can be done months ahead. Store shapes in an airtight container. The icing will keep well so the buttons can be made over a long period of time. If shapes don't come out of the moulds easily, freeze them for 2 minutes, then release the shapes.

THERE ARE NO PIPING SKILLS REQUIRED FOR THIS CAKE – THE RICH EMBROIDERED
EFFECT COMES FROM USING BUTTON MOULDS OF DIFFERENT SHAPES AND SIZES.
THERE ARE LOTS OF DIFFERENT MOULDS AVAILABLE IN CAKE DECORATING SHOPS;
TAKE THE TIME TO MIX AND MATCH THEM TO MAKE THIS CAKE A SUCCESS.

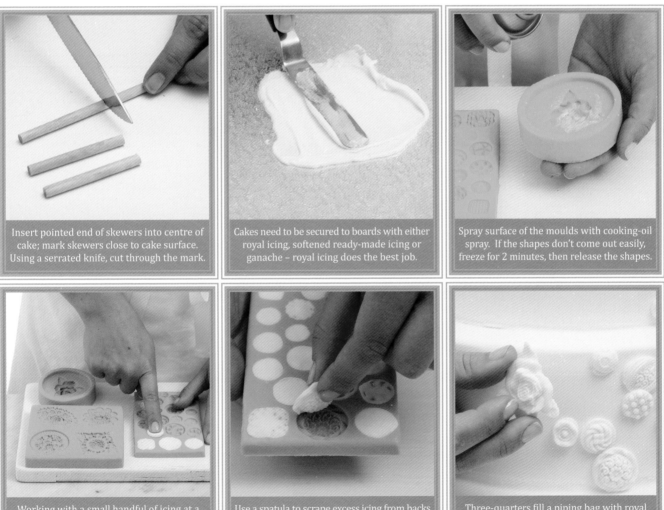

Insert pointed end of skewers into centre of cake; mark skewers close to cake surface. Using a serrated knife, cut through the mark.

Cakes need to be secured to boards with either royal icing, softened ready-made icing or ganache – royal icing does the best job.

Spray surface of the moulds with cooking-oil spray. If the shapes don't come out easily, freeze for 2 minutes, then release the shapes.

Working with a small handful of icing at a time, push enough icing into the lightly-oiled moulds to tightly fill the shapes.

Use a spatula to scrape excess icing from backs of shapes. Bend mould to remove shapes; place on baking-paper-lined tray to dry.

Three-quarters fill a piping bag with royal icing. Pipe dots of icing on the backs of the buttons; position randomly over cake.

BITE-SIZED
Stencilled Squares

ALMOST LIKE PETIT FOURS, THESE LITTLE CAKES WOULD BE GREAT AS PART OF A MENU FOR A STYLISH HIGH TEA. CHANGE THE COLOURS TO SUIT YOUR THEME.

EQUIPMENT
5cm (2-inch) square cutter
4 paper piping bags (page 221)
small stencils (see tips)
small offset metal spatula
16 plain coloured paper cases
30cm (12-inch) square wooden cake board (page 208)
CAKE
shallow 22cm (9-inch) square cake of choice (page 190)
DECORATIONS
250g (8 ounces) ready-made white icing
cornflour (cornstarch)
golden yellow, blue, orange and rose pink food colourings
1 quantity royal icing (page 220)
1 quantity butter cream (page 218)

1 Knead ready-made icing on surface dusted with a little cornflour until icing loses its stickiness. Divide icing into four equal portions: tint yellow, blue, orange and pink. Wrap separately in plastic wrap.

2 Roll each portion, separately, on cornfloured surface into a 3mm (⅛-inch) thickness. Using cutter, cut out four squares from each coloured icing, place on baking-paper-lined tray to dry, about 3 hours or overnight.

3 Divide royal icing evenly into four small bowls, tint using all four colourings. Cover surface of icings with plastic wrap to keep airtight.

4 Using one icing at a time, drop a teaspoon of icing into piping bag. Using corresponding colour, pipe a dot of icing in the corners of the icing squares to anchor stencil in position.

5 Use spatula to spread royal icing thinly but evenly over stencil; scrape away excess icing, gently remove stencil. Wash and dry stencil before using again. Repeat with remaining squares and royal icing. Stand squares about 1 hour or until dry. Carefully remove the anchoring dots from the icing squares after the icing has dried.

6 Trim top of cake so it will sit flat when upside down (page 209). Turn cake upside down, trim sides to make a 20cm (8-inch) square cake. Cut cake into 16 x 5cm (2-inch) squares. Spread butter cream over cake tops; position icing squares on cakes.

7 Place cake squares into paper cases. Secure cakes to board with a little royal icing or butter cream, to stop them sliding off the board.

tips Square paper cases are available in specialty food or kitchen shops, but we found round cases happily change shape to accommodate the square cakes. The stencilled icing squares can be made several weeks ahead; store in an airtight container at room temperature. The cake will become stale within a day of cutting. We used stencils used for dusting cappuccinos; they can be found at many of the larger supermarkets.

Pipe a tiny dot of royal icing in two opposing corners of each square of icing to anchor the stencil in place, if necessary.

Using a spatula, spread royal icing thinly and as evenly as possible over stencil (only cover the one shape). Scrape away excess icing.

Gently and slowly lift the stencil from the icing square. Stand icing 1 hour to dry. Wash and dry stencil before using again.

ALMONDY WEDDING
Cake Biscuits

ALMONDY WEDDING
Cake Biscuits

THESE DELICATE BISCUITS CAN BE COLOURED TO SUIT YOUR THEME; THEY LOOK LOVELY IN ONE COLOUR, OR LAYERED USING DIFFERENT COLOURS, HOWEVER, IT IS QUICKER AND EASIER TO ICE THE BISCUITS IN THE SAME COLOUR.

EQUIPMENT
6.5cm (2½-inch) round cutter
5cm (2-inch) round cutter
3.5cm (1¼-inch) round cutter
6 paper piping bags (page 221)
tweezers
ALMOND BISCUITS
250g (8 ounces) butter
2 teaspoons finely grated
    orange rind
½ cup (110g) caster (superfine)
    sugar
2 egg yolks
2 cups (300g) plain (all-purpose)
    flour
⅓ cup (50g) self-raising flour
½ cup (75g) cornflour (cornstarch)
1 cup (120g) ground almonds
DECORATIONS
2 quantities royal icing (page 220)
pink, blue and yellow food
    colourings
1 tablespoon strained lemon juice
50g (1½ ounce) packet pearlized
    blush sugar pearls

1 Have butter at room temperature.
2 To make almond biscuits: Beat chopped butter, rind, sugar and egg yolks in small bowl with electric mixer until light and fluffy. Transfer mixture to large bowl. Stir in sifted flours, cornflour and ground almonds in two batches.

3 Knead dough on lightly floured surface until smooth; divide in half. Roll both pieces of dough, separately, between sheets of baking paper into 3mm (⅛-inch) thickness; refrigerate 30 minutes.
4 Preheat oven to 180°C/350°F. Line oven trays with baking paper.
5 Using the largest cutter, cut 18 rounds from dough; place on oven trays. Using both medium and small cutters, cut 12 rounds of each from dough, re-rolling scraps as necessary; place on oven trays. Bake biscuits about 15 minutes or until browned lightly. Cool on trays.
6 Divide royal icing equally between three small bowls; tint pale pink, blue and lemon. Cover surface of icing with plastic wrap to keep airtight.
7 Decide how many biscuits are needed of the same colour. Spread biscuits out on a flat surface ready for piping.
8 Use one colour of royal icing at a time: Half-fill one of the piping bags with icing. Pipe an unbroken border of icing around outside edge of the biscuits; stand until set. Wrap piping bag in plastic wrap to keep airtight. Repeat with remaining colours.
9 Using one colour at a time, add a drop or two of lemon juice to the remaining icing in bowl – the icing

should be the consistency of pouring cream. Spoon icing into another paper piping bag; snip the tip from the bag. Pipe icing inside the same-coloured border to "flood" the tops of the biscuits. Stand overnight to set. Repeat with remaining batches of royal icing and biscuits.
10 To make wedding cakes: Stack 3 large biscuits on top of each other, followed by 2 medium and 2 small biscuits, joining each biscuit with a dab of royal icing.
11 Use the reserved icing in piping bags (the normal royal icing, not the runny icing) to decorate the wedding cake biscuits with loops (see tips), one layer at a time. Using tweezers, position pearls before the icing sets.

makes 6
tips To ensure the loops are evenly spaced, pipe small dots of royal icing around the biscuits as a guide, if you like. The biscuits can be finished a week ahead; store them in a single layer, covered, at room temperature. They're not hard to make, but they do require a good dose of patience. The biscuits look pretty stacked on a tiered stemmed cake plate or cupcake stand. The 'pearlized blush sugar pearls' are small edible pearls, and are available from cake decorating suppliers.

THESE BISCUITS USE A TECHNIQUE KNOWN AS 'FLOODING' OR 'RUNOUT';
THIS IS WHEN AN OUTLINE IS FILLED WITH RUNNY ICING. HERE THE BISCUITS
ARE OUTLINED WITH ROYAL ICING AND, WHEN THAT IS DRY, THEY'RE 'FLOODED'
WITH THINNED ROYAL ICING, WHICH BECOMES SMOOTH AND SHINY WHEN SET.
THE BISCUITS ARE QUITE FRAGILE ONCE THEY'VE BEEN DECORATED WITH THE
ROYAL ICING LOOPS AND PEARLS, SO TREAT THEM GENTLY.

Lay biscuits out on a flat surface ready for piping. Divide royal icing between 3 small bowls. Tint icing pink, blue and lemon.

Using one colour at a time, pipe a border of royal icing in an unbroken line around the outside edge of the biscuits; allow to dry.

Stir a drop or two of lemon juice into the royal icing to make it the consistency of pouring cream. Place into the piping bag.

Using sharp scissors, snip the tip from the piping bag. Flood the icing into the centre of the biscuits within the piped border.

Stack 3 large, 2 medium, then 2 small biscuits on top of each other, joining each layer with a little royal icing to secure.

Working with one stack of biscuits at a time; pipe loops around biscuits. Using tweezers, position pearls on icing before it sets.

PALE MINTY GREEN AND SOFT DUSTY PINK BLEND TOGETHER FOR A SWEET OLD-FASHIONED EFFECT. THIS IS DEFINITELY A GIRLY CAKE FOR OLD AND YOUNG ALIKE.

EQUIPMENT
30cm (12-inch) round wooden cake board (page 208)
15cm (6-inch) round wooden cake board (page 208)
smoothing tools
3cm x 3.5cm (1¼-inch x 1½-inch) scalloped cutter
3 wooden skewers
2 paper piping bags (page 221)
tape measure
fine artist's paint brush
2.5cm (1-inch) perspex measure
tweezers

CAKE
deep 20cm (8-inch) round cake of choice (page 190)
deep 15cm (6-inch) round cake of choice (page 190)

DECORATIONS
1kg (2 pounds) ready-made white icing
cornflour (cornstarch)
rose pink and kelly green food colourings
1 quantity royal icing (page 220)
113g (3½-ounce) packet pearlized blush sugar pearls

1 Trim cakes (page 209). Secure large cake to largest board; secure small cake to remaining board (page 209). Prepare cakes for covering with ready-made icing (page 209).

2 Knead ready-made icing on surface dusted with cornflour until icing loses its stickiness. Tint 100g (3 ounces) of the icing pink, enclose in plastic wrap. Tint the remaining icing green.

3 Roll 400g (12½ ounces) of green icing on cornfloured surface until large enough to cover small cake. Using rolling pin, lift icing onto cake; smooth with hands then smoothing tools. Trim icing neatly around base of cake. Use remaining green icing plus any scraps to cover large cake in the same way as the small cake.

4 Carefully press scallop cutter around side and over the top edge of large cake while the icing is still soft. Dry cakes overnight.

5 Push trimmed skewers into centre of large cake to support top tier. Secure small cake to large cake (page 212).

6 Colour half the royal icing the same green as the cakes. Three-quarters fill a piping bag with icing. Pipe green icing around base of each cake. Use fingertip to blend icing into any gaps where cakes join the boards (page 212). Dry cakes overnight.

7 Measure around base of top tier. Roll pink icing on cornfloured surface into 2mm (¹⁄₁₆-inch) thickness, and long enough to wrap around cake. Cut a straight edge down one long side. Brush bottom 2cm (¾-inch) of small cake sparingly with water; secure icing strip around base, trim ends neatly. Use perspex measure and a small sharp knife to trim strip into a 2.5cm-wide ribbon; don't cut into icing underneath.

8 Re-roll pink icing scraps to 3mm (⅛-inch) thick. Using scallop cutter, cut a scallop from the icing; secure to side of small cake with a little water.

9 Tint remaining royal icing pale pink. Half-fill piping bag with icing; pipe decorations onto cake. Pipe a 5cm (2-inch) line of pink icing around base of small cake, position pearls on icing before it sets. Repeat all around cake.

As soon as the cake has been covered with icing, gently press the cutter into the icing starting from the bottom of the cake.

Use the perspex measure and a sharp knife to trim the ribbon into a 2.5cm width. Be careful not to cut through the icing underneath.

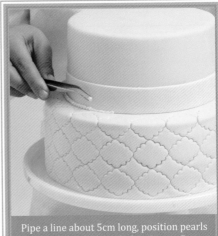

Pipe a line about 5cm long, position pearls with tweezers on icing before it sets. Repeat with icing and pearls all around the cake.

Mark the pattern on the icing before it sets – do it carefully and slowly and you'll be pleased with the outcome. The cake would be suitable for birthdays, christenings, baby showers and kitchen teas. The 'pearlized blush sugar pearls' are small edible pearls, and are available from cake decorating suppliers. The cutter we used came from a kit of patchwork cutters.

CHRISTMAS
Snowflakes

WE LOVE THE SNOWFLAKES ON THIS PRETTY CHRISTMAS CAKE. TRADITIONALLY, WE WOULD USE A RICH FRUIT CAKE, BUT A MUD CAKE WOULD DO JUST AS WELL.

EQUIPMENT
25cm (10-inch) round wooden cake board (page 208)
smoothing tools
set of 3 snowflake plunger cutters (small, medium, large)
fine artist's paint brush
paper piping bag (page 221)
CAKE
deep 20cm (8-inch) round cake of choice (page 190)
DECORATIONS
750g (1½ pounds) ready-made white icing
cornflour (cornstarch)
cornflower blue food colouring
1 teaspoon tylose powder
1 egg white, lightly beaten
½ cup (110g) white sanding sugar
1 quantity royal icing (page 220)
180g (5½ ounces) small persian confetti

1 Trim cake (page 209). Secure cake to board (page 209). Prepare for covering with ready-made icing (page 209).
2 Knead ready-made icing on surface dusted with a little cornflour until icing loses its stickiness. Tint three-quarters of the icing blue with colouring.
3 Roll out blue icing on cornfloured surface into 3mm (⅛-inch) thickness. Using rolling pin, lift icing over cake; smooth with hands then smoothing tools. Trim icing neatly around base of cake.
4 Knead remaining white ready-made icing with tylose powder on surface dusted with cornflour until smooth. Roll out on surface dusted with cornflour into 3mm (⅛-inch) thickness. Use cutters to cut out different-sized snowflakes. Place snowflakes on baking-paper-lined tray to dry overnight.

5 Brush a very thin layer of egg white onto tips and around the centres of snowflake shapes; sprinkle sanding sugar over egg white. Stand the snowflakes for about 1 hour to dry.
6 Meanwhile, three-quarters fill piping bag with royal icing. Pipe a line of icing all the way around base of cake. Position persian confetti on icing before it dries.
7 Secure snowflakes to cake with royal icing; leave to dry for about 1 hour.

tips The sanding sugar gives the snowflakes a lovely texture, however, if you can't find it, don't worry, the snowflakes look divine without it. Snowflakes can be made months ahead; store them in an airtight container at room temperature. Persian confetti is sometimes sold as 'snowfall'. A fine dusting of sifted icing sugar added at the last minute adds to the snowy look.

Using a fine artist's paint brush, brush a very thin layer of egg white onto the tips and around the centres of all the snowflakes.

Sprinkle the centres and tips of the snowflakes with the sanding sugar; stand the snowflakes for about 1 hour or until they are dry.

Pipe royal icing on the back of a snowflake, position on cake; hold large snowflakes for about 5 seconds until they grip the cake.

PINK ON WHITE *Flower Cake*

EQUIPMENT
35cm (14-inch) round wooden cake board (page 208)
20cm (8-inch) round wooden cake board (page 208)
15cm (6-inch) round wooden cake board (page 208)
smoothing tools
6 wooden skewers
fine long wooden skewer
silicone flower mould
small metal spatula
4 small piping bags
small (number 2) plain piping tube

CAKE
deep 25cm (10-inch) round cake of choice (page 190)
deep 20cm (8-inch) round cake of choice (page 190)
deep 15cm (6-inch) round cake of choice (page 190)

DECORATIONS
2kg (4 pounds) ready-made white icing
cornflour (cornstarch)
tylose powder
rose pink food colouring
1 quantity royal icing (page 220)

1 Knead ready-made icing on surface dusted with a little cornflour until icing loses its stickiness. Reserve 200g (6½ ounces) of icing for flowers.

2 Trim cakes (page 209). Secure 25cm cake to largest board; secure remaining cakes to same-sized boards (page 209). Prepare cakes for covering with ready-made icing (page 209).

3 Roll 400g (12½ ounces) of the icing on surface dusted with cornflour until large enough to cover small cake. Using rolling pin, lift icing onto cake; smooth with hands then smoothing tools. Trim icing neatly around base of cake.

4 Use 600g (1¼ pounds) of the icing to cover medium cake in the same way as small cake. Use remaining icing to cover large cake. Reserve icing scraps.

5 Use the fine wooden skewer to mark the icing in random lengths all around cakes before the icing sets. Dry cakes overnight.

6 Push 3 trimmed skewers into centres of large and medium cakes to support top tiers (page 212). Assemble cakes, securing each tier to the tier below (page 212).

7 Knead ½ teaspoon tylose powder into reserved icing and scraps. Divide icing into four portions; colour three portions different shades of pink. Leave remaining portion white. Press small amounts of each coloured icing into flower moulds; using spatula, scrape excess icing from backs of flowers so the shapes are flush with the mould. Bend mould gently to release flowers. Place the flowers, top-side up, on baking-paper-lined tray to dry overnight.

8 Fit piping bag with tube. Half-fill bag with royal icing. Pipe snail trail (page 224) around base of each cake. Pipe white vertical lines in some of the grooves on the cakes. Wash and dry piping tube; place in clean piping bag.

9 Mix leftover icing in piping bag with remaining royal icing; divide between three small bowls. Colour each batch a different shade of pink; cover surface with plastic wrap to keep airtight. Working with one colour at a time, pipe vertical lines in some of the grooves on the cakes. Repeat with remaining icings leaving some grooves plain. Wash and dry piping tube after each colour.

10 Using a few flowers at a time, pipe a little royal icing onto back of flowers; secure over cake in a random pattern.

tips Silicone moulds come in myriad shapes and sizes. The mould we used gave us three different-sized flowers. The 'snail trail' edging (page 224) around the cake bases requires a little practice before you start on the cakes.

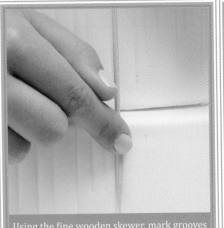
Using the fine wooden skewer, mark grooves of random lengths around the sides of all the cakes. Do this before the icing sets.

Press small amounts of icing into mould. Scrape away excess icing. Remove flowers from mould and allow to dry overnight.

Pipe vertical lines of royal icing into the grooves using white and three shades of pink icing. Leave some grooves without icing.

MINTY FLOCKED
Wedding Cake

SQUARE CAKES HAVE TO BE NEAR-PERFECT TO GIVE CRISP CLEAN LINES.

EQUIPMENT
40cm (16-inch) square wooden cake board (page 208)
25cm (10-inch) square wooden cake board (page 208)
20cm (8-inch) square wooden cake board (page 208)
15cm (6-inch) square wooden cake board (page 208)
smoothing tools
12 wooden skewers
large stencil
fine pearl-headed pins
small offset metal spatula
straight-sided metal scraper
2 paper piping bags (page 221)
craft glue

CAKE
2 x deep 30cm (12-inch) square cakes of choice (page 190)
deep 25cm (10-inch) square cake of choice (page 190)
shallow 25cm (10-inch) square cake of choice (page 190)
shallow 20cm (8-inch) square cake of choice (page 190)
deep 15cm (6-inch) square cake of choice (page 190)
shallow 15cm (6-inch) square cake of choice (page 190)
jam or ganache of choice (page 210)

DECORATIONS
3.5kg (7 pounds) ready-made white icing
cornflour (cornstarch)
green and blue food colouring
2 quantities royal icing (page 220)
2.5m (2½ yards) wide ribbon

1   Trim cakes (page 209). Secure one 30cm cake to largest board (page 209); top with remaining 30cm cake, joining cakes with a little jam or ganache (page 212). Stack and secure the two 25cm and the two 15cm cakes to same-sized boards in the same way. Secure 20cm cake to same-sized board. Prepare cakes for covering with ready-made icing (page 209).

2   Knead ready-made icing on surface dusted with a little cornflour until icing loses its stickiness. Tint icing pale green with colouring. Roll 1.6kg (3¼ pounds) of icing on cornfloured surface until large enough to cover the 30cm cake. Using rolling pin, lift icing onto cake; smooth with hands then smoothing tools. Trim icing neatly around base of cake.

3   Use 500g (1 pound) of the icing to cover the 15cm cake and 400g (12½ ounces) of the icing to cover the 20cm cake in the same way.

4   Use blue colouring to colour the remaining icing and icing scraps a shade of blue-green to tone with the green; use to cover the 25cm cake in the same way as the large cake. Dry cakes overnight.

5   Push 4 trimmed skewers into centres of all cakes except the smallest cake to support the next tier (page 212).

6   To stencil the 30cm (12-inch) cake: Working on one side of the cake at a time, use a wad of damp paper towel to lightly dampen the side of the cake to help hold the stencil in position. Hold stencil against side of cake; secure corners of stencil with pins, if necessary. Use spatula to spread royal icing over entire stencil; remove excess icing back into bowl with metal scraper, gently remove stencil and pins. Wash and dry stencil before using again. Repeat on all sides of the cake. Stand about 1 hour or until dry.

7   Reserve 2 tablespoons of the royal icing. Tint remaining royal icing the same colour as the 20cm cake. Stencil sides in the same way as the large cake.

8   Assemble cakes, securing each tier to the tier below (page 212).

9   Tint the reserved royal icing a blue-green colour to match the 25cm cake. Half-fill piping bags with royal icing to match the cakes; pipe around bases of same-coloured cakes. Use fingertip to blend icing into any gaps where cakes join the boards (page 212). Dry cakes overnight.

10   Trim ribbon to fit around the base of the top tier and the blue-green tier. Secure ends of ribbon with glue. Make small tailored bows (page 226) from ribbon. Glue bows into position over ribbon joins.

tips Covering the large cakes with the soft icing can be a little difficult. Ask someone to help by supporting the icing with their hands as it drapes down the sides of the cake. We used the same stencil on the small cake as we did on the large cake. When stencilling the small cake, rest it on a smaller cake pan to give it a bit of height off the bench. This makes it easier to place the large stencil around the cake before applying the icing.

THE READY-MADE ICING COVERING THE CAKES SHOULD BE DONE AT LEAST A DAY AHEAD AND ALLOWED TO DRY BEFORE APPLYING THE STENCIL. USING A STENCIL ON A CAKE NEEDS A LITTLE PRACTICE; DO THIS ON THE SIDE OF A CAKE PAN TO GET THE FEEL OF JUST HOW MUCH ROYAL ICING TO USE AND HOW TO REMOVE THE STENCIL WITH CONFIDENCE. IF YOU MAKE A MISTAKE USING THE STENCIL, QUICKLY SCRAPE THE ICING OFF THE CAKE BEFORE IT SETS, THEN REPEAT THE STENCILLING.

Working on one side of the cake at time, gently blot the side of the cake with damp absorbent paper towel to lightly moisten the icing.

Position the stencil on the side of the cake. If necessary, secure the stencil to the cake using fine pins at the corners of the stencil.

Using a small offset metal spatula, carefully spread the royal icing as evenly as possible over the stencil along one side of the cake.

Using the metal scraper, scrape excess icing from the stencil and return to the bowl. Press firmly, but not too heavily, against the stencil.

Starting from the end of the stencil, remove the pins, then carefully remove the stencil from the cake by pulling back along the cake.

Secure the ribbon around the cake, then make a small flat bow and glue in position to cover where the ends of the ribbon join.

WEDDING CAKE *Wonder*

ELEGANCE AND SIMPLICITY IS WHAT THIS STUNNING CAKE IS ALL ABOUT. THE STYROFOAM DISCS ARE USED TO SUPPORT THE FLOWERS BETWEEN EACH LAYER.

EQUIPMENT
drill
12mm (½ inch) drill bit with
    centring tip (see tips)
35cm (14-inch) round wooden
    cake board (page 208)
30cm (12-inch) round wooden
    cake board (page 208)
25cm (10-inch) round wooden
    cake board (page 208)
20cm (8-inch) round wooden
    cake board (page 208)
15cm (6-inch) round wooden
    cake board (page 208)
9cm x 20cm (3¾-inch x 8-inch)
    diameter styrofoam disc
9cm x 15cm (3¾-inch x 6-inch)
    diameter styrofoam disc
9cm x 10cm (3¾-inch x 4-inch)
    diameter styrofoam disc
craft glue (or glue gun)
12mm x 60cm (½-inch x 24-inch)
    wooden dowel
smoothing tools
pastry brush
plastic ruler
pizza cutter
pencil
fine pearl-headed pins
small piping bag
small (number 2) plain piping tube
7 wooden skewers
CAKE
deep 25cm (10-inch) round cake
    of choice (page 190)
shallow 25cm (10-inch) round
    cake of choice (page 190)
deep 20cm (8-inch) round cake
    of choice (page 190)
shallow 20cm (8-inch) round cake
    of choice (page 190)
deep 15cm (6-inch) round cake
    of choice (page 190)
shallow 15cm (6-inch) round cake
    of choice (page 190)
jam or ganache of choice (page 210)
DECORATIONS
2.5kg (5 pounds) ready-made
    ivory icing

cornflour (cornstarch)
1 quantity sugar syrup (page 217)
1 quantity royal icing (page 220)
rose pink food colouring
fresh large organic flowers

1 Knead 500g (1 pound) ready-made icing on surface dusted with a little cornflour until icing loses its stickiness. Brush 35cm board with sugar syrup. Roll icing large enough to cover board. Using rolling pin, lift icing onto board; smooth with hands then smoothing tools. Trim icing neatly around base (page 208); use cornfloured fingertip to smooth edge. Stand overnight to dry.

2 Mark the centre of each cake board and styrofoam disc. Except for the 30cm wooden board, drill a 12mm hole through the centre of each disc and each board. Glue the 35cm board on top of the 30cm board (this gives clearance under the board so you can pick it up off the bench). Squeeze glue into hole in the 35cm board; position dowel in the hole. Stand until dry.

3 Trim cakes (page 209). Secure deep 25cm cake to largest board. Secure remaining deep cakes to same-sized boards (page 209). Position shallow cakes on top of same-sized deep cakes; secure with jam or ganache (page 212). Prepare cakes for covering with ready-made icing (page 209).

4 Knead icing on surface dusted with a little cornflour until icing loses its stickiness. Roll 375g (12 ounces) of icing on cornfloured surface until large enough to cover small cake. Using rolling pin, lift icing onto cake; smooth with hands then smoothing tools. Trim icing neatly around base.

5 Use 625g (1¼ pounds) of icing to cover medium cake and use 750g (1½ pounds) of icing to cover large cake in the same way as small cake. Dry cakes overnight.

6 Using one styrofoam disc at a time, brush syrup sparingly around sides of discs. Roll 80g (2½ ounces) icing on cornfloured surface until long enough to wrap around side of smallest disc; using ruler and pizza cutter, trim to fit. Cover side of styrofoam; reserve scraps. Trim away any excess icing on top and bottom of disc. Knead scraps and remaining icing together; cover sides of remaining discs in the same way.

7 Using picture as a guide, draw 'stitch' pattern onto a strip of baking paper large enough to wrap around large cake; attach to cake, marked-side out, using pins. Using a fine pin, mark pattern onto each cake, reducing the length of the paper to fit around the middle cake, then the small cake.

8 Tint royal icing pale pink. Fit piping bag with tube. Three-quarters fill bag with royal icing; pipe pattern onto cakes using pin marks as a guide; leave to dry for at least 1 hour.

9 To assemble the cake: Position the largest styrofoam disc onto the dowel, secure to board with a little royal icing. Next, firmly push the large cake down over the dowel; secure to the disc below with royal icing. Push 3 trimmed skewers into top of large cake. Top with the medium disc then medium cake in the same way; push 3 trimmed skewers into medium cake. Top with the small disc then small cake.

10 Use remaining skewer to pierce holes into side of styrofoam discs; push stems into holes to fill the gaps between the cakes with flowers. Lay more flowers on top of cake. Position flowers on the day of serving.

tips The drill bit should be suitable for drilling wood. Discuss the type of flowers to be used with a florist to make sure they'll stay fresh. Use artificial flowers, if you prefer.

Drill 1cm holes in all the discs and boards except for the 30cm wooden board. Use glue to secure the dowel into position.

Lightly brush the sides of the discs with sugar syrup. Cut strips of icing long and wide enough to wrap around sides of discs.

Use a sharp knife to cut away any excess icing from the top and bottom of each disc. Be careful not to cut into the disc.

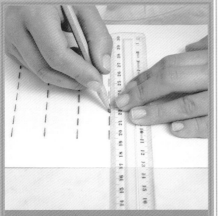

Measure around cake using a band of baking paper; using pencil and ruler, draw 'stitch' markings of varying lengths onto the paper.

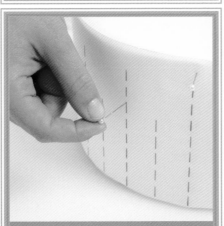

Secure the band of baking paper (marked-side outwards) around the cake with fine pins. Mark the pattern onto the cake with pins.

Remove baking paper. Fit piping bag with tube and, following the pin markings, pipe the pattern onto the cakes. Leave to dry.

Position the largest disc on the dowel; secure to board with royal icing. Spread more royal icing on top of the disc.

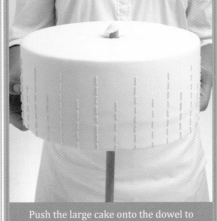

Push the large cake onto the dowel to meet the disc. Push the trimmed skewers into the cake to support the next disc.

Push a wooden skewer into the disc; wriggle it around to make holes large enough to hold the flower stems firmly in position.

DIVINE WHITE SILK
Rose Cake

THIS CAKE IS TOPPED WITH A FABULOUS SILK CABBAGE ROSE, IF YOU PREFER, BUY
FRESH ORGANIC FLOWERS TO DECORATE THE CAKE ON THE DAY OF SERVING.

EQUIPMENT
**30cm (12-inch) round wooden
    cake board (page 208)**
**15cm (6-inch) round wooden
    cake board (page 208)**
smoothing tools
**number 3 strip cutter 7mm
    (¼-inch) wide**
3 wooden skewers
2 paper piping bags (page 221)
white florist's tape
CAKE
**deep 20cm (8-inch) round cake
    of choice (page 190)**
**2 x deep 15cm (6-inch) round
    cakes of choice (page 190)**
jam or ganache of choice (page 210)
DECORATIONS
**1kg (2 pounds) ready-made
    white icing**
cornflour (cornstarch)
green food colouring
1 quantity royal icing (page 220)
1m (1 yard) wide ribbon
1m (1 yard) narrow ribbon
**white silk cabbage rose or
    fresh organic flowers**

1   Trim cakes (page 209). Secure large cake to largest board. Secure one 15cm cake to smaller board (page 209); top with remaining 15cm cake, joining with a little jam or ganache (page 212). Prepare cakes for covering with ready-made icing (pages 209).

2   Knead ready-made icing on surface dusted with a little cornflour until icing loses its stickiness.

3   Tint half the icing pale green; roll icing on cornfloured surface until large enough to cover 20cm cake. Using rolling pin, lift icing onto cake; smooth with hands then smoothing tools. Trim icing neatly around base.

4   Use white icing to cover 15cm cake in the same way. While icing is still soft, use strip cutter to mark grooves into the icing on the top tier. Dry cakes overnight.

5   Push trimmed skewers into centre of large cake to support the top tier. Secure small cake on top of large cake (page 212).

6   Tint half the royal icing green to match the bottom tier. Three-quarters fill a piping bag with icing; pipe around base of cake. Use fingertip to blend icing into any gaps where cake joins the board (page 212). Repeat process using white royal icing for top tier. Dry cakes overnight.

7   Wrap ribbons around base of bottom cake; cut to fit. Secure ends with a little white royal icing.

8   Trim silk flower to fit top of cake. Wrap stem in white florist's tape. Gently prise open flower petals; lay flower on top of cake.

tips The strip cutter, used for marking the icing on the top tier of this cake, is very useful if the icing is not quite perfect. It's important to mark the grooves on the icing before it begins to develop a crust and becomes firm. Position the flower on the day of serving.

Using the strip cutter, gently, but evenly, press it onto the soft icing before the icing begins to dry and develop a crust.

Measure around the base of the bottom tier; cut ribbons to fit. Position and secure ribbons to cake with tiny dabs of royal icing.

Trim the stem, leaves and buds of the silk rose to fit the cake; tape stems with florist's tape. Gently prise open the flower petals.

PEACHES & CREAM
Frilled Cake

PEACHES & CREAM
Frilled Cake

WHILE THIS FRILLY LITTLE CAKE IS IDEAL FOR A BABY SHOWER OR CHRISTENING, IT WOULD ALSO DELIGHT ANY BUDDING PRIMA BALLERINA IN THE FAMILY. USE SHADES OF PINK TO RESEMBLE A TUTU, AND TOP WITH A PAIR OF BALLET SLIPPERS.

EQUIPMENT
20cm (8-inch) square wooden cake board (page 208)
smoothing tools
15cm (6-inch) scalloped edge frill cutter
vinyl mat
frilling tool
medium artist's paint brush
CAKE
deep 15cm (6-inch) square cake of choice (page 190)
DECORATIONS
500g (1 pound) ready-made ivory icing
cornflour (cornstarch)
peach food colouring

1 Trim cake (page 209). Secure cake to board (page 209). Prepare cake for covering with ready-made icing (page 209).

2 Knead three-quarters of the ready-made icing on surface dusted with a little cornflour until icing loses its stickiness. Roll icing on cornfloured surface into 3mm (⅛-inch) thickness. Using rolling pin, lift icing over cake, smooth with hands then smoothing tools. Trim icing neatly around base. Dry cake overnight.

3 Divide remaining icing into 5 equal portions. Working with cornfloured hands, tint 4 portions with peach colouring so that each portion is a slightly darker shade than the last. Leave remaining portion ivory. Wrap portions, separately, in plastic wrap.

4 Roll out darkest shade of icing into 3mm thickness on surface dusted with cornflour. Using frill cutter, cut out 4 scalloped shapes; cover with vinyl mat.

5 Working with one shape at a time on a surface dusted with cornflour, frill the scalloped edge of the shape by rolling the frilling tool backwards and forwards over the edge of the shape. Repeat with remaining shapes.

6 Brush a tiny amount of water 2cm (¾ inch) up from the base of the cake. Position the straight edge of the frilled shape onto the damp area of the cake. (Brush only where the top of the frill is to sit, not the frill itself.) Continue this process around the cake, using one frilled shape for each side.

7 Repeat using remaining portions of icing, ending with the ivory-coloured frill, and overlapping frilled layers slightly, until the sides are completely covered with frills.

tips The frilled strips of icing should still be slightly soft when positioned on the cake. The icing strips will stretch a little to cover the sides of the cake. If you prefer to colour this cake a different colour, you will need to use white ready-made icing, not ivory coloured.

THE CHARM OF THIS DAINTY LITTLE CAKE IS IN THE DELICATE SHADES OF ITS COLOUR ALONG WITH ITS PEACHY FRILLS. THE FRILLS ARE QUITE EASY TO MAKE, HOWEVER, THEY ARE FRAGILE AND MUST BE HANDLED WITH CARE OTHERWISE THEY MAY STRETCH OR TEAR WHEN BEING POSITIONED AROUND THE CAKE.

Divide the icing into 5 equal portions. Using tiny amounts of colouring, tint 4 portions varying shades of peach; leave 1 portion ivory.

Roll out darkest shade of icing on a surface dusted with cornflour into a 3mm thickness, cut out 4 strips using scalloped frill cutter.

Cover 3 strips with vinyl mat. Using frilling tool, roll the tool backwards and forwards over the edge of the remaining strip.

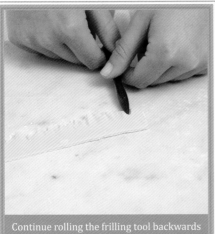

Continue rolling the frilling tool backwards and forwards over one edge of the icing strip until the frill covers the whole edge.

Brush water sparingly about 2cm up from the base of the cake. Only brush where the top of the frill is to sit, not the frill part itself.

Position frill on cake. Continue to make frills in the various shades; position each layer on the cake, with the frill showing beneath.

A POSY
of Daisies

A POSY
of Daisies

THIS CAKE IS SO PRETTY IT REMINDS US OF YOUTH AND SPRING. IT WOULD MAKE A DELIGHTFUL ENGAGEMENT OR 21ST BIRTHDAY CAKE.

EQUIPMENT
2.5cm (1-inch) flower cutter
1.5cm (¾-inch) flower cutter
vinyl mat
flower mat
small ball tool
metal skewer
10cm (4-inch) styrofoam ball
1cm x 20cm (½-inch x 8-inch) wooden dowel
craft glue
small styrofoam block
30cm (12-inch) round wooden cake board (page 208)
15cm (6-inch) round wooden cake board (page 208)
smoothing tools
3 wooden skewers
paper piping bag (page 221)
pastry brush

CAKE
deep 20cm (8-inch) round cake of choice (page 190)
deep 15cm (6-inch) round cake of choice (page 190)
1 quantity sugar syrup (page 217)

DECORATIONS
150g (4½ ounces) modelling paste
cornflour (cornstarch)
1m (1 yard) narrow white ribbon
1kg (2 pounds) ready-made white icing
lemon yellow food colouring
1 quantity royal icing (page 220)

1 Knead modelling paste on surface dusted with a little cornflour until paste loses its stickiness. Roll paste out on cornfloured surface into 1mm (¹/₃₂-inch) thickness. Using both cutters, cut out 5 flowers of each size at a time. Cover paste with vinyl mat to prevent it drying out.

2 Place 5 flowers on the flower mat; using the ball tool, press into the centre of each flower, in a circular motion, until the flower has thinned out and curled into a cup shape. Place the flowers on a fine wire rack or a baking-paper-lined tray to dry. Repeat process until all the paste is used.

3 Push the metal skewer halfway into the styrofoam ball and wriggle it around to create a hole large enough to push the dowel into. Place a little glue around one end of the dowel, push dowel into hole in the ball. Stand 1 hour to dry. Spread a little glue along the back of the ribbon. Starting at the top of the dowel, wrap ribbon around the dowel. Allow to dry; stand ball upright in the styrofoam block to support it.

4 Trim cakes (page 209). Secure large cake to largest board; secure small cake to remaining board (page 209). Prepare cakes for covering with ready-made icing (page 209).

5 Knead ready-made icing on surface dusted with a little cornflour until icing loses its stickiness. Tint icing pale yellow.

6 Roll 300g (9½ ounces) of the icing on cornfloured surface until large enough to cover small cake. Using rolling pin, lift icing onto cake; smooth with hands then smoothing tools. Trim icing neatly around base.

7 Using 500g (1 pound) of the icing, cover large cake in the same way. Dry cakes overnight.

8 Push trimmed skewers into centre of large cake to support the top tier (page 212). Secure small cake to large cake (page 212).

9 Tint royal icing yellow to match cakes. Three-quarters fill piping bag with royal icing; pipe around base of each cake. Use fingertip to blend icing into any gaps where cakes join the boards (page 212). Dry overnight.

10 Pipe yellow centres into each of the flowers with royal icing; stand 3 hours or overnight to dry.

11 Brush styrofoam ball lightly with sugar syrup. Roll out remaining yellow icing until large enough to cover the ball. Using rolling pin, lift icing onto ball; smooth with hands then smoothing tools. Trim icing neatly around base of the ball.

12 Push dowel through the centre of the top cake until it reaches the board below. Using small and large flowers, pipe a dot of royal icing onto the back of a flower, position on the ball. Continue positioning flowers to cover the ball. Leave assembled cake to dry overnight.

13 Using picture as a guide, use flowers to decorate both cakes.

tips Modelling paste is also sold as 'petal paste', 'flower moulding paste' and 'gum paste'.

THERE ARE NO SPECIAL PIPING SKILLS REQUIRED FOR THIS CAKE, BUT COVERING THE BALL CAN BE A LITTLE TRICKY. DRAPE THE ROLLED READY-MADE ICING OVER THE BALL – IT WILL HANG WITH LOOSE FOLDS. GENTLY, WITHOUT STRETCHING, EASE THE FOLDS OUT OF THE ICING AS YOU PRESS THE ICING ONTO AND AROUND THE BALL. TRIM OFF EXCESS ICING AT THE BASE OF THE BALL. THERE SHOULD BE NO CREASES IN THE ICING IF DONE CORRECTLY.

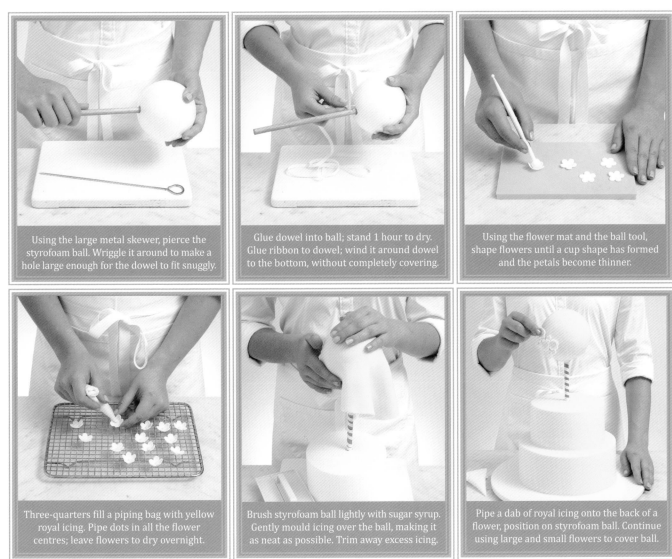

Using the large metal skewer, pierce the styrofoam ball. Wriggle it around to make a hole large enough for the dowel to fit snuggly.

Glue dowel into ball; stand 1 hour to dry. Glue ribbon to dowel; wind it around dowel to the bottom, without completely covering.

Using the flower mat and the ball tool, shape flowers until a cup shape has formed and the petals become thinner.

Three-quarters fill a piping bag with yellow royal icing. Pipe dots in all the flower centres; leave flowers to dry overnight.

Brush styrofoam ball lightly with sugar syrup. Gently mould icing over the ball, making it as neat as possible. Trim away excess icing.

Pipe a dab of royal icing onto the back of a flower, position on styrofoam ball. Continue using large and small flowers to cover ball.

Latte Lace CAKE

EQUIPMENT
40cm (16-inch) square wooden cake board (page 208)
25cm (10-inch) square wooden cake board (page 208)
20cm (8-inch) square wooden cake board (page 208)
15cm (6-inch) square wooden cake board (page 208)
10cm (4-inch) square wooden cake board (page 208)
smoothing tools
16 wooden skewers
3 paper piping bags (page 221)
lace patterns (page 228)

CAKE
2 x deep 30cm (12-inch) square cakes of choice (page 190)
deep 25cm (10-inch) square cake of choice (page 190)
deep 20cm (8-inch) square cake of choice (page 190)
shallow 20cm (8-inch) square cake of choice (page 190)
shallow 15cm (6-inch) square cake of choice (page 190)
deep 10cm (4-inch) square cake of choice (page 190)
shallow 10cm (4-inch) square cake of choice (page 190)
jam or ganache of choice (page 210)

DECORATIONS
3.5kg (7 pounds) ready-made ivory icing
cornflour (cornstarch)
brown food colouring
1 quantity royal icing (page 220)
300g (9½ ounces) white chocolate Melts
1.5m (1½ yards) wide ribbon

1   Trim cakes (page 209). Secure one 30cm cake to largest board (page 209); top with remaining 30cm cake, joining cakes with a little jam or ganache (page 212). Join the two 20cm cakes and the two 10cm cakes in the same way, securing cakes to same-sized boards (page 209). Secure 25cm and 15cm cakes to same-sized boards. Prepare cakes for covering with ready-made icing (page 209).

2   Knead 1kg (2 pounds) ready-made icing on surface dusted with a little cornflour until icing loses its stickiness. Tint light brown with colouring.

3   Knead one-third of the icing on cornfloured surface. Roll icing until large enough to cover the 15cm cake. Using rolling pin, lift icing onto cake; smooth with hands then smoothing tools. Trim icing neatly around base of cake. Use remaining icing and scraps to cover the 25cm cake.

4   Knead remaining ivory icing on surface dusted with cornflour; tint a darker shade of brown than the previous cakes. Use 350g (11 ounces) of the icing to cover the 10cm cake; use 700g (1½ pounds) to cover the 20cm cake; use the remaining icing, plus scraps, to cover the 30cm cake. Dry cakes overnight.

5   Push 4 trimmed skewers into centre of all cakes except the top cake to support the next tier (page 212).

6   Assemble cakes, securing each tier to the tier below (page 212).

7   Tint royal icing to match the two colours of the cakes. Three-quarters fill two piping bags with each of the coloured royal icings; pipe around base of each cake to match the icing. Use fingertip to blend icing into any gaps where cakes join the boards. Dry cakes overnight.

8   Trace lace patterns onto baking paper; turn paper over. Melt chocolate (page 222). Half-fill piping bag with chocolate, snip tip off bag. Carefully pipe pattern onto baking paper; stand until set.

9   Pipe small dots of chocolate onto backs of chocolate lace; carefully secure lace to cake. Wrap ribbon around base of large cake; secure with royal icing.

Carefully trace the lace patterns for the cakes onto sheets of baking paper; turn paper over so tracings are on the other side.

Half-fill a paper piping bag with melted chocolate; pipe chocolate over patterns, then stand about 5 minutes or until set.

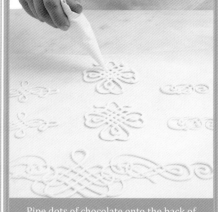

Pipe dots of chocolate onto the back of one piece of lace; position on cake. Repeat process to cover cake with lace pattern.

If you prefer, draw patterns of your own to suit the purpose of the cake. You will need to pipe extra chocolate lace in case of breakages. The chocolate will set quite quickly so, if you break any of the piped patterns, simply re-melt the chocolate and pipe the pattern again.

SOME OF THE CAKES IN THIS CHAPTER are easy until you get to the HAND-MADE FLOWERS – THESE NEED practise, skill and patience – YOU CAN USE SILK OR FRESH FLOWERS in their place. Think of READY-MADE ICING AND MODELLING paste as play dough and let YOUR IMAGINATION RUN LOOSE.

CHAPTER THREE

EXPERT

BOWTIE
Mini Cakes

EQUIPMENT
6.5cm (2¾-inch) round cutter
9 x 7cm (2¾-inch) round cardboard
   cake boards (page 208)
5cm (2-inch) round cutter
tape measure
plastic ruler
pizza cutter
vinyl mat
fine artist's paint brush
plaque plunger cutter
CAKE
2 x shallow 20cm (8-inch) square
   cakes of choice (page 190)
1 quantity ganache of choice
   (page 210)
1 quantity sugar syrup (page 217)
DECORATIONS
2kg (4 pounds) ready-made
   white icing
tylose powder
cornflour (cornstarch)
ivory, black and rose pink food
   colouring

1 Trim tops of cakes so they sit flat when upside-down (page 209). Turn cakes upside-down. Using 6.5cm cutter, cut nine rounds from each cake. Secure nine cakes to cardboards (page 209) with a little ganache (see tips). Spread tops of cakes with more ganache; top with remaining nine cakes. Spread cakes lightly, but evenly, all over with remaining ganache. Stand overnight at a cool room temperature.
2 Knead 400g (12½ ounces) of the ready-made icing with ½ teaspoon tylose on cornfloured surface until smooth. Roll icing on cornfloured surface into 3mm (⅛-inch) thickness. Using 6.5cm cutter, cut nine rounds from the icing. Reserve icing scraps. Place rounds on baking-paper-lined trays; stand 2 hours or until dry.

3 Colour 300g (9½ ounces) of the ready-made icing ivory with a little colouring. Knead icing with ½ teaspoon tylose on lightly cornfloured surface until smooth. Roll icing on cornfloured surface into 3mm thickness. Using 5cm cutter, cut nine rounds from icing. Place rounds on baking-paper-lined trays; stand 2 hours or until dry.
4 Brush cakes lightly all over with sugar syrup. Knead remaining white icing on cornfloured surface until icing loses its stickiness.
5 Measure and note height and circumference of cake. Roll icing into 3mm thickness on cornfloured surface until large enough to cover sides of all cakes; using ruler and pizza cutter, cut nine rectangles of required size to cover cakes, re-rolling icing as necessary. Cover eight rectangles with vinyl mat. Cover cake with icing rectangle, as pictured; trim end neatly, join ends with a little water. The icing should cover the edge of the cardboard. Repeat with remaining cakes and icing. Reserve icing scraps.
6 Brush the backs of the ivory rounds with a little water; position on top of the white rounds.
7 Combine reserved icing scraps with another 100g of icing; colour black. Knead in a pinch of tylose on cornfloured surface. Roll out about one-third of the icing on cornfloured surface into 3mm thickness. Using pizza cutter and plastic ruler; cut out nine 5mm x 5cm (¼-inch x 2-inch) strips of icing. Brush a little water on the backs of the strips, position on top and over sides of ivory rounds.

8 To make bows: Knead black icing scraps together on cornfloured surface; roll into 3mm thickness. Using pizza cutter and plastic ruler cut nine 5mm x 8cm (¼-inch x 3¼-inch) strips of icing; secure to centre of black strips on rounds with a little water. Brush a little water over centre of strip, bring each end in to meet in the middle to make loops of bows. Cover joins with small strips of black icing secured across the centre of the bow with a little water. Secure rounds to cakes.
9 Roll remaining white icing into 3mm thickness on cornfloured surface. Using plaque cutter, cut out nine plaques. Brush backs with a little water, secure on cakes.
10 Colour white icing scraps pink, roll out on cornfloured surface into 3mm thickness; cut out heart shapes (see tips).
11 Roll remaining black icing with scraps on cornfloured surface into 3mm thickness, cut out letters about 1cm (½-inch) high (see tips).
12 Position and secure letters and hearts to plaque with a little water.

makes 9
tips If necessary, cut the cake boards to the same size as the base of the cakes. The boards should be invisible after the ready-made icing is wrapped around the cakes. Make templates for your chosen letters and a small heart shape for the cakes, or buy small alphabet and heart-shaped cutters from cake decorating suppliers.

YOU'LL NEED A FAIRLY SOLID CAKE, SUCH AS A FRUIT OR MUD CAKE, TO SUPPORT THE WEIGHT OF THE ICING. IF USING FRUIT OR MUD CAKES, THEY CAN BE COMPLETED AT LEAST A MONTH AHEAD; STORE IN AN AIRTIGHT CONTAINER AT ROOM TEMPERATURE.

Using 6.5cm cutter, cut out 9 rounds from each cake. Join rounds with a little ganache. Secure cylinders to boards with ganache.

Knead ½ teaspoon tylose into white icing, roll out on lightly cornfloured surface. Cut out 9 x 6.5cm rounds from icing.

Spread cakes all over with ganache; stand overnight. Brush sugar syrup lightly over cakes, then cover with a length of icing.

Join ivory rounds to white rounds with a little water. Secure black icing ribbon to rounds. Brush centre of ribbon with water.

Cut a narrow strip of black icing, long enough to make both loops of bow. Join ends to centre of ribbon to make loops with a little water.

Cut a short strip of black icing just long enough to cover the joins of the bows. Secure into position with a little water.

WEDDING CAKE
Pops

WEDDING CAKE
Pops

EQUIPMENT
20cm x 30cm (8-inch x 12-inch) rectangular cake pan
20cm (8-inch) styrofoam block
2.5cm (1-inch) round cutter
3cm (1¼-inch) round cutter
3.5cm (1½-inch) round cutter
5cm (2-inch) round cutter
18 long thin toothpicks
18 x 30cm (12-inch) cake pop sticks
paper piping bag (page 221)
tweezers
metal skewer
ruler
CAKE
5 cups firmly packed butter cake crumbs
½ quantity butter cream (page 218)
DECORATIONS
3 x 375g (12-ounce) packets white chocolate Melts
golden yellow and black food colourings
1 quantity royal icing (page 220)
1 packet 2mm (¹⁄₁₆-inch) white sugar pearls
9 white sugar flowers
50g (1½ ounces) ready-made white icing
cornflour (cornstarch)
4m (4 yards) narrow ribbon

1 Grease and line a rectangular slice pan with baking paper. Combine cake crumbs and butter cream in medium bowl. Press mixture evenly into pan; cover, freeze 1 hour or refrigerate overnight until firm.

2 Stir two-thirds of the chocolate in medium heatproof bowl over medium saucepan of simmering water until smooth (don't let water touch base of bowl). Transfer to tall narrow heatproof glass or jug.

3 Meanwhile, use a sharp pointed knife to make 18 small holes, about 5cm (2 inches) apart, in styrofoam.

4 To make all cake pops: For the hats, use 3cm cutter to cut 18 rounds from the cake crumb mixture. For the wedding cakes, cut 9 x 2.5cm rounds, 9 x 3.5cm rounds and 9 x 5cm rounds.

5 To make wedding cake pops: Dip the end of a toothpick into melted white chocolate; push about halfway into the middle of a 2.5cm round. Repeat with remaining toothpicks and remaining 2.5cm and 3.5cm rounds. Freeze cakes about 5 minutes.

6 Dip the end of a cake pop stick into white chocolate; push stick all the way through 5cm round, extending about 4.5cm (1¾-inch) past the top of the cake. Repeat with remaining cake pop sticks and remaining 5cm rounds. Freeze cakes about 5 minutes.

7 Dip wedding cake rounds in melted chocolate to coat; rock back and forth, don't twist or cakes will break (re-melt chocolate as necessary). Stand upright in styrofoam, refrigerate until set.

8 To assemble wedding cakes; scrape away any excess visible chocolate from the toothpicks or cake pop sticks to prevent damaging any of the tiers. Remove 3.5cm rounds from toothpicks, carefully push onto cake pop sticks on top of the 5cm rounds. Repeat with 2.5cm rounds. Use a little re-melted white chocolate to join tiers together.

9 Use a tiny bit of yellow colouring to tint the royal icing the same colour as the chocolate on the wedding cakes (see tips). Half-fill paper piping bag with icing, use to fill any gaps between tiers of cakes; smooth with fingertip.

10 Pipe tiny dots around base of 2.5cm and 3.5cm tiers, about 5cm at a time; using tweezers, position pearls in wet icing. Repeat all the way around cakes. Secure flowers to cakes with a little royal icing.

11 To make top hats: Melt remaining chocolate; use black colouring to tint chocolate grey. Transfer chocolate to tall narrow heatproof glass or jug. Dip end of cake pop stick into chocolate; push stick through 2 x 3cm rounds about halfway into the top round. Join rounds with a little melted chocolate; freeze cakes about 5 minutes. Dip hats in melted grey chocolate to coat (re-melt chocolate, if necessary); stand upright in styrofoam, refrigerate until set.

12 To make brims for hats: re-melt grey chocolate as necessary, spread onto a sheet of baking paper about 2mm (¹⁄₁₆-inch) thick. Stand about 10 minutes or until almost set.

13 Use 5cm-round cutter to cut 9 rounds from chocolate. Use a metal skewer to pierce a hole through the centre of the rounds (heat skewer if the chocolate has become too hard); thread onto cake pop sticks. Secure with chocolate. Return cake pop sticks to styrofoam, refrigerate until set.

14 Knead ready-made icing on surface dusted with cornflour until icing loses its stickiness. Roll icing on surface dusted with cornflour until 2mm thick. Cut icing into 9 strips, measuring 1cm x 8cm (½-inch x 3¼-inches) (they should be long enough to wrap around the hat). Secure bands to hats with a little royal icing.

15 Tie small bows (page 226) around cake pop sticks.

tips Cut out cake rounds as close as possible. Squash and press remaining cake mixture together, freeze and cut out more shapes, if necessary. Because the royal icing is very white, and the white chocolate is a creamy colour, it is necessary to tint the icing with a tiny bit of yellow colouring to give it a creamy colour so it blends with the white chocolate. Re-melt chocolate as necessary (page 222).

STORE THE WEDDING CAKE POPS AT A COOL ROOM TEMPERATURE, STANDING UP IN STYROFOAM, COVERED, TO PROTECT THEM FROM DUST. OR, STORE THEM FLAT IN AIRTIGHT CONTAINERS. THE CAKE POPS ARE FIDDLY TO MAKE, BUT ARE WELL WORTH THE EFFORT. WE USED LITTLE SUGAR ROSES, BOUGHT FROM THE SUPERMARKET, TO DECORATE THE TOP OF THE WEDDING CAKES.

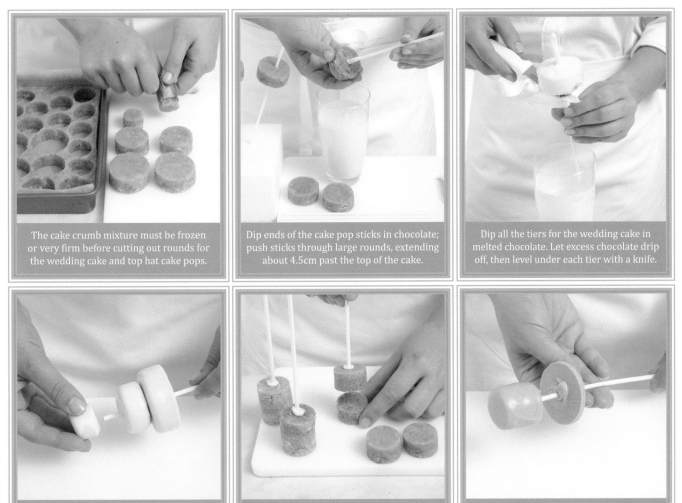

The cake crumb mixture must be frozen or very firm before cutting out rounds for the wedding cake and top hat cake pops.

Dip ends of the cake pop sticks in chocolate; push sticks through large rounds, extending about 4.5cm past the top of the cake.

Dip all the tiers for the wedding cake in melted chocolate. Let excess chocolate drip off, then level under each tier with a knife.

Push the medium and small tiers onto the extended cake pop stick; secure the tiers together with a little melted chocolate.

Push two of the cake rounds for the top hats onto a cake pop stick to form the hats. Join rounds with a little melted chocolate.

Push a round of chocolate onto cake pop stick to make the brim of the hat. Secure brim to hat with a little melted chocolate.

DUSKY ROSE *Cake*

EQUIPMENT
12 lengths 18-gauge floral wire
long-nosed pliers
flower glue (page 227)
styrofoam block
vinyl mat
3cm (1-inch), 4cm (1½-inch),
   5.5cm (2¾-inch) round cutters
flower mat
ball tool
fine artist's paint brush
small non-stick rolling pin
12-hole round-based, shallow
   (1 tablespoon/20ml) patty pan
stamens
1.5cm (¾-inch) 4-petal blossom
   cutter
florist's tape
45cm (18-inch) round wooden
   cake board (page 208)
18cm (6-inch) round wooden
   cake board (page 208)
smoothing tools
3 wooden skewers
paper piping bag (page 221)
CAKE
deep 22cm (9-inch) round cake
   of choice (page 190)
deep 18cm (7-inch) round cake
   of choice (page 190)
DECORATIONS
2 quantities modelling paste
   (page 227)
rose pink and purple food colouring
cornflour (cornstarch)
2kg (4 pounds) ready-made
   white icing
1 quantity royal icing (page 220)

1 To make roses: Cut two lengths of wire into 3 x 12cm (4¾-inch) lengths each. Make small hook at one end of each piece of wire using pliers.
2 Reserve 100g of modelling paste for blossoms. Colour one-third of the remaining paste dark pink, use to make 6 centres for 4 roses and 2 buds: Roll a marble-sized piece of paste into a rounded cone shape; dip hooked end of wire into flower glue, push halfway into broad end of cone. Push wire into styrofoam; dry overnight. Make 5 more centres in the same way.

3 When working with petals and blossoms, work with one at a time, and keep the remaining petals and blossoms covered with a vinyl mat.
4 Roll remaining dark pink paste on a cornfloured surface into 3mm (⅛-inch) thickness; using the 3cm cutter, cut out 3 petals, place on flower mat. Use ball tool to thin top of petal. Brush bottom third of petal lightly with flower glue; wrap around a bud. Secure and wrap remaining 2 petals around bud in the same way. Stand in styrofoam to dry overnight. Make 5 more buds in the same way. Reserve icing scraps.
5 Knead icing scraps into one-third of the remaining paste; use colouring to tint to a shade slightly lighter than the buds, if necessary. Roll paste on cornfloured surface until 3mm thick; cut out 3 x 4cm petals.
6 Use rolling pin to thin top half of petal; place petal on flower mat, use ball tool to curl edge of petal. Secure around rose bud with flower glue. Repeat with the remaining 2 petals, overlapping each petal; dry overnight. Make 5 more buds in the same way.
7 Knead icing scraps into remaining paste; use colouring to tint to a paler shade than previous layer of petals.
8 To make the rose: Roll and cut out 5 petals using the 5.5cm cutter. Use rolling pin to thin top half of petals; place petals on flower mat, use ball tool to curl edge. Place petals in cornfloured patty pan until edges of petals begin to firm. Glue in position around previous petals, overlapping each petal. Make 3 more roses the same way.
9 Make cup shapes from foil so the outside petals are supported by foil. Place rose in foil cup, poke wire through foil. Suspend a wire cake rack above bench so the rose wire can sit in rack unimpeded while the rose is drying.
10 To make blossoms: Cut 10 pieces of wire into 6 equal lengths each. Cut 30 of the stamens in half. Roll half the reserved paste into a 3mm thickness; using 1.5cm cutter, cut out 30 blossoms.

11 Place 5 blossoms on flower mat (keep remainder under vinal mat); shape petals with ball tool. Dab a dot of flower glue in centre of blossom; poke a stamen through the glue. Repeat with remaining blossoms. Roll out remaining paste and make a further 30 blossoms. Dry blossoms overnight.
12 Gather five blossoms together, position a piece of wire close to the bottom of the blossom, secure stamens to wire with florist's tape.
13 Trim cakes (page 209). Secure large cake to large board; secure small cake to small board. Prepare for covering with ready-made icing (page 209).
14 Tint white ready-made icing mauve with purple colouring. Knead icing on cornfloured surface until icing loses its stickiness. Roll one-quarter of the icing on cornfloured surface until large enough to cover small cake. Use rolling pin to lift icing onto cake; smooth with hands then smoothing tools. Trim icing neatly around base; reserve scraps.
15 Use half the remaining icing to cover large cake in the same way as the small cake; dry cakes overnight.
16 Push trimmed skewers into centre of large cake to support top tier (page 212). Secure small cake on top of large cake (page 212).
17 Tint royal icing mauve to match cakes. Three-quarters fill piping bag with icing; pipe around base of each cake. Use fingertip to blend icing into any gaps where cakes join the board (page 212). Dry cakes overnight.
18 Knead reserved mauve icing and icing scraps on cornfloured surface. Roll icing large enough to make a 15cm x 30cm rectangle. Gently fold icing into three pleats. Gather and pinch ends together and, using picture as a guide, position and secure draped icing to cake with a little water; stand overnight to dry.
19 Position roses and blossoms, by gently pushing wires into cake.

Cut 2 lengths of wire into 3 x 12cm lengths. Using pliers, bend each piece of wire into a loop at one end to make a small hook.

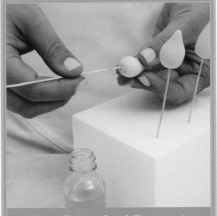

Roll a small piece of modelling paste into a cone shape. Dip hooked end of wire into flower glue, push into cone; dry overnight.

For each rose, cut out 3 x 3cm petals. Roll out the top half of each petal thinly, frill with a ball tool, then glue around the 'bud'.

Cut out 3 x 4cm petals for each rose, roll and frill the tops of each petal thinly. Position and secure on rose with flower glue.

Using the blossom cutter, cut 30 blossoms from modelling paste. Place 5 blossoms on flower mat; shape using the ball tool.

Dab a tiny dot of flower glue in the centre of a blossom; pull end of stamen through blossom to secure the tip on the glue.

Gather five of the blossoms together, secure the stamens to a piece of wire by firmly wrapping with a single layer of florist's tape.

Roll mauve icing on a cornfloured surface into a 15cm x 30cm (6-inch x 12-inch) rectangle; gently fold the icing into three large pleats.

Gently drape the icing over the cake. Gather the ends together and secure the ends of the icing to the cake with a little water.

TRADITIONAL
Wedding Cake

TRADITIONAL Wedding Cake

EQUIPMENT
**45cm (18-inch) round wooden
  cake board (page 208)**
**30cm (12-inch) round wooden
  cake board (page 208)**
**25cm (10-inch) round wooden
  cake board (page 208)**
**20cm (8-inch) round wooden
  cake board (page 208)**
**15cm (6-inch) round wooden
  cake board (page 208)**
smoothing tools
quilting tool
tape measure
embossed rolling pin
plastic ruler
pizza cutter
small non-stick rolling pin
12 wooden skewers
paper piping bag (page 221)
small piping bag
small (number 2) plain piping tube
tweezers
craft glue
CAKE
**deep 35cm (14-inch) round cake
  of choice (page 190)**
**deep 30cm (12-inch) round cake
  of choice (page 190)**
**deep 25cm (10-inch) round cake
  of choice (page 190)**
**deep 20cm (8-inch) round cake
  of choice (page 190)**
**deep 15cm (6-inch) round cake
  of choice (page 190)**
DECORATIONS
**4.3kg (9½ pounds) ready-made
  white icing**
cornflour (cornstarch)
2 quantities royal icing (page 220)
**2 tablespoons pearlized blush
  sugar pearls**
1m (1 yard) narrow ribbon

1 Trim cakes (page 209). Secure 35cm cake to largest board; secure remaining cakes to the same-sized boards (page 209). Prepare cakes for covering with ready-made icing (page 209).

2 Knead ready-made icing on surface dusted with a little cornflour until icing loses its stickiness.

3 Roll 1.2kg (2½ pounds) of icing on cornfloured surface until large enough to cover the 35cm cake. Using rolling pin, lift icing onto cake; smooth with hands then smoothing tools. Trim icing neatly around base. Use quilting tool to mark pattern on side of cake.

4 Use 600g (1¼ pounds) of icing to cover the 25cm cake in the same way. Use quilting tool to mark pattern on cake, the same way as the 35cm cake.

5 Use 800g (1½ pounds) of icing to cover the 30cm cake; 500g (1 pound) of icing to cover the 20cm cake; and 300g (9½ ounces) of icing to cover the 15cm cake in the same way. Dry cakes overnight.

6 Use the tape measure to measure the circumference of the 30cm cake. Roll 500g of the remaining icing into a strip about 8cm (3¼ inches) wide, 5cm (2 inches) thick, and long enough to wrap around the cake. Use the embossed rolling pin to mark a pattern onto the strip of icing. Use the ruler and the pizza cutter to cut a straight edge down one long side of the strip.

7 Lightly blot dried icing around the side of the 30cm cake with damp kitchen paper to hold the strip of icing in place. Carefully roll the icing strip, embossed-side in, around the small rolling pin. Position the rolling pin so that the straight edge of the icing is flush with the bottom and side of the cake. Unroll icing onto side of cake.

8 Use a sharp knife to trim the excess icing flush with the top edge of the cake. Use fingertip to gently blend the soft icing edge with the firm icing on the top of the cake. Leave to dry 3 hours or overnight.

9 Use remaining 375g (12 ounces) of icing to make embossed strip to cover side of the 20cm cake in the same way.

10 Push 3 trimmed skewers into the centres of all the cakes except the smallest cake to support the next tier (page 212). Assemble cakes, securing each tier to the tier below (page 212). Half-fill paper piping bag with royal icing; pipe around base of each cake. Use fingertip to blend icing into any gaps where cakes join the boards. Dry cakes overnight.

11 Fit piping bag with piping tube. Half-fill bag with royal icing. Pipe dots onto six joins at time on the quilting pattern; use tweezers to position pearls on dots. Continue this way on the 35cm and 25cm quilted cakes.

12 Pipe over some of the embossed pattern on the 20cm and 30cm cakes. Leave all cakes to dry overnight.

13 Wrap and secure ribbon to top cake tier with a little royal icing. Use ribbon to make bow (page 226); secure bow to ribbon with a little craft glue.

tips Keep in a cool dark dust-free place. This cake is extremely heavy to lift and move, especially if the cakes are fruit cakes. You will need two people to lift the cake. The 'pearlized blush sugar pearls' are small edible pearls, and are available from cake decorating suppliers.

HERE WE HAVE A BEAUTIFUL TRADITIONAL FIVE-TIER WEDDING CAKE.
THE PIPING TECHNIQUES USED FOR THIS CAKE ARE RELATIVELY SIMPLE, BUT
THE PIPING NEEDS TO BE REALLY GOOD FOR THE CAKE TO LOOK WONDERFUL.

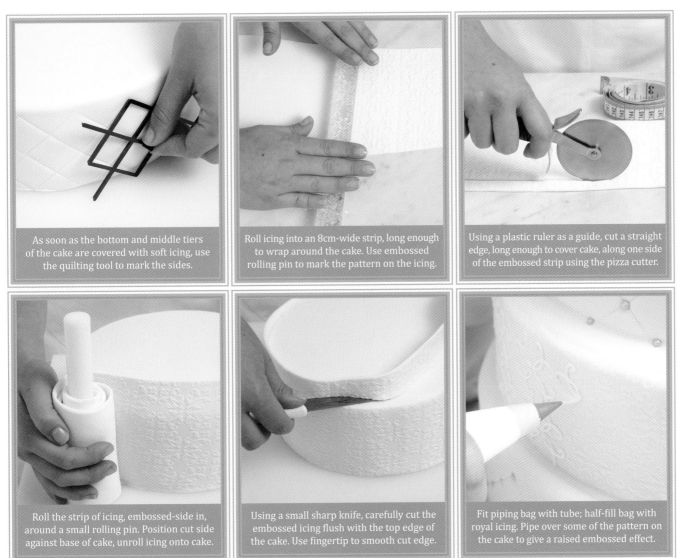

As soon as the bottom and middle tiers of the cake are covered with soft icing, use the quilting tool to mark the sides.

Roll icing into an 8cm-wide strip, long enough to wrap around the cake. Use embossed rolling pin to mark the pattern on the icing.

Using a plastic ruler as a guide, cut a straight edge, long enough to cover cake, along one side of the embossed strip using the pizza cutter.

Roll the strip of icing, embossed-side in, around a small rolling pin. Position cut side against base of cake, unroll icing onto cake.

Using a small sharp knife, carefully cut the embossed icing flush with the top edge of the cake. Use fingertip to smooth cut edge.

Fit piping bag with tube; half-fill bag with royal icing. Pipe over some of the pattern on the cake to give a raised embossed effect.

The croquembouche can be completed up to 12 hours ahead and kept in a refrigerated cool room (most catering venues have these). Don't make the croquembouche in humid weather as the humidity will affect the spun sugar, the toffee, and the crispness of the puffs. We used a huge mould for this impressive croquembouche, but there are smaller moulds available to buy or hire.

CROQUEMBOUCHE

CROQUEMBOUCHE

EQUIPMENT
**60cm (24-inch) deep
croquembouche mould
(diameter 32cm/12¾ inches)
large piping bag
5mm (¼-inch) plain piping tube
candy or digital thermometer
35cm (16-inch) round wooden
cake board (page 208)
masking tape
2 wooden spoons
modified wire whisk (see page 155)**
PROFITEROLES (1 QUANTITY)
**½ cup (125ml) water
60g (2 ounces) butter
1 tablespoon caster (superfine)
sugar
½ cup (75g) baker's flour
3 eggs**
CRÈME PÂTISSIÈRE (1 QUANTITY)
**1 cup (250ml) milk
⅓ cup (75g) caster (superfine) sugar
1 teaspoon vanilla extract
2 tablespoons cornflour
(cornstarch)
3 egg yolks**
TOFFEE (1 QUANTITY)
**2 cups (440g) white (granulated)
sugar
1 cup (250ml) water**
DECORATIONS
fresh organic or sugar flowers

1 Make profiteroles and crème pâtissière.
2 Grease and line croquembouche mould with strips of baking paper as neatly as possible.
3 Fit piping bag with tube, spoon crème pâtissière into bag; pipe into profiteroles.
4 Make one batch of toffee. Use a fork to hold filled profiteroles, dip quickly into hot toffee; place into mould (do not leave any large gaps between profiteroles). Repeat to completely fill mould with profiteroles; stand about 1 hour or until set.
5 Gently turn croquembouche onto board. Make another batch of toffee. Drizzle toffee as evenly as possible over croquembouche.

6 Using masking tape, secure two wooden spoons about 60cm (2 feet) apart on bench, placing spoons so that the handles overhang the edge of the bench. Place newspaper on floor under handles to catch any toffee drips. Make another batch of toffee; cool for about 3 minutes or until toffee is slightly thickened. Dip ends of modified whisk into hot toffee and wave the whisk back and forth over the spoon handles to make spun toffee threads.
7 Carefully lift spun toffee onto croquembouche; position flowers.

profiteroles Preheat oven to 200°C/400°F. Grease and line oven trays. Combine the water, finely chopped butter and caster sugar in medium saucepan; bring to the boil. Add flour, beat with a wooden spoon over heat until mixture comes away from base and side of pan and forms a smooth ball. Transfer mixture to medium bowl; continue beating with wooden spoon until mixture cools slightly. Beat in two of the eggs, one at a time. Lightly beat the third egg in a cup, gradually beat in egg, a bit at a time, until the mixture becomes glossy and gently folds over when the wooden spoon is lifted out of the mixture (you may not need to use all the egg). Drop level tablespoons of mixture onto trays about 5cm (2 inches) apart. Bake 10 minutes. Reduce oven temperature to 180°C/350°F; bake a further 15 minutes. Cut a small opening in the base of each profiterole; bake a further 10 minutes or until profiteroles are dry and crisp. Cool on trays. You need to make 20 quantities of the profiterole recipe to fill this sized croquembouche mould.

crème pâtissière Combine milk, sugar and extract in small saucepan; bring to the boil. Meanwhile, whisk cornflour with egg yolks in medium heatproof bowl; gradually whisk in hot milk mixture. Return mixture to pan; stir over medium-high heat until mixture boils and thickens. Cover surface of mixture with plastic wrap; refrigerate 2 hours. You will need to make 20 quantities to fill the profiteroles.

toffee Combine sugar and the water in large saucepan; stir over high heat without boiling until sugar dissolves. Bring to the boil; boil, without stirring, until toffee reaches a temperature of 150°C/300°F on a candy or digital thermometer, or becomes a light golden brown in colour. Remove from heat, allow bubbles to subside before using. You need about 5 quantities of toffee for the croquembouche; make each batch as you need it.

tips Have a bowl of cold tap water on the bench in case of any accidental burns when dipping the puffs. If burned, immediately plunge fingers into the water. The profiteroles can be made well in advance. You need about 400 to fill the mould we used – make sure they've completely dried out in the oven then cooled before storing. Unfilled profiteroles can be stored in an airtight container for up to 4 weeks, or can be frozen for up to 3 months. It's best to make the toffee, one batch at a time, as you need it. Digital thermometers are easier to read and quicker to use than candy thermometers (see page 219).

Line well-greased croquembouche mould as neatly as possible with long strips of baking paper. Cut the paper to fit the mould.

Fit the piping bag with the tube then half fill the bag with crème pâtissèrie. Fill the profiteroles through the hole in the bottom.

Using a fork to hold each profiterole, carefully and quickly dip profiterole into the toffee, hold until toffee drips subside.

Place profiterole into mould immediately after dipping it; pack profiteroles as evenly as possible without squashing them.

Turn croquembouche onto board, remove mould and paper. Drizzle more toffee as evenly as possible over croquembouche.

Modifying a wire whisk will make it easier to make the spun toffee: just snip off the rounded ends of the wire using wire cutters.

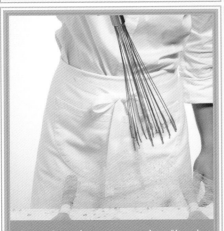

Secure 2 wooden spoons on edge of bench. Dip ends of whisk into toffee, wave whisk over spoon handles to make spun toffee.

Carefully gather spun toffee and gently wrap around the croquembouche. Make as much toffee as is needed to wrap around the tower.

Position flowers on spun toffee. If using sugar flowers, position them with a little of the warmed toffee leftover from coating the puffs.

YELLOW PEONY
Rose Cake

While making the cake is easy – making the peony rose is not; it is an advanced technique. Once the petals are made, it's a matter of carefully assembling them. It would be wise to buy all the bits and pieces listed, to make the challenge easier.

YELLOW PEONY
Rose Cake

EQUIPMENT

12cm (4¾-inch) length 18-gauge floral wire

long-nosed pliers

white florist's tape

pasta machine (see tips)

vinyl mat

small, medium, large and extra large peony cutters

wire cutters

7 lengths x 26-gauge floral wire

flower glue (page 227)

2 x 12-hole round-based, shallow (1 tablespoon/20ml) patty pans

peony petal veiner

flower mat

ball tool

fine artist's paint brush

35cm (14-inch) square wooden cake board (page 208)

20cm (8-inch) square wooden cake board (page 208)

15cm (6-inch) square wooden cake board (page 208)

smoothing tools

8 wooden skewers

3 paper piping bags (page 221)

craft glue

CAKE

deep 25cm (10-inch) square cake of choice (page 190)

deep 20cm (8-inch) square cake of choice (page 190)

deep 15cm (6-inch) square cake of choice (page 190)

DECORATIONS

1 bundle small white stamens

100g (3 ounces) modelling paste

ivory and lemon yellow food colouring

cornflour (cornstarch)

yellow petal dust

2kg (4 pounds) ready-made white icing

1 quantity royal icing (page 220)

4m (4 yards) wide ribbon

1 To make peony: Make a small hook in one end of the 18-gauge wire using pliers, don't fully close it. Fold the bunch of stamens in half, pull the centre of the stamens into the hook; close the hook by twisting the wire together with pliers. Secure stamens to wire with florist's tape.

2 Tint modelling paste ivory. Knead paste on surface dusted with a little cornflour until smooth. Roll paste on cornfloured surface until thin enough to be rolled through a pasta machine set on the thickest setting (see tips). Cover paste with vinyl mat.

3 Using petal cutters, cut 3 small, 5 medium, 5 large and 7 extra large petals from paste; cover with vinyl mat.

4 Using wire cutters, cut each piece of 26-gauge wire into 3 even lengths. Work with one petal at a time, keeping remaining petals covered with vinyl mat. Thread one petal onto one piece of wire by dipping one end of wire into flower glue and gently pushing wire into pointed end of petal, one-third of the way into petal.

5 Dust patty pans lightly with cornflour. Dust petal veiner with cornflour; press wired petal in petal veiner. Place petal onto flower mat; frill edge of petal by gently rolling ball tool over edge of petal. Place petal into patty pan to dry overnight. Repeat with remaining petals.

6 To colour petals, combine a pinch of petal dust with a pinch of cornflour. Using paint brush, brush dust into centres of petals and stamens.

7 To assemble peony: Gently bend wire on a small petal to a 45 degree angle, hold against base of prepared flower centre (with stamens), secure by wrapping florist's tape once around wires. Repeat with remaining small petals, spacing evenly around centre of peony.

8 Continue wiring the petals in the same way using medium, then large, then extra large petals; placing each layer of petals evenly around flower centre slightly below the previous layer of petals.

9 Trim cakes (page 209). Secure 25cm cake to largest board; secure remaining cakes to same-sized boards (page 209). Prepare cakes for covering with ready-made icing (page 209).

10 Knead ready-made icing on cornfloured surface until icing loses its stickiness. Tint 500g (1 pound) icing very pale yellow, 700g (1½ pounds) a slightly darker yellow shade, and the remaining icing a darker shade again. Enclose, separately, in plastic wrap.

11 Roll pale yellow icing on surface dusted with cornflour until large enough to cover small cake. Using rolling pin, lift icing onto cake; smooth with hands then smoothing tools. Trim icing neatly around base of cake.

12 Knead pale yellow icing scraps into medium-yellow icing; use to cover medium cake in the same way as small cake. Knead icing scraps into darkest yellow icing and use to cover the large cake in the same way. Dry cakes overnight.

13 Push 4 trimmed skewers into centres of large and medium cakes to support the next tier (page 212).

14 Assemble cakes, securing each tier to the tier below (page 212).

15 Divide royal icing into 3 bowls; tint each to match colour of the cakes. Half-fill piping bags to match cakes; pipe around bases of same-coloured cakes. Use fingertip to blend icing into any gaps where cakes join the boards (page 212). Dry overnight.

16 Trim ribbon to fit around bases of all tiers. Secure ends neatly with glue.

17 Gently push stem of peony into top of cake just before serving.

tips The petals can be made by rolling the icing out thinly to 2mm (¹⁄₁₆-inch), rather than rolling through the pasta machine, however, the machine gives great results. The flower can be made months ahead; keep it in an airtight container at a cool room temperature.

Using pliers, make a small hook on the end of the piece of 18-gauge wire. It should be barely large enough to hold the bunch of stamens.

Fold the stamens in half and pull the centre of the stamens into the hook. Twist wire with pliers to hold the stamens securely in place.

Firmly wrap the florist's tape around the stamens to secure them to the wire. Only wrap the base of the stamens to the wire.

Roll the modelling paste through the pasta machine. Cut out 3 small, 5 medium, 5 large and 7 extra large petals from the paste.

Using a piece of 26-gauge wire, dip end of the wire into flower glue, push wire a third of the way into the pointy end of the petal.

Dust the petal-veiner with cornflour; working with one petal at a time, press the wired petal in petal-veiner to create veins in icing.

Place petal on the flower mat, frill the edge of the petal using the ball tool. Place petal in cornfloured patty pan to dry overnight.

Use equal amounts of combined petal dust and cornflour, and brush lightly onto petals, graduating the colour from dark to light.

Bend wire on a small petal to 45 degrees, tape onto wire holding the stamens. Wire all petals in the same way, from small to extra large.

SILHOUETTE
Spectacular

SILHOUETTE
Spectacular

BLACK AND WHITE MAY BE CONSIDERED NEUTRAL COLOURS, BUT THEY BRING A BOLD LOOK TO THIS CAKE. THE COLOURS COMPLEMENT EACH OTHER, GIVING THIS CAKE CLEAN CLASSIC LINES THAT HAVE PLENTY OF 'WOW' FACTOR.

EQUIPMENT
30cm (12-inch) round wooden
    cake board (page 208)
pastry brush
1 quantity sugar syrup (page 217)
smoothing tools
stencil
medium offset metal spatula
6 wooden skewers
2 x 18cm (7-inch) round wooden
    cake boards (page 208)
fine pearl-headed pins
straight-sided metal scraper
paper piping bag (page 221)
small shallow bowls
3 lengths 18-gauge floral wire
wire cutters
CAKE
2 x deep 18cm (7-inch) round
    cakes of choice (page 190)
1 shallow 18cm (7-inch) round
    cake of choice (page 190)
jam or ganache of choice (page 210)
DECORATIONS
2.5kg (5 pounds) ready-made
    white icing
cornflour (cornstarch)
1 quantity royal icing (page 220)
black food colouring
tylose powder
1m (1 yard) narrow ribbon

1 Knead 500g (1 pound) ready-made icing on surface dusted with a little cornflour until icing loses its stickiness. Brush the large wooden board with sugar syrup. Roll icing large enough to cover board. Using rolling pin, lift icing onto board; smooth with hands then smoothing tools. Trim icing neatly around base of board (page 208); then smooth edge with cornfloured fingertip. Stand overnight to dry.

2 Reserve half the royal icing; cover surface to keep airtight. Use a damp paper towel to dampen the icing on board (this helps hold the stencil in position). Hold stencil against icing on board, use spatula to spread royal icing over entire stencil, scrape away excess, return to bowl; gently remove stencil. Wash and dry stencil before reusing. Repeat until board is stencilled all over. Stand 1 hour or until dry. Cover surface of leftover royal icing in bowl.

3 Trim cakes (page 209). Secure one deep cake to stencilled board (page 209); push 3 trimmed skewers into centre of cake (page 212).

4 Secure remaining cakes to smaller boards; push 3 trimmed skewers into centre of deep cake and secure to top of cake on stencilled board. Secure the shallow cake on top of the cake stack. Prepare cake for covering with ready-made icing (page 209).

5 Knead 1.5kg (3 pounds) ready-made icing on surface dusted with a little cornflour until icing loses its stickiness. Roll icing on cornfloured surface until large enough to cover cake. Using rolling pin, lift icing onto cake; smooth with hands then smoothing tools. Trim icing neatly around base of cake. Dry overnight.

6 Secure stencil around lower third of cake with pins. Use spatula to spread royal icing over stencil, remove excess icing with scraper; return to bowl. Gently remove pins and stencil; wash and dry stencil before using again. Repeat until stencil is completed around the lower third of the cake. Stand about 1 hour to dry.

7 Half-fill piping bag with royal icing; pipe around base of cake. Use fingertip to blend icing into any gaps where cake joins the board (page 212). Dry cake overnight.

8 Tint any leftover royal icing black; cover surface to keep airtight.

9 Lightly dust shallow bowls with cornflour.

10 Knead remaining ready-made icing with a pinch of tylose on cornfloured surface until icing loses its stickiness. Roll icing on cornfloured surface into 2mm ($^1/_{16}$-inch) thickness. Roll icing into a rectangle about 25cm x 35cm (10-inch x 14-inch). Use damp paper towel to dampen the icing to help hold the stencil in position. Place stencil over icing, spread evenly with black royal icing, scrape away excess icing, return to bowl; gently remove stencil. Wash and dry stencil before reusing to stencil over another area.

11 Use a sharp pointed knife to cut icing into 6 random-sized elliptical shapes before the royal icing dries. Drape shapes in shallow bowls; stand overnight to dry.

12 Cut wire into 18cm (7¼-inch) lengths, then bend in half. Secure wire to backs of shapes with royal icing. Place on baking-paper-lined tray to dry overnight.

13 Push wired shapes into top of cake on day of serving (keep in an airtight container until ready to use). Wrap ribbon around base of cake; secure ends with a dab of royal icing.

AS WITH THE 'POSY OF DAISIES' CAKE (PAGE 130), THIS CAKE CAN BE A LITTLE TRICKY TO COVER. DRAPE THE ROLLED READY-MADE ICING OVER THE CAKE – IT WILL HANG WITH LOOSE FOLDS. GENTLY, WITHOUT STRETCHING, EASE THE FOLDS OUT OF THE ICING AS YOU PRESS THE ICING AROUND THE CAKE. TRIM OFF EXCESS ICING AT THE BASE OF THE CAKE. THERE SHOULD BE NO PLEATS OR CREASES IN THE ICING IF DONE CORRECTLY. IF YOU USE THE SAME RECIPE FOR ALL THREE CAKES, YOU CAN SIMPLY JOIN THE CAKES WITH JAM OR GANACHE, AND NOT USE THE CAKE BOARDS BETWEEN THE LAYERS. HOWEVER, IF YOU WANT TO USE DIFFERENT CAKES FOR THE LAYERS – USE THE CAKE BOARDS UNDER EACH CAKE TO MAKE SERVING THE CAKES EASIER.

Use spatula to spread royal icing over the ready-made icing on board; remove stencil. Repeat until board is stencilled all over.

Roll out a strip of ready-made icing; dampen with a paper towel to hold the stencil in place. Spread stencil evenly with black royal icing.

Carefully remove the stencil from icing. Wash and dry the stencil before using again. Stencil all over the rectangle of icing.

Using a sharp pointed knife, cut out 6 random-sized elliptical shapes. Do this quickly and evenly before the royal icing sets.

Drape the shapes in and over the sides of the lightly cornfloured shallow bowls (stencilled-side up). Stand the shapes overnight to dry.

Bend the wire in half and secure to the backs of the dried shapes with royal icing. When dry, position the shapes in the top of the cake.

GIFT BOX
for Baby

GIFT BOX
for Baby

ALTHOUGH THIS CAKE IS A LABOUR OF LOVE, IT'S WORTH EVERY BIT OF EFFORT.

EQUIPMENT
35cm (14-inch) square wooden
   cake board (page 208)
smoothing tools
pasta machine (see tips)
1.4cm (¾-inch) and 4.5cm
   (1¾-inch) perspex measures
vinyl mat
fine artist's paint brush
stitching tool
alphabet cutters
paper piping bag (page 221)
CAKE
2 x deep 20cm (8-inch) square
   cakes of choice (page 190)
jam or ganache of choice (page 210)
DECORATIONS
2kg (4 pounds) ready-made
   white icing
cornflour (cornstarch)
kelly green food colouring
1 quantity royal icing (page 220)
tylose powde*r*

1 Trim cakes (page 209). Secure one cake to wooden board (page 209); top with remaining cake, joining cakes with a little jam or ganache (page 212). Prepare cake for covering with ready-made icing (page 209).
2 Knead ready-made icing on surface dusted with a little cornflour until icing loses its stickiness. Tint three-quarters of the icing pale green.
3 Roll 1kg (2 pounds) of the green icing on cornfloured surface until large enough to cover cake. Using rolling pin, lift icing onto cake; smooth with hands then smoothing tools. Trim icing neatly around base of cake. Dry cake overnight. Knead green icing scraps into remaining green icing.

4 Using apricot-sized pieces of both the green and white icing, roll out each icing, separately, into a rectangle the width of the pasta machine. Feed pieces through the pasta machine set on the thickest setting (see tips).
5 Using the 1.4cm perspex measure as a guide, cut 15cm (6-inch) lengths of green and white icing, each 1.4cm wide. You need 7 strips of each coloured icing for each side of the cake. Cover icing strips with vinyl mat to prevent drying out. Roll any icing scraps into same-coloured icing; cover, separately, with plastic wrap.
6 Brush a little water onto the sides of the cake, secure icing strips to all sides of the cake, alternating colours.
7 Before the icing strips dry, Use 1.4cm perspex measure to mark sides of cake for lid. Dry cake overnight.
8 To make the lid: Brush a little water onto the area where the box lid will sit. Roll out remaining white icing on cornfloured surface until large enough to cover top of cake and extend over the sides to cover marked area for lid. Using rolling pin, lift icing onto cake; smooth with hands then smoothing tools. Use 1.4cm measure to mark the sides of the lid. Cut off excess icing with a sharp knife. Reserve icing scraps. Use stitching tool to mark pattern around bottom edge of lid. Dry cake overnight.
9 To make the plaque: Roll scraps of white icing on surface dusted with cornflour into 6cm x 16cm (2½-inch x 6½-inch) rectangle. Use stitching tool to mark edges. Roll half the remaining green icing into a 3mm (⅛-inch)

thickness; use alphabet cutters to cut out letters. Outline letters with stitching tool. Half-fill piping bag with royal icing; secure letters to plaque with icing. Leave to dry overnight.
10 To make bow: Knead ¼ teaspoon tylose into remaining green icing. Roll out half the icing on surface dusted with cornflour into 3mm (⅛-inch) thickness. Using 4.5cm perspex measure, cut 5 strips of icing 4.5cm wide and 20cm long (1¾-inches x 8-inches). Run stitching tool along both edges of all strips. Fold strips in half to make loops, secure ends with a little water. Cut end into "V" shapes, turn loops on their side on a baking-paper-lined tray to dry overnight.
11 Roll out remaining green icing, cut 4 strips of icing 4.5cm x 20cm long (1¾-inches x 8-inches). Run the stitching tool along both edges of all strips. Using picture as a guide, secure the icing strips to four sides of the cake with a little water. Roll scraps of icing long enough to make 2 tails for the bows; cut "V" shapes into ends, secure to top of cake with a little royal icing. Position dried loops on cake to finish the bow; secure with royal icing.

tips The strips of icing can be made by rolling the icing out thinly to 2mm, however, rolling the icing through a pasta machine results in the icing being an even thickness all over. To make this cake look really good, it has to look very square. Measure all the strips precisely.

Set pasta machine to thickest setting. Roll a piece of icing into a rectangle the same width as the machine, feed through the machine.

Cut strips of green and white icing long enough to cover each side of the cake. Secure alternate coloured strips to cake with water.

Use a perspex measure to mark icing around the sides of the box where the lid will sit. Brush a little water over this area of the box.

Roll icing out until it covers the top and sides of the cake. Use ruler to mark the sides of the lid. Cut off excess icing with a sharp knife.

Make the plaque from scraps of white icing. Cut out letters from green icing. Use the stitching tool to mark the plaque and letters.

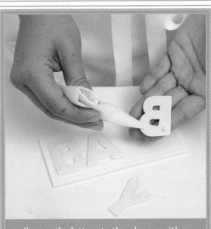

Secure the letters to the plaque with a little royal icing. Stand the plaque on a baking-paper-lined tray to dry overnight.

Mark strips for bow with the stitching tool. Join ends of strips with water, trim ends into a "V" shape. Turn loops on sides to dry.

Roll strips of icing for the ribbon and tails for the bow, mark with stitching tool; position and secure to the cake with a little water.

Half-fill a paper piping bag with royal icing. Pipe dots of icing onto the ribbon to secure the loops of the bow on the cake.

BRIDAL
Mosaic Squares

TO ACHIEVE THEIR CRISP, CLEAN LOOK, THE ICING SQUARES MUST BE PERFECTLY SQUARE AND THE PIPING NEAT AND TIDY. PRACTISE PIPING ON A FLAT SURFACE TO LEARN HOW TO CONTROL THE PRESSURE ON THE PIPING BAG FOR GOOD RESULTS.

EQUIPMENT
patchwork cutter trellis
star template (page 229)
fine pearl-headed pin
small piping bag
small (number 2) plain piping tube
paper piping bag (page 221)
small metal spatula
28cm (11-inch) square wooden cake board (page 208)
CAKE
deep 25cm (10-inch) square cake of choice (page 190)
DECORATIONS
350g (11 ounces) ready-made ivory icing
cornflour (cornstarch)
1 quantity royal icing (page 220)
1 packet small pearlized blush sugar pearls
1 tablespoon strained lemon juice
1 quantity white chocolate ganache (page 210)

1   Knead ready-made icing on surface dusted with a little cornflour until icing loses its stickiness; roll out on surface dusted with cornflour into 3mm (⅛-inch) thickness. Cut 9 x 7.5cm (3-inch) squares from icing. Use the patchwork cutter to mark pattern on icing while icing is still soft. Place squares on baking-paper-lined tray to dry overnight.
2   Cut around star template, place on top of dried icing square. Scratch outline into icing with a fine pin.
3   Fit piping bag with tube, half-fill bag with royal icing. Using picture as a guide, pipe patterns onto icing squares; pipe over patchwork outline. Position pearls, if using, on royal icing before it dries. Stand overnight to dry.
4   For star shape, add a drop or two of lemon juice to the remaining royal icing – icing should be the consistency of pouring cream. Spoon icing into paper piping bag; snip tip from bag. Pipe the icing inside the star points to "flood" the star. Flood icing into

any other shape as required. Stand overnight to set.
5   Trim cake top so it sits flat when turned upside down. Turn cake upside down, cut into 9 x 7.5cm squares.
6   Spread cakes evenly all over with ganache; freeze 10 minutes. Smooth ganache with a hot dry metal spatula.
7   Position cakes on board, top cakes with icing squares.

tips The icing squares can be made months ahead. Store them in a single layer (to protect the delicate piping) in airtight containers. Trim and cut the cakes a day ahead. Cover the cakes evenly with ganache to keep them as fresh as possible. Store them at a cool room temperature. The patchwork cutter is also known as a 'quilting embosser'. The 'pearlized blush sugar pearls' are small edible pearls, and are available from cake decorating suppliers.

Hold the piping bag at a 45 degree angle. Squeeze the bag firmly with an even pressure. Pipe a tiny dot of icing at the starting point.

Continue to keep a firm pressure on the piping bag, lift the line of icing about 5mm (¼-inch) from the surface of the icing square.

Keeping the pressure even, touch down with the tip of the piping tube on the end of the icing square. Repeat to cover the square.

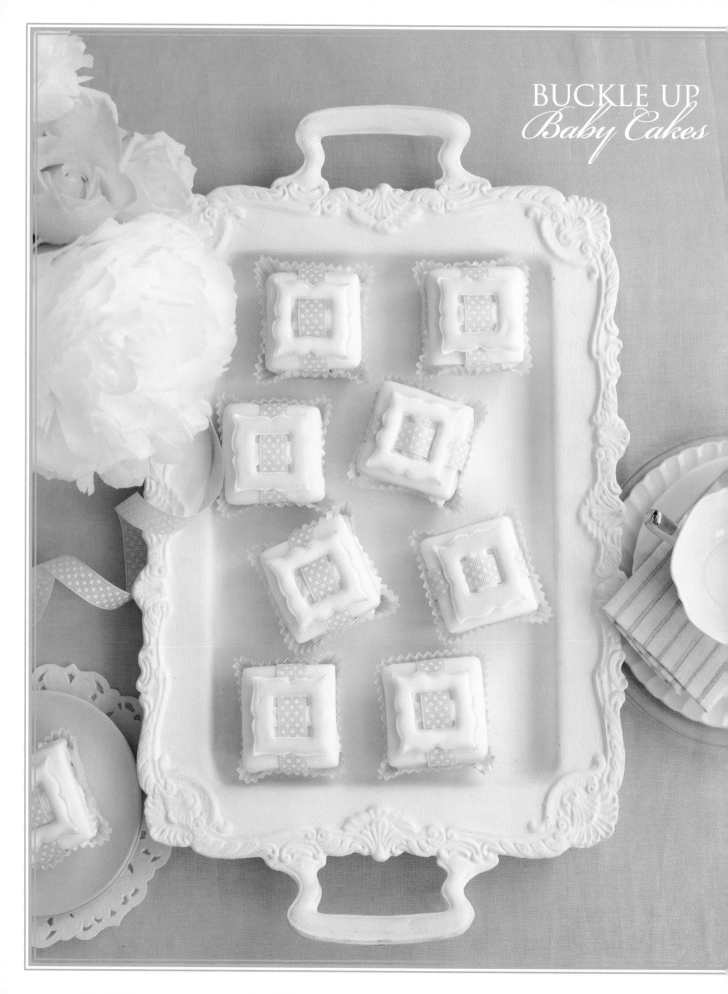

BUCKLE UP
Baby Cakes

THESE LITTLE BUCKLES ARE SO TRENDY YOUR BABY WILL MAKE THE FASHION PAGES.
THE BUCKLES CAN BE A LITTLE FIDDLY TO MAKE AND, BECAUSE THEY'RE QUITE
DELICATE, IT'S BEST TO MAKE A FEW MORE JUST IN CASE ANY BREAKAGES OCCUR.

EQUIPMENT
5cm (2-inch) square cutter
buckle template (page 229)
4 paper piping bags (page 221)
16 plain yellow paper cases
CAKE
shallow 23cm (9-inch) square
 cake of choice (page 190)
DECORATIONS
1kg (2 pounds) ready-made
 white icing
cornflour (cornstarch)
1 quantity royal icing (page 220)
lemon yellow food colouring
1 tablespoon strained lemon juice
2 egg whites
3m x 18mm (3 yards) wide ribbon

1 Knead a quarter of the ready-made icing on surface dusted with a little cornflour until icing loses its stickiness. Roll 200g (6½ ounces) of the icing on surface dusted with cornflour until 3mm (⅛-inch) thick. Using cutter, cut 16 x 5cm (2-inch) squares from icing. Transfer squares to baking-paper-lined tray to dry. Reserve icing scraps.
2 Using buckle template, trace 16 buckles onto baking paper. Turn paper over, place on a flat surface.

3 Tint half the royal icing yellow. Three-quarters fill piping bag with yellow icing; snip tip off bag. Pipe around the inside and outside edges of 8 buckles in unbroken lines. Spoon white royal icing into another piping bag, repeat to make 8 white buckles. Allow buckles to dry.
4 Add a drop or two of lemon juice to the remaining white royal icing – icing should be the consistency of pouring cream. Spoon icing into another paper piping bag; snip tip from bag. Using picture as a guide, pipe icing into the yellow buckles by piping into the space to flood the area. Repeat with the yellow royal icing and white buckles. Allow the buckles to dry overnight.
5 Trim cake into a 20cm (8-inch) square; cut cake into 16 x 5cm (2-inch) squares. Transfer cakes to wire rack; place rack over a tray. Secure icing squares to tops of all cakes with a little royal icing.
6 Chop half the remaining ready-made icing (including scraps) into medium heatproof bowl; add one lightly beaten egg white. Stir mixture over medium saucepan of simmering water (don't let water touch base of bowl). Gradually stir in about 1 tablespoon of warm water until the mixture becomes smooth and of a thick, slightly runny, (but not too runny) coating consistency. Do not over-heat the mixture.

7 Carefully pour the mixture over eight of the cake squares, covering the tops and sides of the cakes completely. Repeat process with remaining icing, egg white and water. Stand cakes about 1 hour or until the icing feels firm.
8 Cut ribbon into lengths long enough to extend over sides of each cake. Thread through the buckles. Place each cake into a paper case. Place a buckle on each cake, push the ribbon down the sides of the cakes. Push the paper cases against the icing on the cakes to form a seal.

makes 16
tips The squares of icing and the buckles can be made at least 2 weeks ahead. Make a few more buckles to allow for breakages. Square paper cases are available in specialty food or kitchen shops, but we found round paper cases happily change shape to accommodate the square cakes. You could also secure the icing squares to the cakes using a little jam or lemon curd, if you prefer. The cakes can be completed up to 2 days ahead.

USE A MOIST CAKE, SUCH AS A WHITE MUD CAKE, FOR THIS RECIPE. MAKE SURE THAT THE CAKE IS COVERED WITH ICING AND THE PAPER CASES ARE PRESSED FIRMLY AROUND THE CAKES AS THIS WILL HELP TO KEEP THEM FRESH FOR A DAY OR SO.

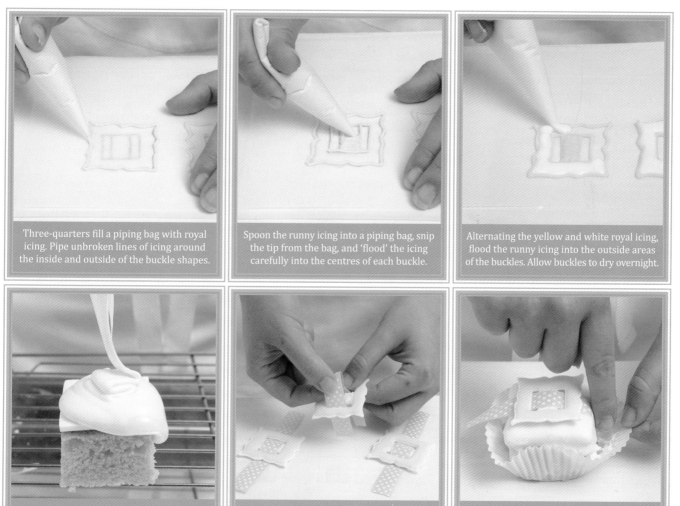

Three-quarters fill a piping bag with royal icing. Pipe unbroken lines of icing around the inside and outside of the buckle shapes.

Spoon the runny icing into a piping bag, snip the tip from the bag, and 'flood' the icing carefully into the centres of each buckle.

Alternating the yellow and white royal icing, flood the runny icing into the outside areas of the buckles. Allow buckles to dry overnight.

Heat ready-made icing gently with egg white and water until pourable. Stand cake squares on wire rack over tray; pour over icing.

Cut ribbon into lengths long enough to extend over top and two sides of each cake. Carefully position ribbon through all the buckles.

Position buckles on cakes, push end of ribbon onto sides of cakes. Press paper cases firmly onto icing on all sides of each cake to seal.

KITCHEN TEA
Biscuits

THESE PRETTY TEACUPS AND TEAPOTS ARE VERSATILE LITTLE BISCUITS – THEY'D BE
PERFECT TO SERVE AT A KITCHEN TEA, BUT WOULD ALSO BE GREAT AT A LITTLE GIRL'S
FIRST TEA PARTY, OR AS A DELICIOUS GIFT TO TAKE TO A HOUSE-WARMING PARTY.

EQUIPMENT
oven trays
6cm x 9cm (2½-inch x 3¾-inch)
teacup cutter
6.5cm x 7.5cm (2¾-inch x 3-inch)
teapot cutter
pastry brush
small piping bag
small (number 2) plain piping tube
1.4cm (¾-inch) blossom cutter
2.5cm (1-inch) blossom cutter
tweezers
BISCUITS
125g (4 ounces) butter
2 eggs
1 teaspoon vanilla extract
⅔ cup (150g) caster (superfine)
sugar
1⅓ cups (200g) self-raising flour
1 cup (150g) plain (all-purpose)
flour
DECORATIONS
500g (1 pound) ready-made
white icing
cornflour (cornstarch)
mauve, rose pink, sky blue, leaf
green and golden yellow food
colourings
1 egg white, beaten lightly
1 quantity royal icing (page 220)
2 teaspoons pearlized blush sugar
pearls

1 Have butter and eggs at room
temperature.
2 To make biscuits: Beat butter,
extract and sugar in small bowl with
electric mixer until combined. Beat
in eggs, one at a time; beat only until
combined. (Do not overbeat; mixture
will curdle at this stage, but will come
together later.) Transfer mixture to
large bowl. Stir in sifted flours in two
batches; mix to a soft dough. Knead
dough on floured surface until smooth;
cover, refrigerate 30 minutes.
3 Preheat oven to 180°C/350°F.
Grease and line oven trays with
baking paper.
4 Roll dough between sheets of
baking paper until 5mm (¼-inch)
thick. Using teacup and teapot
cutters, cut 10 of each shape from
dough, re-rolling dough as necessary.
5 Place shapes, about 2.5cm (1-inch)
apart, on trays. Bake about 15 minutes
or until biscuits are firm and browned
lightly. Stand biscuits on trays for
5 minutes; lift onto wire racks to cool.
6 Knead ready-made icing on surface
dusted with a little cornflour until
icing loses its stickiness. Divide icing
into 5 equal portions. Tint each
portion with one of the colourings;
enclose, separately, in plastic wrap.
7 Roll each icing portion, separately,
on cornfloured surface until 3mm
(⅛-inch) thick. Using cutters, cut

10 teacups and 10 teapots from
icings, re-rolling icing as necessary.
Reserve all icing scraps, enclose,
separately, in plastic wrap.
8 Working with 2 or 3 shapes at a
time, lightly brush tops of biscuits
with egg white; position icing shapes
on biscuits.
9 Fit piping bag with tube. Fill the
bag three-quarters full with royal
icing; pipe outlines and lines on
biscuits, as pictured.
10 Re-roll icing scraps on surface
dusted with cornflour until 1mm
(¹⁄₃₂-inch) thick; using blossom
cutters, cut 20 small and 10 large
blossoms from icing. Secure 10 small
blossoms to large blossoms with a
little royal icing; secure to teapot
biscuits. Secure remaining small
blossoms to teacup biscuits with a
little royal icing.
11 Pipe a dot of royal icing in the
centre of each flower; using tweezers,
position a pearl in flower centre. Pipe
dots around flowers on teapots; pipe
dots in teapot lids.

makes 20

tips You could use a paper piping
bag without a tube to pipe the
decorations on the biscuits. The
'pearlized blush sugar pearls' are
small edible pearls, and are available
from cake decorating suppliers.

ONCE DECORATED AND DRIED, LAYER THE BISCUITS CAREFULLY BETWEEN SHEETS OF BAKING PAPER IN AN AIRTIGHT CONTAINER. THEY WILL KEEP FOR ABOUT 4 WEEKS AT ROOM TEMPERATURE. THE ONLY TRICKY PART TO MAKING THESE BISCUITS IS THE PIPING; PRACTISE ON A FLAT SURFACE FIRST, BEFORE PIPING ONTO THE BISCUITS.

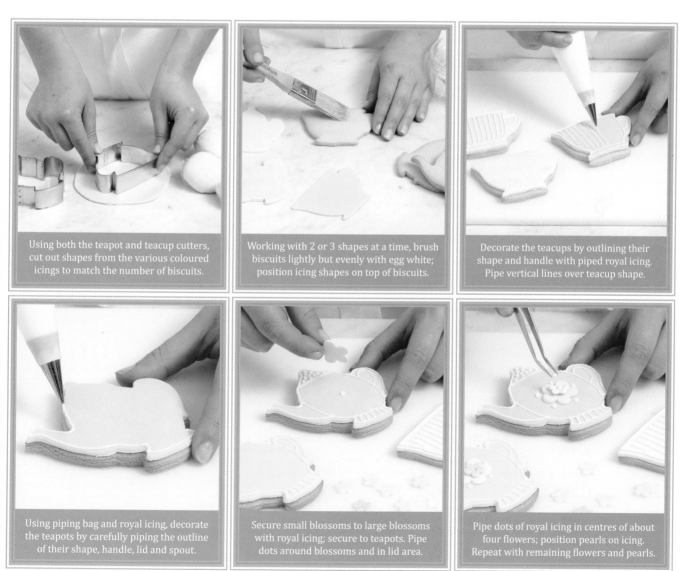

Using both the teapot and teacup cutters, cut out shapes from the various coloured icings to match the number of biscuits.

Working with 2 or 3 shapes at a time, brush biscuits lightly but evenly with egg white; position icing shapes on top of biscuits.

Decorate the teacups by outlining their shape and handle with piped royal icing. Pipe vertical lines over teacup shape.

Using piping bag and royal icing, decorate the teapots by carefully piping the outline of their shape, handle, lid and spout.

Secure small blossoms to large blossoms with royal icing; secure to teapots. Pipe dots around blossoms and in lid area.

Pipe dots of royal icing in centres of about four flowers; position pearls on icing. Repeat with remaining flowers and pearls.

BOOTIES
for Baby

We love this cake with its little boots on top, it's a perfect christening cake. The patterned roller and ball tool make the plaques very easy to make. Shaping the booties is a little harder, but well worth the effort. You can buy ready-made booties from some cake decorating suppliers.

BOOTIES
for Baby

EQUIPMENT

EQUIPMENT
30cm (14-inch) round wooden cake board (page 208)
12cm (5-inch) round wooden cake board (page 208)
smoothing tools
3 wooden skewers
paper piping bag (page 221)
plastic ruler
ball tool
quilted pattern rolling pin
bootie pattern template (page 229)
vinyl mat
fine artist's paint brush
metal skewer

CAKE
deep 20cm (8-inch) octagonal cake of choice (page 190)
deep 15cm (6-inch) octagonal cake of choice (page 190)

DECORATIONS
1.5kg (3 pounds) ready-made white icing
cornflour (cornstarch)
teal food colouring
1 quantity royal icing (page 220)
100g (3 ounces) modelling paste

1 Trim cakes (page 209). Secure large cake to largest board; secure small cake to remaining board (page 209). Prepare cakes for covering with ready-made icing (page 209).

2 Knead ready-made icing on surface dusted with a little cornflour until icing loses its stickiness. Tint 1.25kg (2½ pounds) of the icing pale teal with colouring.

3 Roll 500g (1 pound) of the pale teal icing on cornfloured surface until large enough to cover small cake. Using rolling pin, lift icing onto cake; smooth with hands then smoothing tools. Trim icing neatly around base; reserve icing scraps.

4 Use 750g (1½ pounds) of the pale teal icing to cover large cake in the same way as the small cake. Dry cakes overnight. Reserve icing scraps.

5 Push trimmed skewers into centre of large cake to support the top tier. Secure small cake on top of large cake (page 212).

6 Tint royal icing pale teal to match cakes. Three-quarters fill piping bag with royal icing; pipe around base of each cake. Use fingertip to blend icing into any gaps where cakes join the boards (page 212). Dry overnight.

7 Knead half the remaining pale teal icing with reserved icing scraps on surface dusted with a little cornflour. Roll icing on cornfloured surface into 4mm (¼-inch) thickness. Using ruler and sharp knife, cut out eight 6cm x 8cm (2½-inch x 3¼-inch) rectangles from icing. Using ball tool, gently rub edges of rectangles to make a frill. Place on baking-paper-lined tray to dry overnight.

8 Firmly roll patterned rolling pin over remaining pale teal icing (re-roll icing as necessary); cut out eight 4cm x 4.5cm (1½-inch x 1¾-inch) rectangles from icing. Place on baking-paper-lined trays to dry overnight.

9 Roll remaining ready-made white icing on cornfloured surface into 4mm thickness. Using ruler and sharp knife, cut out four 6.5cm x 5.5cm (2¾-inch x 2¼-inch) rectangles from icing. Using ball tool, gently rub edges of rectangles to make a frill. Place on baking-paper-lined tray to dry overnight.

10 Firmly roll the patterned rolling pin over remaining white icing (re-roll the icing as necessary); cut out eight 4.5cm x 6cm (1¾-inch x 2½-inch) rectangles from icing. Place on baking-paper-lined tray; stand overnight to dry.

11 Using picture as a guide, join the plain rectangles to the frilled rectangles with a little royal icing contrasting the colours and matching the small and large rectangles.

12 Knead modelling paste on surface dusted with cornflour until it loses its stickiness. Tint half the paste the same teal colour as the cake covering. Cover paste with plastic wrap when not using.

13 Make one bootie at a time: Roll teal modelling paste on surface dusted with cornflour until 1mm (¹⁄₃₂-inch) thick. Using template, carefully cut out one of each shape. Cover paste with vinyl mat to prevent drying out while making the bootie. Lightly brush a little water onto edge of sole of bootie, attach front of bootie to sole; carefully mould edges together into shape bootie.

14 Attach heel section to back of bootie with a little water. Using the skewer, make 4 holes for the shoelace (two on each side). Using tip of a fork, press around edge where booties and the sole join.

15 Roll 10g (½ ounce) of the white modelling paste on cornfloured surface into an oval shape about 3mm (⅛-inch) thick and slightly larger than the pattern for the sole. Attach to bottom of bootie with a little water. Place bootie on baking-paper-lined tray to dry overnight. Repeat to make second bootie.

16 To make laces: Roll small pieces of white modelling paste into thin bootlace lengths. Attach to booties with a little water.

17 Using a little royal icing, secure panels around sides of cakes and booties to top of cake.

Cut out 8 teal and 4 white rectangles from the icing; leave plain. Use the ball tool to frill the edges of the rectangles.

Roll teal icing out on surface dusted with cornflour into 3mm thickness. Roll quilted rolling pin firmly over icing to create pattern.

Using a plastic ruler and a sharp knife, cut out eight 4cm x 4.5cm patterned rectangles from the teal-coloured icing.

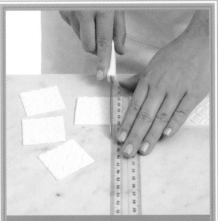

Roll quilted rolling pin firmly over white icing to create pattern. Cut eight 6cm x 4.5cm patterned rectangles from icing.

Join 4 patterned teal rectangles to 4 frilled white rectangles; join 8 patterned white rectangles to 8 frilled blue rectangles.

Tint modelling paste and roll to 3mm thick. Using pattern, cut out one of each shape. Cover with vinyl mat while making bootie.

Brush water sparingly over front edge of sole. Attach front of bootie to sole; gently mould edges together to make bootie shape.

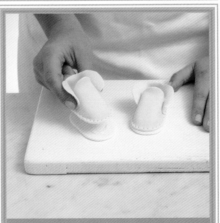

Cut white modelling paste into an oval shape slightly larger than the sole of the bootie; secure to base of bootie with a little water.

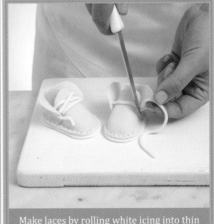

Make laces by rolling white icing into thin bootlace shapes; position so it appears they are threaded through the holes for laces.

PRETTY PINK
Boxes & Bows

EQUIPMENT
**30cm (12-inch) square wooden
   cake board (page 208)**
**15cm (6-inch) square wooden
   cake board (page 208)**
**10cm (4-inch) square wooden
   cake board (page 208)**
smoothing tools
**2.5cm (1-inch), 3cm (1¼-inch)
   and 3.5cm (1½-inch)
   perspex measures**
fine artist's paint brush
stitching tool
8 wooden skewers
3 paper piping bags (page 221)
vinyl mat
tape measure
cotton wool
CAKE
**deep 20cm (8-inch) square cake
   of choice (page 190)**
**shallow 20cm (8-inch) square cake
   of choice (page 190)**
**deep 15cm (6-inch) square cake
   of choice (page 190)**
**deep 10cm (4-inch) square cake
   of choice (page 190)**
jam or ganache of choice (page 210)
DECORATIONS
**3.3kg (6¾ pounds) ready-made
   white icing**
cornflour (cornstarch)
rose pink food colouring
1 quantity royal icing (page 220)
tylose powder

1   Trim cakes (page 209). Secure deep 20cm cake to largest board (page 209); top with remaining 20cm cake, joining cakes with jam or ganache (page 212). Secure remaining cakes to same-sized boards. Prepare cakes for covering with ready-made icing (page 209).

2   Reserve 500g (1 pound) of the ready-made icing for bow. Knead 1.5kg (3 pounds) of remaining icing on surface dusted with a little cornflour until icing loses its stickiness. Tint pale pink with colouring. Reserve 500g for box lid.

3   Roll remaining pale pink icing on cornfloured surface until large enough to cover largest cake. Using rolling pin, lift icing onto cake; smooth with hands then smoothing tools. Trim icing around base. Reserve icing scraps. Use 3.5cm perspex measure to mark sides of cake where lid will cover sides of box.

4   Tint 500g of the remaining white icing medium pink. Reserve 200g for box lid. Roll remaining medium pink icing on surface dusted with a little cornflour until large enough to cover small cake in the same way as the large cake. Reserve scraps. Use 2.5cm perspex measure to mark sides of cake for lid.

5   Tint remaining icing a darker pink. Reserve 300g (9½ ounces) for box lid. Roll remaining icing on cornfloured surface until large enough to cover medium cake in the same way as the large cake. Reserve scraps. Use 3cm perspex measure to mark sides of cake for lid. Dry cakes overnight.

6   To make lids: Work with one cake at a time, using matching reserved icing and scraps, and corresponding perspex measure. Lightly brush a little water in marked area for lid. Roll icing out on cornfloured surface until large enough to cover top of cake and extend over sides to cover marked area. Use perspex measure and a sharp knife to cut away excess icing. Reserve scraps. Smooth icing with hands then smoothing tools.

7   Using the stitching tool, mark around the bottom edge of all lids.

8   Push 4 trimmed skewers into centres of large and medium cakes to support the next tier (page 212). Assemble cakes, securing each tier to the tier below (page 212).

9   Divide royal icing into three bowls, tint to match cakes. Half-fill each of the piping bags with royal icing; pipe

around base of same-coloured cake. Use fingertip to blend icing into any gaps where cakes join the boards (page 212). Dry cakes overnight.

10   To make ribbons: Take tiny pieces of the reserved icing scraps, roll into tiny balls. Place balls under vinyl mat. Knead two-thirds of the white icing on cornfloured surface until icing loses its stickiness.

11   Measure height of stacked cakes, roll out icing long enough to match height of cakes. Place dots randomly over icing; gently roll over the dots to push them into the icing. Cut a 3cm-wide rectangle of the required length. Secure ribbon to cakes with a little royal icing. Repeat process to make three more ribbons.

12   To make bow: Make more tiny pink balls, place under vinyl mat. Knead ½ teaspoon tylose into the remaining white icing on cornfloured surface. Roll icing on cornfloured surface until large enough to cut out a 10cm x 30cm (4-inch x 12-inch) strip and a 2.5cm x 20cm (1-inch x 8-inch) strip. Roll balls into icing the same way as the ribbon. Place large strip under vinyl mat. To make tails for bow, cut the small strip of icing in half crossways; cut 'V's into ends. Secure tails to cake with royal icing. Pinch the blunt ends of the tails to make narrower.

13   Cut the large strip of icing in half crossways. Place cotton wool on both rectangles of icing, fold icing over to enclose cotton wool, join edges with a little water. Gently pleat edges together. Stand each bow on one end almost touching; cover join with a scrap of icing, secure with a little water. Stand overnight to dry.

14   Remove cotton wool from bow when dry. Position bow on cake, secure with a little royal icing.

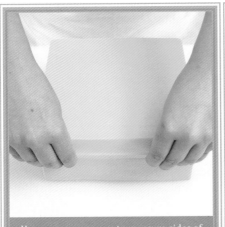

Use perspex measure to measure sides of cakes for lids. Press the measure into the icing to mark the area before the icing sets.

Brush marked areas on sides of cakes with a little water. Cover cakes with reserved icing extending icing over sides; trim excess icing.

Smooth the icing with the smoothing tools. Make the lids as square as possible, then use the stitching tool to mark pattern on lids.

Using reserved scraps of all the icings, roll tiny balls of random sizes in palm of your hand. Keep the balls under the vinyl mat.

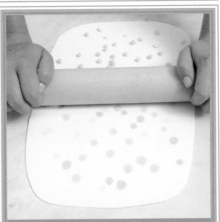

Place the coloured icing balls randomly over the white icing. Gently roll over the balls with a rolling pin pressing the balls into the icing.

Make the ribbons and tails for the bow; secure to cake stack with royal icing. Pinch blunt ends of tails to make them narrower.

Cut the large strip of icing in half crossways. Position cotton wool on each rectangle; fold over icing, joining edges with water.

Gently pinch and pleat joined edges of both rectangles to make the two halves of the bow narrow enough to join together.

Push the halves of the bow together while standing the bow on its side. Cover the join with a scrap of icing. Push bow into shape.

MAGNOLIA *&* *Pearls*

EQUIPMENT

12cm (4¾-inch) 18-gauge floral wire
long nose pliers; wire cutters
3 lengths 26-gauge floral wire
flower glue (page 227)
fine artist's paint brush
magnolia cutter set
vinyl mat
12-hole round-based, shallow
    (1 tablespoon/20ml) patty pan
flower mat
ball tool
small non-stick rolling pin
white florist's tape
30cm (12-inch) round wooden
    cake board (page 208)
smoothing tools
paper piping bag (page 221)
tweezers

CAKE

deep 20cm (8-inch) round cake
    of choice (page 190)
shallow 20cm (8-inch) round cake
    of choice (page 190)
jam or ganache of choice (page 210)

DECORATIONS

100g (3 ounces) modelling paste
tylose powder
cornflour (cornstarch)
yellow and pink petal dust
800g (1½ pounds) ready-made
    ivory icing
1 quantity royal icing (page 220)
ivory food colouring
15g (½ ounce) large ivory pearls
15g (½ ounce) small grey pearls

1 To make magnolia: Make a small hook in one end of the 18-gauge wire using pliers. Cut each 26-gauge wire into 3 even lengths.

2 Knead modelling paste with a pinch of tylose on cornfloured surface until paste loses its stickiness.

3 To make flower centre, roll a piece of paste into a ball the size of a large marble. Dip wire hook into flower glue; push into ball of paste. Use small scissors to snip the paste into small points; dry upright overnight. Dust centre with yellow petal dust.

4 Roll paste 3mm (⅛-inch) thick on cornfloured surface. Using cutters, cut 3 small and 5 large petals. Cover petals with vinyl mat. Dust pan with cornflour.

5 Dip one end of a piece of wire into glue; gently push wire into pointed end of small petal. Working with one small petal at a time, place petal on flower mat, use ball tool to frill the edge. Dry petals overnight in pan. Combine a pinch each of cornflour and pink petal dust; use to brush insides of petals.

6 To make large petals, insert wire one-third of the way through pointed end. Using small rolling pin, roll top two-thirds of petals to make larger. Frill edge of petals on flower mat using ball tool. Dry overnight in patty pan.

7 To assemble magnolia: See steps 7 and 8 of *Yellow Peony Rose Cake* (page 158) for full assembly instructions. Using tape, secure wired small petals, one at a time, to wired flower centre. Attach large petals in the same way.

8 Trim cakes (page 209). Secure deep cake to wooden board (page 209); top with remaining cake, joining cakes with a little jam or ganache (page 212). Prepare cake for covering with ready-made icing (page 209).

9 Knead ready-made icing on cornfloured surface until icing loses its stickiness. Roll icing on cornfloured surface until large enough to cover cake. Using rolling pin, lift icing onto cake; smooth with hands then smoothing tools. Trim icing neatly around base of cake.

10 Tint royal icing ivory. Half-fill piping bag with icing; pipe around base of cake. Use fingertip to blend icing into any gap where cake joins the board (page 212). Dry overnight.

11 Pipe a line of icing round base of cake. Use tweezers to position large pearls on icing. Pipe small dots of icing, a few at a time, between first row of pearls; position small pearls. Repeat to make 5 rows of large pearls and 4 rows of small pearls. Position magnolia in cake.

Make a hook on the end of a piece of wire, push into large-marble sized ball of paste, snip with scissors to make flower centre.

Dip wire into the glue, then push the wire a third of the way through petal from pointed end. Roll top two-thirds of the petal thinly.

Position 3 petals around centre of magnolia. Position and secure one large petal at a time around centre. Secure wire with florist's tape.

The magnolia is made in much the same way as the peony on page 158; check the finer details there. The magnolia can be made months ahead; store in an airtight container. The pearls should be positioned a day or two before the cake is needed to preserve their lustre. Position the magnolia on the day of serving.

THE
MECHANICS

Butter Cake

INGREDIENTS	DEEP 10CM (4-INCH) ROUND	DEEP 12CM (5-INCH) ROUND	SHALLOW 15CM (6-INCH) ROUND	DEEP 15CM (6-INCH) ROUND	SHALLOW 18CM (7-INCH) ROUND	DEEP 18CM (7-INCH) ROUND	SHALLOW 20CM (8-INCH) ROUND
BUTTER	50g (1½oz)	60g (2oz)	60g (2oz)	100g (3oz)	100g (3oz)	125g (4oz)	125g (4oz)
VANILLA EXTRACT	¼ teaspoon	½ teaspoon	½ teaspoon	½ teaspoon	½ teaspoon	1 teaspoon	1 teaspoon
CASTER (SUPERFINE) SUGAR	¼ cup	⅓ cup	⅓ cup	½ cup	½ cup	¾ cup	¾ cup
EGGS (60g/2oz)	1	1	1	1	1	2	2
SELF-RAISING FLOUR	⅔ cup	¾ cup	¾ cup	1¼ cups	1¼ cups	1½ cups	1½ cups
MILK	2 tablespoons	¼ cup	¼ cup	⅓ cup	⅓ cup	½ cup	½ cup
BAKING TIME (approx)	30 minutes	40 minutes	40 minutes	35 minutes	35 minutes	55 minutes	40 minutes

INGREDIENTS	DEEP 20CM (8-INCH) ROUND	DEEP 22CM (9-INCH) ROUND	SHALLOW 25CM (10-INCH) ROUND	DEEP 25CM (10-INCH) ROUND	DEEP 30CM (12-INCH) ROUND	DEEP 35CM (14-INCH) ROUND
BUTTER	185g (6oz)	250g (8oz)	250g (8oz)	375g (12oz)	625g (1¼lb)	740g (1½lb)
VANILLA EXTRACT	1½ teaspoons	2 teaspoons	2 teaspoons	3 teaspoons	1 tablespoon	1½ tablespoons
CASTER (SUPERFINE) SUGAR	1 cup	1½ cups	1½ cups	2½ cups	3¾ cups	4 cups
EGGS (60g/2oz)	3	4	4	6	10	12
SELF-RAISING FLOUR	2¼ cups	3 cups	3 cups	4½ cups	7½ cups	9 cups
MILK	¾ cup	1 cup	1 cup	1½ cups	2½ cups	3 cups
BAKING TIME (approx)	1 hour	1¼ hours	45 minutes	1½ hours	1¾ hours	2 hours

INGREDIENTS	SHALLOW 10CM (4-INCH) SQUARE	DEEP 10CM (4-INCH) SQUARE	SHALLOW 15CM (6-INCH) SQUARE	DEEP 15CM (6-INCH) SQUARE	SHALLOW 18CM (7-INCH) SQUARE	DEEP 18CM (7-INCH) SQUARE	SHALLOW 20CM (8-INCH) SQUARE
BUTTER	60g (2oz)	65g (2oz)	100g (3oz)	125g (4oz)	125g (4oz)	185g (6oz)	185g (6oz)
VANILLA EXTRACT	½ teaspoon	½ teaspoon	½ teaspoon	1 teaspoon	1 teaspoon	1½ teaspoons	1½ teaspoons
CASTER (SUPERFINE) SUGAR	⅓ cup	⅓ cup	½ cup	¾ cup	¾ cup	1 cup	1 cup
EGGS (60g/2oz)	1	1	1	2	2	3	3
SELF-RAISING FLOUR	¾ cup	¾ cup	1¼ cups	1½ cups	1½ cups	2¼ cups	2¼ cups
MILK	¼ cup	¼ cup	⅓ cup	½ cup	½ cup	¾ cup	¾ cup
BAKING TIME (approx)	30 minutes	30 minutes	45 minutes	55 minutes	45 minutes	1 hour	45 minutes

INGREDIENTS	DEEP 20CM (8-INCH) SQUARE	SHALLOW 22CM (9-INCH) SQUARE	DEEP 22CM (9-INCH) SQUARE	SHALLOW 25CM (10-INCH) SQUARE	DEEP 25CM (10-INCH) SQUARE	DEEP 30CM (12-INCH) SQUARE
BUTTER	250g (8oz)	250g (8oz)	375g (12oz)	375g (12oz)	625g (1¼lb)	740g (1½lb)
VANILLA EXTRACT	2 teaspoons	2 teaspoons	3 teaspoons	3 teaspoons	1 tablespoon	1½ tablespoons
CASTER (SUPERFINE) SUGAR	1½ cups	1½ cups	2½ cups	2½ cups	3¾ cups	4 cups
EGGS (60g/2oz)	4	4	6	6	10	12
SELF-RAISING FLOUR	3 cups	3 cups	4½ cups	4½ cups	7½ cups	9 cups
MILK	1 cup	1 cup	1½ cups	1½ cups	2½ cups	3 cups
BAKING TIME (approx)	1¼ hours	1 hour	1½ hours	1¼ hours	1¾ hours	2 hours

INGREDIENTS	DEEP 18CM (7-INCH) HEART SHAPED	DEEP 15CM (6-INCH) OCTAGONAL	DEEP 20CM (8-INCH) OCTAGONAL	12-HOLE MUFFIN PAN (⅓-CUP/80ML)
BUTTER	125g (4oz)	125g (4oz)	250g (8oz)	185g (6oz)
VANILLA EXTRACT	1 teaspoon	1 teaspoon	2 teaspoons	1½ teaspoons
CASTER (SUPERFINE) SUGAR	¾ cup	¾ cup	1½ cups	1 cup
EGGS (60g/2oz)	2	2	4	3
SELF-RAISING FLOUR	1½ cups	1½ cups	3 cups	2¼ cups
MILK	½ cup	½ cup	1 cup	¾ cup
BAKING TIME (approx)	1 hour	1 hour	1¼ hours	20 minutes

WE USED 7.5CM (3-INCH) DEEP CAKE PANS WITH STRAIGHT SIDES. BUTTER, EGGS AND MILK SHOULD BE AT ROOM TEMPERATURE FOR BEST RESULTS. THE IMPERIAL MEASUREMENTS USED HERE ARE AN APPROXIMATION ONLY.

1 Preheat oven to 180°C/350°F. Grease and line base and side(s) of cake pan with baking paper, extending paper 5cm (2 inches) above side(s).

2 Beat butter, extract and sugar in bowl with electric mixer until light and fluffy. Beat in eggs, one at a time. Transfer mixture to larger bowl; stir in sifted flour and milk, in two batches. Spread mixture into pan.

3 Bake cake for the time given in chart. Cover cake with foil halfway through baking if cake is over-browning, or lower the oven temperature by 10-20 degrees if cake is over 20cm.

4 Test cake by inserting a skewer into centre of cake; if cooked, skewer will be clean, if there is cake mixture on the skewer, bake cake a further 10 minutes before testing again.

5 Stand cake in the pan for 10 to 30 minutes, depending on the size of cake, before turning, top-side down, onto wire rack to cool.

tip The cake will keep well for 2 days in an airtight container, or can be frozen for 3 months.

Raspberry Hazelnut Cake

INGREDIENTS	DEEP 10CM (4-INCH) ROUND	DEEP 12CM (5-INCH) ROUND	SHALLOW 15CM (6-INCH) ROUND	DEEP 15CM (6-INCH) ROUND	SHALLOW 18CM (7-INCH) ROUND	DEEP 18CM (7-INCH) ROUND	SHALLOW 20CM (8-INCH) ROUND
BUTTER	55g (2oz)	80g (2½oz)	80g (2½oz)	110g (3½oz)	110g (3½oz)	165g (5oz)	165g (5oz)
CASTER (SUPERFINE) SUGAR	½ cup	¾ cup	¾ cup	1 cup	1 cup	1¼ cups	1¼ cups
EGGS (60g/2oz)	1	2	2	3	3	4	4
PLAIN (ALL-PURPOSE) FLOUR	¼ cup	⅓ cup	⅓ cup	½ cup	½ cup	¾ cup	¾ cup
SELF-RAISING FLOUR	1½ tablespoons	2 tablespoons	2 tablespoons	¼ cup	¼ cup	⅓ cup	⅓ cup
GROUND HAZELNUTS	¼ cup	⅓ cup	⅓ cup	½ cup	½ cup	¾ cup	¾ cup
SOUR CREAM	2 tablespoons	¼ cup	¼ cup	⅓ cup	⅓ cup	½ cup	½ cup
FRESH OR FROZEN RASPBERRIES	65g (2oz)	100g (3oz)	100g (3oz)	130g (4oz)	130g (4oz)	190g (6oz)	190g (6oz)
BAKING TIME (approx)	50 minutes	1¼ hours	1 hour	1¼ hours	1¼ hours	1½ hours	1 hour

INGREDIENTS	DEEP 20CM (8-INCH) ROUND	DEEP 22CM (9-INCH) ROUND	SHALLOW 25CM (10-INCH) ROUND	DEEP 25CM (10-INCH) ROUND	DEEP 30CM (12-INCH) ROUND	DEEP 35CM (14-INCH) ROUND
BUTTER	220g (7oz)	275g (9oz)	275g (9oz)	385g (12oz)	550g (1lb)	880g (1¾lb)
CASTER (SUPERFINE) SUGAR	1¾ cups	2 cups	2 cups	3 cups	4½ cups	7 cups
EGGS (60g/2oz)	5	6	6	9	13	20
PLAIN (ALL-PURPOSE) FLOUR	1 cup	1¼ cups	1¼ cups	1¾ cups	2½ cups	4 cups
SELF-RAISING FLOUR	½ cup	⅔ cup	⅔ cup	¾ cup	1¼ cups	2 cups
GROUND HAZELNUTS	1 cup	1¼ cups	1¼ cups	1¾ cups	2½ cups	4 cups
SOUR CREAM	⅔ cup	¾ cup	¾ cup	1 cup	1⅔ cups	2⅔ cups
FRESH OR FROZEN RASPBERRIES	260g (8½oz)	325g (10½oz)	325g (10½oz)	450g (14½oz)	650g (1¼lb)	1kg (2lb)
BAKING TIME (approx)	1¾ hours	2 hours	1½ hours	2½ hours	3 hours	3½ hours

INGREDIENTS	SHALLOW 10CM (4-INCH) SQUARE	DEEP 10CM (4-INCH) SQUARE	SHALLOW 15CM (6-INCH) SQUARE	DEEP 15CM (6-INCH) SQUARE	SHALLOW 18CM (7-INCH) SQUARE	DEEP 18CM (7-INCH) SQUARE	SHALLOW 20CM (8-INCH) SQUARE
BUTTER	55g (2oz)	80g (2½oz)	110g (3½oz)	165g (5oz)	165g (5oz)	220g (7oz)	220g (7oz)
CASTER (SUPERFINE) SUGAR	½ cup	¾ cup	1 cup	1¼ cups	1¼ cups	1¾ cups	1¾ cups
EGGS (60g/2oz)	1	2	3	4	4	5	5
PLAIN (ALL-PURPOSE) FLOUR	¼ cup	⅓ cup	½ cup	¾ cup	¾ cup	1 cup	1 cup
SELF-RAISING FLOUR	1½ tablespoons	2 tablespoons	¼ cup	⅓ cup	⅓ cup	½ cup	½ cup
GROUND HAZELNUTS	¼ cup	⅓ cup	½ cup	¾ cup	¾ cup	1 cup	1 cup
SOUR CREAM	2 tablespoons	¼ cup	⅓ cup	½ cup	½ cup	⅔ cup	⅔ cup
FRESH OR FROZEN RASPBERRIES	65g (2oz)	100g (3oz)	130g (4oz)	190g (6oz)	190g (6oz)	260g (8½oz)	260g (8½oz)
BAKING TIME (approx)	45 minutes	1 hour	1¼ hours	1½ hours	1 hour	1¾ hours	1¼ hours

INGREDIENTS	DEEP 20CM (8-INCH) SQUARE	SHALLOW 22CM (9-INCH) SQUARE	DEEP 22CM (9-INCH) SQUARE	SHALLOW 25CM (10-INCH) SQUARE	DEEP 25CM (10-INCH) SQUARE	DEEP 30CM (12-INCH) SQUARE
BUTTER	275g (9oz)	275g (9oz)	385g (12oz)	385g (12oz)	550g (1lb)	880g (1¾lb)
CASTER (SUPERFINE) SUGAR	2 cups	2 cups	3 cups	3 cups	4½ cups	7 cups
EGGS (60g/2oz)	6	6	9	9	13	20
PLAIN (ALL-PURPOSE) FLOUR	1¼ cups	1¼ cups	1¾ cups	1¾ cups	2½ cups	4 cups
SELF-RAISING FLOUR	⅔ cup	⅔ cup	¾ cup	¾ cup	1¼ cups	2 cups
GROUND HAZELNUTS	1¼ cups	1¼ cups	1¾ cups	1¾ cups	2½ cups	4 cups
SOUR CREAM	¾ cup	¾ cup	1 cup	1 cup	1⅔ cups	2⅔ cups
FRESH OR FROZEN RASPBERRIES	325g (10½oz)	325g (10½oz)	450g (14½oz)	450g (14½oz)	650g (1¼lb)	1kg (2lb)
BAKING TIME (approx)	2 hours	1¾ hours	2½ hours	2¼ hours	3 hours	3½ hours

INGREDIENTS	DEEP 18CM (7-INCH) HEART SHAPED	DEEP 15CM (6-INCH) OCTAGONAL	DEEP 20CM (8-INCH) OCTAGONAL	12-HOLE MUFFIN PAN (⅓-CUP/80ML)
BUTTER	165g (5oz)	165g (5oz)	275g (9oz)	220g (7oz)
CASTER (SUPERFINE) SUGAR	1¼ cups	1¼ cups	2 cups	1¾ cups
EGGS (60g/2oz)	4	4	6	5
PLAIN (ALL-PURPOSE) FLOUR	¾ cup	¾ cup	1¼ cups	1 cup
SELF-RAISING FLOUR	⅓ cup	⅓ cup	⅔ cup	½ cup
GROUND HAZELNUTS	¾ cup	¾ cup	1¼ cups	1 cup
SOUR CREAM	½ cup	½ cup	¾ cup	⅔ cup
FRESH OR FROZEN RASPBERRIES	190g (6oz)	190g (6oz)	325g (10½oz)	260g (8½oz)
BAKING TIME (approx)	1½ hours	1½ hours	2 hours	35 minutes

WE USED 7.5CM (3-INCH) DEEP CAKE PANS WITH STRAIGHT SIDES. THE BUTTER, EGGS AND SOUR CREAM SHOULD BE AT ROOM TEMPERATURE FOR BEST RESULTS. THE IMPERIAL MEASUREMENTS USED HERE ARE AN APPROXIMATION ONLY.

1 Preheat oven to 160°C/325°F. Grease and line base and side(s) of cake pan with baking paper, extending paper 5cm (2 inches) above side(s).

2 Beat butter and sugar in bowl with electric mixer until light and fluffy. Beat in eggs, one at a time. (Mixture will curdle at this stage but will come together later.)

3 Transfer mixture to a larger bowl; stir in the sifted flours and ground hazelnuts, sour cream and berries. Spread mixture into pan.

4 Bake cake for the time given in chart. Cover cake with foil halfway through baking if cake is over-browning, or lower the oven temperature by 10-20 degrees if cake is over 20cm.

5 Test cake by inserting a skewer into centre of cake; if cooked, skewer will be clean, if there is cake mixture on the skewer, bake cake a further 10 minutes before testing again.

6 Stand cake in the pan for 10 to 30 minutes, depending on the size of the cake, before turning, top-side down, onto wire rack to cool.

tips If using frozen berries do not thaw them; frozen berries are less likely to "bleed" into the cake mixture. The cake will keep well for 3 days in an airtight container, or can be frozen for 3 months.

Poppy seed and Orange Cake

INGREDIENTS	DEEP 10CM (4-INCH) ROUND	DEEP 12CM (5-INCH) ROUND	SHALLOW 15CM (6-INCH) ROUND	DEEP 15CM (6-INCH) ROUND	SHALLOW 18CM (7-INCH) ROUND	DEEP 18CM (7-INCH) ROUND	SHALLOW 20CM (8-INCH) ROUND
POPPY SEEDS	2 tablespoons	¼ cup	¼ cup	⅓ cup	⅓ cup	½ cup	½ cup
MILK	3 teaspoons	1 tablespoon	1 tablespoon	1½ tablespoons	1½ tablespoons	2 tablespoons	2 tablespoons
BUTTER	45g (1½oz)	70g (2½oz)	70g (2½oz)	100g (3oz)	100g (3oz)	140g (4½oz)	140g (4½oz)
ORANGE RIND	1½ teaspoons	2 teaspoons	2 teaspoons	3 teaspoons	3 teaspoons	1 tablespoon	1 tablespoon
CASTER (SUPERFINE) SUGAR	¼ cup	⅓ cup	⅓ cup	½ cup	½ cup	¾ cup	¾ cup
EGGS (60g/2oz)	1	2	2	2	2	3	3
SELF-RAISING FLOUR	½ cup	⅔ cup	⅔ cup	1 cup	1 cup	1¼ cups	1¼ cups
PLAIN (ALL-PURPOSE) FLOUR	1½ tablespoons	2 tablespoons	2 tablespoons	¼ cup	¼ cup	⅓ cup	⅓ cup
GROUND ALMONDS (MEAL)	1½ tablespoons	2 tablespoons	2 tablespoons	¼ cup	¼ cup	⅓ cup	⅓ cup
ORANGE JUICE	1½ tablespoons	2 tablespoons	2 tablespoons	¼ cup	¼ cup	⅓ cup	⅓ cup
BAKING TIME (approx)	30 minutes	45 minutes	40 minutes	50 minutes	40 minutes	1 hour	45 minutes

INGREDIENTS	DEEP 20CM (8-INCH) ROUND	DEEP 22CM (9-INCH) ROUND	SHALLOW 25CM (10-INCH) ROUND	DEEP 25CM (10-INCH) ROUND	DEEP 30CM (12-INCH) ROUND	DEEP 35CM (14-INCH) ROUND
POPPY SEEDS	¾ cup	1 cup	1 cup	1 cup	1¾ cups	2 cups
MILK	2½ tablespoons	⅓ cup	⅓ cup	⅓ cup	½ cup	1 cup
BUTTER	175g (5½oz)	285g (9oz)	285g (9oz)	300g (9½oz)	370g (12oz)	740g (1½lb)
ORANGE RIND	1 tablespoon	1½ tablespoons	1½ tablespoons	¼ cup	⅓ cup	⅓ cup
CASTER (SUPERFINE) SUGAR	1 cup	1⅓ cups	1⅓ cups	1⅔ cups	2 cups	4 cups
EGGS (60g/2oz)	4	4	4	5	6	12
SELF-RAISING FLOUR	1⅓ cups	1½ cups	1½ cups	3⅔ cups	3 cups	6 cups
PLAIN (ALL-PURPOSE) FLOUR	½ cup	⅔ cup	⅔ cup	¾ cup	1 cup	2 cups
GROUND ALMONDS (MEAL)	½ cup	⅔ cup	⅔ cup	¾ cup	1 cup	2 cups
ORANGE JUICE	½ cup	⅔ cup	⅔ cup	¾ cup	1 cup	2 cups
BAKING TIME (approx)	1 hour	1¼ hours	1 hour	1¼ hours	1½ hours	1¾ hours

INGREDIENTS	SHALLOW 10CM (4-INCH) SQUARE	DEEP 10CM (4-INCH) SQUARE	SHALLOW 15CM (6-INCH) SQUARE	DEEP 15 CM (6-INCH) SQUARE	SHALLOW 18CM (7-INCH) SQUARE	DEEP 18CM (7-INCH) SQUARE	SHALLOW 20CM (8-INCH) SQUARE
POPPY SEEDS	2 tablespoons	¼ cup	⅓ cup	½ cup	½ cup	¾ cup	¾ cup
MILK	3 teaspoons	1 tablespoon	1½ tablespoons	2 tablespoons	2 tablespoons	2½ tablespoons	2½ tablespoons
BUTTER	45g (1½oz)	70g (2½oz)	100g (3oz)	140g (4½oz)	140g (4½oz)	175g (5½oz)	175g (5½oz)
ORANGE RIND	1½ teaspoons	2 teaspoons	3 teaspoons	1 tablespoon	1 tablespoon	1 tablespoon	1 tablespoon
CASTER (SUPERFINE) SUGAR	¼ cup	⅓ cup	½ cup	¾ cup	¾ cup	1 cup	1 cup
EGGS (60g/2oz)	1	2	2	3	3	4	4
SELF-RAISING FLOUR	½ cup	⅔ cup	1 cup	1¼ cups	1¼ cups	1⅓ cups	1⅓ cups
PLAIN (ALL-PURPOSE) FLOUR	1½ tablespoons	2 tablespoons	¼ cup	⅓ cup	⅓ cup	½ cup	½ cup
GROUND ALMONDS (MEAL)	1½ tablespoons	2 tablespoons	¼ cup	⅓ cup	⅓ cup	½ cup	½ cup
ORANGE JUICE	1½ tablespoons	2 tablespoons	¼ cup	⅓ cup	⅓ cup	½ cup	½ cup
BAKING TIME (approx)	35 minutes	45 minutes	50 minutes	45 minutes	45 minutes	1 hour	45 minutes

INGREDIENTS	DEEP 20CM (8-INCH) SQUARE	SHALLOW 22CM (9-INCH) SQUARE	DEEP 22CM (9-INCH) SQUARE	SHALLOW 25CM (10-INCH) SQUARE	DEEP 25CM (10-INCH) SQUARE	DEEP 30CM (12-INCH) SQUARE
POPPY SEEDS	1 cup	1 cup	1 cup	1 cup	1⅓ cups	2 cups
MILK	⅓ cup	⅓ cup	½ cup	½ cup	½ cup	1 cup
BUTTER	285g (9oz)	285g (9oz)	325g (10½oz)	325g (10½oz)	370g (12oz)	740g (1½lb)
ORANGE RIND	1½ tablespoons	1½ tablespoons	2 tablespoons	2 tablespoons	¼ cup	⅓ cup
CASTER (SUPERFINE) SUGAR	1⅓ cups	1⅓ cups	1¾ cups	1¾ cups	2 cups	4 cups
EGGS (60g/2oz)	4	4	6	6	6	12
SELF-RAISING FLOUR	1½ cups	1½ cups	2¾ cups	2¾ cups	3 cups	6 cups
PLAIN (ALL-PURPOSE) FLOUR	⅔ cup	⅔ cup	1 cup	1 cup	1 cup	2 cup
GROUND ALMONDS (MEAL)	⅔ cup	⅔ cup	1 cup	1 cup	1 cup	2 cup
ORANGE JUICE	⅔ cup	⅔ cup	1 cup	1 cup	1 cup	2 cup
BAKING TIME (approx)	1¼ hours	1 hour	1½ hours	1¼ hours	1¼ hours	1¾ hours

INGREDIENTS	DEEP 18CM (7-INCH) HEART SHAPED	DEEP 15CM (6-INCH) OCTAGONAL	DEEP 20CM (8-INCH) OCTAGONAL	12-HOLE MUFFIN PAN (⅓-CUP/80ML)
POPPY SEEDS	½ cup	½ cup	¾ cup	¾ cup
MILK	2 tablespoons	2 tablespoons	2½ tablespoons	2½ tablespoons
BUTTER	140g (4½oz)	140g (4½oz)	175g (5½oz)	175g (5½oz)
ORANGE RIND	1 tablespoon	1 tablespoon	1 tablespoon	1 tablespoon
CASTER (SUPERFINE) SUGAR	¾ cup	¾ cup	1 cup	1 cup
EGGS (60g/2oz)	3	3	4	4
SELF-RAISING FLOUR	1¼ cups	1¼ cups	1⅓ cups	1⅓ cups
PLAIN (ALL-PURPOSE) FLOUR	⅓ cup	⅓ cup	½ cup	½ cup
GROUND ALMONDS (MEAL)	⅓ cup	⅓ cup	½ cup	½ cup
ORANGE JUICE	⅓ cup	⅓ cup	½ cup	½ cup
BAKING TIME (approx)	45 minutes	45 minutes	1 hour	25 minutes

WE USED 7.5CM (3-INCH) DEEP CAKE PANS WITH STRAIGHT SIDES. BUTTER AND EGGS SHOULD BE AT ROOM TEMPERATURE FOR BEST RESULTS. THE IMPERIAL MEASUREMENTS USED HERE ARE AN APPROXIMATION ONLY.

1   Preheat oven to 180°C/350°F. Grease and line base and side(s) of cake pan with baking paper, extending paper 5cm (2 inches) above side(s).
2   Combine seeds and milk in a small bowl, stand 20 minutes.
3   Meanwhile, beat butter, rind and sugar in a bowl with an electric mixer until light and fluffy. Beat in eggs, one at a time, until just combined between additions.
4   Transfer mixture to a larger bowl. Stir in the sifted flours, ground almonds, juice and the poppy seed mixture. Spread mixture into pan.
5   Bake cake for the time given in chart. Cover cake with foil halfway through baking if cake is over-browning, or lower the oven temperature by 10-20 degrees if cake is over 20cm.
6   Test cake by inserting a skewer into centre of cake; if cooked, skewer will be clean, if there is cake mixture on the skewer, bake cake a further 10 minutes before testing again.
7   Stand cake in the pan for 10 to 30 minutes, depending on the size of the cake, before turning, top-side down, onto wire rack to cool.

tip   The cake will keep well for 2 days in an airtight container, or can be frozen for 3 months.

Coconut Cake

INGREDIENTS	DEEP 10CM (4-INCH) ROUND	DEEP 12CM (5-INCH) ROUND	SHALLOW 15CM (6-INCH) ROUND	DEEP 15CM (6-INCH) ROUND	SHALLOW 18CM (7-INCH) ROUND	DEEP 18CM (7-INCH) ROUND	SHALLOW 20CM (8-INCH) ROUND
BUTTER	60g (2oz)	90g (3oz)	90g (3oz)	125g (4oz)	125g (4oz)	185g (6oz)	185g (6oz)
COCONUT ESSENCE	½ teaspoon	¾ teaspoon	¾ teaspoon	1 teaspoon	1 teaspoon	1½ teaspoons	1½ teaspoons
CASTER (SUPERFINE) SUGAR	½ cup	¾ cup	¾ cup	1 cup	1 cup	1½ cups	1½ cups
COCONUT CREAM	⅓ cup	½ cup	½ cup	¾ cup	¾ cup	1 cup	1 cup
SELF-RAISING FLOUR	½ cup	¾ cup	¾ cup	1 cup	1 cup	1½ cups	1½ cups
EGG WHITES	2	2	2	3	3	4	4
BAKING TIME (approx)	50 minutes	1¼ hours	50 minutes	1¼ hours	1 hour	1¼ hours	1 hour

INGREDIENTS	DEEP 20CM (8-INCH) ROUND	DEEP 22CM (9-INCH) ROUND	SHALLOW 25CM (10-INCH) ROUND	DEEP 25CM (10-INCH) ROUND	DEEP 30CM (12-INCH) ROUND	DEEP 35CM (14-INCH) ROUND
BUTTER	250g (8oz)	310g (10oz)	310g (10oz)	500g (1lb)	750g (1½lb)	1kg (2lb)
COCONUT ESSENCE	2 teaspoons	2½ teaspoons	2½ teaspoons	3 teaspoons	1 tablespoon	1 tablespoon
CASTER (SUPERFINE) SUGAR	2 cups	2½ cups	2½ cups	4 cups	6 cups	8 cups
COCONUT CREAM	1½ cups	1¾ cups	1¾ cups	3 cups	4½ cups	6 cups
SELF-RAISING FLOUR	2¼ cups	3 cups	3 cups	4½ cups	6¾ cups	9 cups
EGG WHITES	6	7	7	12	18	24
BAKING TIME (approx)	1½ hours	1¾ hours	1¼ hours	2¼ hours	2½ hours	3 hours

INGREDIENTS	SHALLOW 10CM (4-INCH) SQUARE	DEEP 10CM (4-INCH) SQUARE	SHALLOW 15CM (6-INCH) SQUARE	DEEP 15 CM (6-INCH) SQUARE	SHALLOW 18CM (7-INCH) SQUARE	DEEP 18CM (7-INCH) SQUARE	SHALLOW 20CM (8-INCH) SQUARE
BUTTER	60g (2oz)	90g (3oz)	80g (2½oz)	185g (6oz)	185g (6oz)	250g (8oz)	250g (8oz)
COCONUT ESSENCE	½ teaspoon	¾ teaspoon	½ teaspoon	1½ teaspoons	1½ teaspoons	2 teaspoons	2 teaspoons
CASTER (SUPERFINE) SUGAR	½ cup	¾ cup	⅔ cup	1½ cups	1½ cups	2 cups	2 cups
COCONUT CREAM	⅓ cup	½ cup	½ cup	1 cup	1 cup	1½ cups	1½ cups
SELF-RAISING FLOUR	½ cup	¾ cup	¾ cup	1½ cups	1½ cups	2¼ cups	2¼ cups
EGG WHITES	2	2	2	4	4	6	6
BAKING TIME (approx)	40 minutes	1 hour	1¼ hours	1¼ hours	1 hour	1½ hours	1½ hours

INGREDIENTS	DEEP 20CM (8-INCH) SQUARE	SHALLOW 22CM (9-INCH) SQUARE	DEEP 22CM (9-INCH) SQUARE	SHALLOW 25CM (10-INCH) SQUARE	DEEP 25CM (10-INCH) SQUARE	DEEP 30CM (12-INCH) SQUARE
BUTTER	310g (10oz)	310g (10oz)	500g (1lb)	500g (1lb)	750g (1½lb)	1kg (2lb)
COCONUT ESSENCE	2½ teaspoons	2½ teaspoons	3 teaspoons	3 teaspoons	1 tablespoon	1 tablespoon
CASTER (SUPERFINE) SUGAR	2½ cups	2½ cups	4 cups	4 cups	6 cups	8 cups
COCONUT CREAM	1¾ cups	1¾ cups	3 cups	3 cups	4½ cups	6 cups
SELF-RAISING FLOUR	3 cups	3 cups	4½ cups	4½ cups	6¾ cups	9 cups
EGG WHITES	7	7	12	12	18	24
BAKING TIME (approx)	1½ hours	1 hour	2¼ hours	1¾ hours	1½ hours	3 hours

INGREDIENTS	DEEP 18CM (7-INCH) HEART SHAPED	DEEP 15CM (6-INCH) OCTAGONAL	DEEP 20 CM (8-INCH) OCTAGONAL	12-HOLE MUFFIN PAN (⅓-CUP/80ML)
BUTTER	185g (6oz)	185g (6oz)	310g (10oz)	250g (8oz)
COCONUT ESSENCE	1½ teaspoons	1½ teaspoons	2½ teaspoons	2 teaspoons
CASTER (SUPERFINE) SUGAR	1½ cups	1½ cups	2½ cups	2 cups
COCONUT CREAM	1 cup	1 cup	1¾ cups	1½ cups
SELF-RAISING FLOUR	1½ cups	1½ cups	3 cups	2¼ cups
EGG WHITES	4	4	7	6
BAKING TIME (approx)	1½ hours	1½ hours	1¾ hours	45 minutes

WE USED 7.5CM (3-INCH) DEEP CAKE PANS WITH STRAIGHT SIDES. BUTTER AND EGG WHITES SHOULD BE AT ROOM TEMPERATURE FOR BEST RESULTS. WE USED CANNED COCONUT CREAM. THE IMPERIAL MEASUREMENTS USED HERE ARE AN APPROXIMATION ONLY.

1 Preheat oven to 160°C/325°F. Grease and line base and side(s) of cake pan with baking paper, extending paper 5cm (2 inches) above side(s).

2 Beat butter, essence and sugar in bowl with electric mixer until light and fluffy. Transfer mixture to a larger bowl; stir in coconut cream and sifted flour, in two batches.

3 Beat egg whites in bowl (see tips) with electric mixer until soft peaks form. Fold egg whites into coconut mixture, in two batches. Spread mixture into pan.

4 Bake cake for the time given in chart. Cover cake with foil halfway through baking if cake is over-browning, or lower the oven temperature by 10-20 degrees if cake is over 20cm.

5 Test cake by inserting a skewer into centre of cake; if cooked, skewer will be clean, if there is cake mixture on the skewer, bake cake a further 10 minutes before testing again.

6 Cool cake in pan.

tips The egg whites need to be beaten in a narrow bowl so that the beaters are well down in the egg whites to create the necessary volume. If beating large quantities of egg whites, say, more than 10, beat them in 2 or more batches. This cake is quite soft, and needs to be cooled in the pan before turning out. The cake will keep well for 3 days in an airtight container, or it can be frozen for 3 months.

Carrot Cake

INGREDIENTS	DEEP 10CM (4-INCH) ROUND	DEEP 12CM (5-INCH) ROUND	SHALLOW 15CM (6-INCH) ROUND	DEEP 15CM (6-INCH) ROUND	SHALLOW 18CM (7-INCH) ROUND	DEEP 18CM (7-INCH) ROUND	SHALLOW 20CM (8-INCH) ROUND
SELF-RAISING FLOUR	¼ cup	⅓ cup	⅓ cup	½ cup	½ cup	¾ cup	1 cup
PLAIN (ALL-PURPOSE) FLOUR	2 tablespoons	¼ cup	¼ cup	⅓ cup	⅓ cup	½ cup	½ cup
BICARBONATE OF SODA	¼ teaspoon	¼ teaspoon	¼ teaspoon	½ teaspoon	½ teaspoon	½ teaspoon	½ teaspoon
MIXED SPICE	½ teaspoon	1 teaspoon	1 teaspoon	1 teaspoon	1 teaspoon	2 teaspoons	2 teaspoons
LIGHT BROWN SUGAR	2 tablespoons	¼ cup	¼ cup	⅓ cup	⅓ cup	½ cup	½ cup
COARSELY GRATED CARROT	½ cup	¾ cup	¾ cup	1 cup	1 cup	1½ cups	1½ cups
VEGETABLE OIL	1½ tablespoons	¼ cup	¼ cup	⅓ cup	⅓ cup	½ cup	½ cup
EGGS (60g/2oz)	1	1	1	1	1	2	2
SOUR CREAM	1½ tablespoons	¼ cup	¼ cup	⅓ cup	⅓ cup	½ cup	½ cup
BAKING TIME (approx)	50 minutes	1 hour	30 minutes	1 hour	45 minutes	1¼ hours	1 hour

INGREDIENTS	DEEP 20CM (8-INCH) ROUND	DEEP 22CM (9-INCH) ROUND	SHALLOW 25CM (10-INCH) ROUND	DEEP 25CM (10-INCH) ROUND	DEEP 30CM (12-INCH) ROUND	DEEP 35CM (14-INCH) ROUND
SELF-RAISING FLOUR	1 cup	1½ cups	1½ cups	1¾ cups	3 cups	4 cups
PLAIN (ALL-PURPOSE) FLOUR	⅔ cup	1 cup	1 cup	1¼ cups	2 cups	2⅔ cups
BICARBONATE OF SODA	¾ teaspoon	1 teaspoon	1 teaspoon	1¼ teaspoons	2 teaspoons	3 teaspoons
MIXED SPICE	2 teaspoons	3 teaspoons	3 teaspoons	1 tablespoon	2 tablespoons	2 tablespoons
LIGHT BROWN SUGAR	¾ cup	1 cup	1 cup	1¼ cups	2 cups	3 cups
COARSELY GRATED CARROT	2 cups	3 cups	3 cups	3¾ cups	6 cups	8 cups
VEGETABLE OIL	⅔ cup	1 cup	1 cup	1¼ cups	2 cups	2⅔ cups
EGGS (60g/2oz)	3	4	4	5	8	12
SOUR CREAM	⅔ cup	1 cup	1 cup	1¼ cups	2 cups	2⅔ cups
BAKING TIME (approx)	1½ hours	1¾ hours	1¾ hours	2 hours	2½ hours	3¼ hours

INGREDIENTS	SHALLOW 10CM (4-INCH) SQUARE	DEEP 10CM (4-INCH) SQUARE	SHALLOW 15CM (6-INCH) SQUARE	DEEP 15 CM (6-INCH) SQUARE	SHALLOW 18CM (7-INCH) SQUARE	DEEP 18CM (7-INCH) SQUARE	SHALLOW 20CM (8-INCH) SQUARE
SELF-RAISING FLOUR	¼ cup	⅓ cup	½ cup	¾ cup	¾ cup	1 cup	1 cup
PLAIN (ALL-PURPOSE) FLOUR	2 tablespoons	¼ cup	⅓ cup	½ cup	½ cup	⅔ cup	⅔ cup
BICARBONATE OF SODA	¼ teaspoon	¼ teaspoon	½ teaspoon	½ teaspoon	½ teaspoon	¾ teaspoon	¾ teaspoon
MIXED SPICE	½ teaspoon	1 teaspoon	1 teaspoon	2 teaspoons	2 teaspoons	2 teaspoons	2 teaspoons
LIGHT BROWN SUGAR	2 tablespoons	¼ cup	⅓ cup	½ cup	½ cup	¾ cup	¾ cup
COARSELY GRATED CARROT	½ cup	¾ cup	1 cup	1½ cups	1½ cups	2 cups	2 cups
VEGETABLE OIL	1½ tablespoons	¼ cup	⅓ cup	½ cup	½ cup	⅔ cup	⅔ cup
EGGS (60g/2oz)	1	1	1	2	2	3	3
SOUR CREAM	1½ tablespoons	¼ cup	⅓ cup	½ cup	½ cup	⅔ cup	⅔ cup
BAKING TIME (approx)	40 minutes	1 hour	1 hour	1¼ hours	50 minutes	1½ hours	1 hour

INGREDIENTS	DEEP 20CM (8-INCH) SQUARE	SHALLOW 22CM (9-INCH) SQUARE	DEEP 22CM (9-INCH) SQUARE	SHALLOW 25CM (10-INCH) SQUARE	DEEP 25CM (10-INCH) SQUARE	DEEP 30CM (12-INCH) SQUARE
SELF-RAISING FLOUR	1½ cups	1½ cups	1¾ cups	1¾ cups	3 cups	4 cups
PLAIN (ALL-PURPOSE) FLOUR	1 cup	1 cup	1¼ cups	1¼ cups	2 cups	2⅔ cups
BICARBONATE OF SODA	1 teaspoon	1 teaspoon	1¼ teaspoons	1¼ teaspoons	2 teaspoons	3 teaspoons
MIXED SPICE	3 teaspoons	3 teaspoons	1 tablespoon	1 tablespoon	2 tablespoons	2 tablespoons
LIGHT BROWN SUGAR	1 cup	1 cup	1¼ cups	1¼ cups	2 cups	3 cups
COARSELY GRATED CARROT	3 cups	3 cups	3¾ cups	3¾ cups	6 cups	8 cups
VEGETABLE OIL	1 cup	1 cup	1¼ cups	1¼ cups	2 cups	2⅔ cups
EGGS (60g/2oz)	4	4	5	5	8	12
SOUR CREAM	1 cup	1 cup	1¼ cups	1¼ cups	2 cups	2⅔ cups
BAKING TIME (approx)	1¾ hours	1 hour	2 hours	1¾ hours	2½ hours	3¼ hours

INGREDIENTS	DEEP 18CM (7-INCH) HEART SHAPED	DEEP 15CM (6-INCH) OCTAGONAL	DEEP 20 CM (8-INCH) OCTAGONAL	12-HOLE MUFFIN PAN (⅓-CUP/80ML)
SELF-RAISING FLOUR	¾ cup	¾ cup	1½ cups	1 cup
PLAIN (ALL-PURPOSE) FLOUR	½ cup	½ cup	1 cup	⅔ cup
BICARBONATE OF SODA	½ teaspoon	½ teaspoon	1 teaspoon	¾ teaspoon
MIXED SPICE	2 teaspoons	2 teaspoons	3 teaspoons	2 teaspoons
LIGHT BROWN SUGAR	½ cup	½ cup	1 cup	¾ cup
COARSELY GRATED CARROT	1½ cups	1½ cups	3 cups	2 cups
VEGETABLE OIL	½ cup	½ cup	1 cup	⅔ cup
EGGS (60g/2oz)	2	2	4	3
SOUR CREAM	½ cup	½ cup	1 cup	⅔ cup
BAKING TIME (approx)	1¼ hours	1¼ hours	1¾ hours	30 minutes

We used 7.5cm (3-inch) deep cake pans with straight sides. Eggs and sour cream should be at room temperature for best results. Brown sugar and carrot should be firmly packed into measuring cup. Imperial measurements are an approximation only.

1 Preheat oven to 160°C/325°F. Grease and line base and side(s) of cake pan with baking paper, extending paper 5cm (2 inches) above side(s).
2 Sift flours, soda, spice and sugar into bowl. Add carrot; stir in combined oil, eggs and sour cream (do not over-mix). Spread mixture into pan.
3 Bake cake for the time given in chart. Cover cake with foil halfway through baking if cake is over-browning, or lower the oven temperature by 10-20 degrees if cake is over 20cm.
4 Test cake by inserting a skewer into centre of cake; if cooked, skewer will be clean, if there is cake mixture on the skewer, bake cake a further 10 minutes before testing again.
5 Stand cake in the pan for 10 to 30 minutes, depending on the size of cake, before turning, top-side down, onto wire rack to cool.

tip The cake will keep well for 5 days in an airtight container, or can be frozen for 3 months.

White Chocolate Mud Cake

INGREDIENTS	DEEP 10CM (4-INCH) ROUND	DEEP 12CM (5-INCH) ROUND	SHALLOW 15CM (6-INCH) ROUND	DEEP 15CM (6-INCH) ROUND	SHALLOW 18CM (7-INCH) ROUND	DEEP 18CM (7-INCH) ROUND	SHALLOW 20CM (8-INCH) ROUND
BUTTER	60g (2oz)	85g (3oz)	85g (3oz)	125g (4oz)	125g (4oz)	165g (5oz)	165g (5oz)
WHITE EATING CHOCOLATE	35g (1oz)	45g (1½oz)	45g (1½oz)	75g (2½oz)	75g (2½oz)	100g (3oz)	100g (3oz)
CASTER (SUPERFINE) SUGAR	½ cup	⅔ cup	⅔ cup	1 cup	1 cup	1⅓ cups	1⅓ cups
MILK	¼ cup	⅓ cup	⅓ cup	½ cup	½ cup	⅔ cup	⅔ cup
PLAIN (ALL-PURPOSE) FLOUR	⅓ cup	½ cup	½ cup	¾ cup	¾ cup	1 cup	1 cup
SELF-RAISING FLOUR	1 tablespoon	2 tablespoons	2 tablespoons	¼ cup	¼ cup	⅓ cup	⅓ cup
VANILLA EXTRACT	¼ teaspoon	¼ teaspoon	¼ teaspoon	½ teaspoon	½ teaspoon	½ teaspoon	½ teaspoon
EGGS (60g/2oz)	1	1	1	1	1	1	1
BAKING TIME (approx)	50 minutes	1 hour	50 minutes	1½ hours	1¼ hours	1¾ hours	1¼ hours

INGREDIENTS	DEEP 20CM (8-INCH) ROUND	DEEP 22CM (9-INCH) ROUND	SHALLOW 25CM (10-INCH) ROUND	DEEP 25CM (10-INCH) ROUND	DEEP 30CM (12-INCH) ROUND	DEEP 35CM (14-INCH) ROUND
BUTTER	250g (8oz)	335g (10½oz)	335g (10½oz)	375g (12oz)	625g (1¼lb)	1kg (2lb)
WHITE EATING CHOCOLATE	150g (4½oz)	200g (6½oz)	200g (6½oz)	225g (7oz)	375g (12oz)	600g (1¼lb)
CASTER (SUPERFINE) SUGAR	2 cups	2⅔ cups	2⅔ cups	3 cups	5 cups	8 cups
MILK	1 cup	1½ cups	1½ cups	1½ cups	2½ cups	4 cups
PLAIN (ALL-PURPOSE) FLOUR	1½ cups	2 cups	2 cups	2¼ cups	3¾ cups	6 cups
SELF-RAISING FLOUR	½ cup	⅔ cup	⅔ cup	¾ cup	1¼ cups	2 cups
VANILLA EXTRACT	1 teaspoon	1 teaspoon	1 teaspoon	1½ teaspoons	2½ teaspoons	1 tablespoon
EGGS (60g/2oz)	2	3	3	3	5	8
BAKING TIME (approx)	1¾ hours	2 hours	1¾ hours	2½ hours	3½ hours	4½ hours

INGREDIENTS	SHALLOW 10CM (4-INCH) SQUARE	DEEP 10CM (4-INCH) SQUARE	SHALLOW 15CM (6-INCH) SQUARE	DEEP 15CM (6-INCH) SQUARE	SHALLOW 18CM (7-INCH) SQUARE	DEEP 18CM (7-INCH) SQUARE
BUTTER	60g (2oz)	85g (3oz)	125g (4oz)	165g (5oz)	165g (5oz)	250g (8oz)
WHITE EATING CHOCOLATE	35g (1oz)	45g (1½oz)	75g (2½oz)	100g (3oz)	100g (3oz)	150g (4½oz)
CASTER (SUPERFINE) SUGAR	½ cup	⅔ cup	1 cup	1⅓ cups	1⅓ cups	2 cups
MILK	¼ cup	⅓ cup	½ cup	⅔ cup	⅔ cup	1 cup
PLAIN (ALL-PURPOSE) FLOUR	⅓ cup	½ cup	¾ cup	1 cup	1 cup	1½ cups
SELF-RAISING FLOUR	1 tablespoon	2 tablespoons	¼ cup	⅓ cup	⅓ cup	½ cup
VANILLA EXTRACT	¼ teaspoon	¼ teaspoon	½ teaspoon	½ teaspoon	½ teaspoon	1 teaspoon
EGGS (60g/2oz)	1	1	1	1	1	2
BAKING TIME (approx)	50 minutes	1 hour	1¼ hours	1¾ hours	1½ hours	1¾ hours

INGREDIENTS	SHALLOW 20CM (8-INCH) SQUARE	DEEP 20CM (8-INCH) SQUARE	SHALLOW 22CM (9-INCH) SQUARE	DEEP 22CM (9-INCH) SQUARE	SHALLOW 25CM (10-INCH) SQUARE	DEEP 25CM (10-INCH) SQUARE	DEEP 30CM (12-INCH) SQUARE
BUTTER	250g (8oz)	335g (10½oz)	335g (10½oz)	375g (12oz)	375g (12oz)	500g (1lb)	750g (1½lb)
WHITE EATING CHOCOLATE	150g (4½oz)	200g (6½oz)	200g (6½oz)	225g (7oz)	225g (7oz)	300g (9½oz)	450g (14½oz)
CASTER (SUPERFINE) SUGAR	2 cups	2⅔ cups	2⅔ cups	3 cups	3 cups	4 cups	6 cups
MILK	1 cup	1½ cups	1½ cups	1½ cups	1½ cups	2 cups	3 cups
PLAIN (ALL-PURPOSE) FLOUR	1½ cups	2 cups	2 cups	2¼ cups	2¼ cups	3 cups	4½ cups
SELF-RAISING FLOUR	½ cup	⅔ cup	⅔ cup	¾ cup	¾ cup	1 cup	1½ cups
VANILLA EXTRACT	1 teaspoon	1 teaspoon	1 teaspoon	1½ teaspoons	1½ teaspoons	2 teaspoons	3 teaspoons
EGGS (60g/2oz)	2	3	3	3	3	4	6
BAKING TIME (approx)	1¾ hours	2 hours	1½ hours	2½ hours	2 hours	3 hours	4 hours

INGREDIENTS	DEEP 18CM (7-INCH) HEART SHAPED	DEEP 15CM (6-INCH) OCTAGONAL	DEEP 20CM (8-INCH) OCTAGONAL	12-HOLE MUFFIN PAN (⅓-CUP/80ML)
BUTTER	165g (5oz)	165g (5oz)	335g (10½oz)	250g (8oz)
WHITE EATING CHOCOLATE	100g (3oz)	100g (3oz)	200g (6½oz)	150g (4½oz)
CASTER (SUPERFINE) SUGAR	1⅓ cups	1⅓ cups	2⅔ cups	2 cups
MILK	⅔ cup	⅔ cup	1½ cups	1 cup
PLAIN (ALL-PURPOSE) FLOUR	1 cup	1 cup	2 cups	1½ cups
SELF-RAISING FLOUR	⅓ cup	⅓ cup	⅔ cup	½ cup
VANILLA EXTRACT	½ teaspoon	½ teaspoon	1 teaspoon	1 teaspoon
EGGS (60g/2oz)	1	1	3	2
BAKING TIME (approx)	1¾ hours	1¾ hours	2 hours	45 minutes

WE USED 7.5CM (3-INCH) DEEP CAKE PANS WITH STRAIGHT SIDES. EGGS SHOULD BE AT ROOM TEMPERATURE FOR BEST RESULTS. THE IMPERIAL MEASUREMENTS USED HERE ARE AN APPROXIMATION ONLY.

1 Preheat oven to 160°C/325°F. Grease and line base and side(s) of cake pan with baking paper, extending paper 5cm (2 inches) above side(s).

2 Combine chopped butter, broken chocolate, sugar and milk in a saucepan; stir over low heat until mixture is smooth. Transfer mixture to a bowl; cool 15 minutes.

3 Whisk in sifted flours, extract and lightly beaten eggs. Pour mixture into pan.

4 Bake the cake for the time given in chart. Cover cake with foil halfway through baking if the cake is over-browning, or lower the oven temperature by 10-20 degrees if cake is over 20cm.

5 Cake will develop a thick sugary crust during baking (cracks are normal); test for firmness by touching with fingers about 5 minutes before the end of baking time, then, test with a skewer. If cooked, skewer will be clean, if there is cake mixture on the skewer, bake cake a further 10 minutes before testing again.

6 Cool cake in pan.

tip The cake will keep well for 1 week in an airtight container, or can be frozen for 3 months.

Dark Chocolate Mud Cake

INGREDIENTS	DEEP 10CM (4-INCH) ROUND	DEEP 12CM (5-INCH) ROUND	SHALLOW 15CM (6-INCH) ROUND	DEEP 15CM (6-INCH) ROUND	SHALLOW 18CM (7-INCH) ROUND	DEEP 18CM (7-INCH) ROUND	SHALLOW 20CM (8-INCH) ROUND
BUTTER	85g (3oz)	125g (4oz)	125g (4oz)	175g (5½oz)	175g (5½oz)	225g (7oz)	225g (7oz)
DARK EATING CHOCOLATE	135g (4oz)	185g (6oz)	185g (6oz)	270g (8½oz)	270g (8½oz)	360g (11½oz)	360g (11½oz)
INSTANT COFFEE GRANULES	1½ teaspoons	2 teaspoons	2 teaspoons	3 teaspoons	3 teaspoons	1 tablespoon	1 tablespoon
WATER	¼ cup	⅓ cup	⅓ cup	½ cup	½ cup	¾ cup	¾ cup
LIGHT BROWN SUGAR	¼ cup	⅓ cup	⅓ cup	½ cup	½ cup	¾ cup	¾ cup
PLAIN (ALL-PURPOSE) FLOUR	⅓ cup	½ cup	½ cup	¾ cup	¾ cup	1 cup	1 cup
SELF-RAISING FLOUR	1½ tablespoons	2 tablespoons	2 tablespoons	¼ cup	¼ cup	¼ cup	¼ cup
EGGS (60g/2oz)	1	1	1	1	1	2	2
COFFEE-FLAVOURED LIQUEUR	1½ tablespoons	2 tablespoons	2 tablespoons	¼ cup	¼ cup	¼ cup	¼ cup
BAKING TIME (approx)	1½ hours	1¾ hours	1½ hours	2 hours	1½ hours	2 hours	2 hours

INGREDIENTS	DEEP 20CM (8-INCH) ROUND	DEEP 22CM (9-INCH) ROUND	SHALLOW 25CM (10-INCH) ROUND	DEEP 25CM (10-INCH) ROUND	DEEP 30CM (12-INCH) ROUND	DEEP 35CM (14-INCH) ROUND
BUTTER	395g (12½oz)	430g (14oz)	430g (14oz)	525g (1lb)	900g (1¾lb)	1.5kg (3lb)
DARK EATING CHOCOLATE	625g (1¼lb)	675g (1¼lb)	675g (1¼lb)	840g (1¾lb)	1.5kg (3lb)	2.5kg (5½lb)
INSTANT COFFEE GRANULES	1½ tablespoons	1½ tablespoons	1½ tablespoons	2 tablespoons	⅓ cup	½ cup
WATER	1 cup	1¼ cups	1¼ cups	1½ cups	2⅔ cups	4 cups
LIGHT BROWN SUGAR	1 cup	1¼ cups	1¼ cups	1½ cups	2⅔ cups	4 cups
PLAIN (ALL-PURPOSE) FLOUR	1½ cups	1¾ cups	1¾ cups	2 cups	3½ cups	6 cups
SELF-RAISING FLOUR	⅓ cup	½ cup	½ cup	½ cup	1 cup	1⅓ cups
EGGS (60g/2oz)	3	4	4	4	7	12
COFFEE-FLAVOURED LIQUEUR	⅓ cup	⅓ cup	⅓ cup	½ cup	1 cup	1⅓ cups
BAKING TIME (approx)	2½ hours	2¾ hours	2¼ hours	3¼ hours	4¼ hours	5 hours

INGREDIENTS	SHALLOW 10CM (4-INCH) SQUARE	DEEP 10CM (4-INCH) SQUARE	SHALLOW 15CM (6-INCH) SQUARE	DEEP 15CM (6-INCH) SQUARE	SHALLOW 18CM (7-INCH) SQUARE	DEEP 18CM (7-INCH) SQUARE
BUTTER	60g (2oz)	110g (3½oz)	125g (4oz)	225g (7oz)	225g (7oz)	395g (12½oz)
DARK EATING CHOCOLATE	90g (3oz)	180g (5½oz)	185g (6oz)	360g (11½oz)	360g (11½oz)	625g (1¼lb)
INSTANT COFFEE GRANULES	1 teaspoon	2 teaspoons	2 teaspoons	1 tablespoon	1 tablespoon	1½ tablespoons
WATER	1½ teaspoons	⅓ cup	⅓ cup	¾ cup	¾ cup	1 cup
LIGHT BROWN SUGAR	2 tablespoons	⅓ cup	⅓ cup	¾ cup	¾ cup	1 cup
PLAIN (ALL-PURPOSE) FLOUR	2 tablespoons	½ cup	½ cup	1 cup	1 cup	1½ cups
SELF-RAISING FLOUR	1 tablespoon	1½ tablespoons	2 tablespoons	¼ cup	¼ cup	⅓ cup
EGGS (60g/2oz)	1	1	1	2	2	3
COFFEE-FLAVOURED LIQUEUR	1 tablespoon	1½ tablespoons	2 tablespoons	¼ cup	¼ cup	⅓ cup
BAKING TIME (approx)	1¼ hours	1¼ hours	1¾ hours	2¼ hours	2 hours	2½ hours

INGREDIENTS	SHALLOW 20CM (8-INCH) SQUARE	DEEP 20CM (8-INCH) SQUARE	SHALLOW 22CM (9-INCH) SQUARE	DEEP 22CM (9-INCH) SQUARE	SHALLOW 25CM (10-INCH) SQUARE	DEEP 25CM (10-INCH) SQUARE	DEEP 30CM (12-INCH) SQUARE
BUTTER	395g (12½oz)	430g (14oz)	430g (14oz)	525g (1lb)	525g (1lb)	750g (1½lb)	1kg (2lb)
DARK EATING CHOCOLATE	625g (1¼lb)	675g (1¼lb)	675g (1¼lb)	840g (1¾lb)	840g (1¾lb)	1.2kg (2½lb)	1.7kg (3½lb)
INSTANT COFFEE GRANULES	1½ tablespoons	1½ tablespoons	1½ tablespoons	2 tablespoons	2 tablespoons	¼ cup	⅓ cup
WATER	1 cup	1¼ cups	1¼ cups	1½ cups	1½ cups	2¼ cups	3 cups
LIGHT BROWN SUGAR	1 cup	1¼ cups	1¼ cups	1½ cups	1½ cups	2¼ cups	3 cups
PLAIN (ALL-PURPOSE) FLOUR	1½ cups	1¾ cups	1¾ cups	2 cups	2 cups	3 cups	4 cups
SELF-RAISING FLOUR	⅓ cup	½ cup	½ cup	½ cup	½ cup	¾ cup	1 cup
EGGS (60g/2oz)	3	4	4	4	4	6	8
COFFEE-FLAVOURED LIQUEUR	⅓ cup	⅓ cup	⅓ cup	½ cup	½ cup	¾ cup	1 cup
BAKING TIME (approx)	2¼ hours	2¾ hours	2¼ hours	3¼ hours	3 hours	3¾ hours	4¾ hours

INGREDIENTS	DEEP 18CM (7-INCH) HEART SHAPED	DEEP 15CM (6-INCH) OCTAGONAL	DEEP 20CM (8-INCH) OCTAGONAL	12-HOLE MUFFIN PAN (⅓-CUP/80ML)
BUTTER	225g (7oz)	225g (7oz)	430g (14oz)	395g (12½oz)
DARK EATING CHOCOLATE	360g (11½oz)	360g (11½oz)	675g (1¼lb)	625g (1¼lb)
INSTANT COFFEE GRANULES	1 tablespoon	1 tablespoon	1½ tablespoons	1½ tablespoons
WATER	¾ cup	¾ cup	1¼ cups	1 cup
LIGHT BROWN SUGAR	¾ cup	¾ cup	1¼ cups	1 cup
PLAIN (ALL-PURPOSE) FLOUR	1 cup	1 cup	1¾ cups	1½ cups
SELF-RAISING FLOUR	¼ cup	¼ cup	½ cup	⅓ cup
EGGS (60g/2oz)	2	2	4	3
COFFEE-FLAVOURED LIQUEUR	¼ cup	¼ cup	⅓ cup	⅓ cup
BAKING TIME (approx)	2 hours	2 hours	2¾ hours	45 minutes

WE USED 7.5CM (3-INCH) DEEP CAKE PANS WITH STRAIGHT SIDES. EGGS SHOULD BE AT ROOM TEMPERATURE FOR BEST RESULTS. THE LIGHT BROWN SUGAR SHOULD BE FIRMLY PACKED INTO THE MEASURING CUP. USE SOFT LIGHT BROWN SUGAR IN THIS RECIPE, NOT SOFT DARK BROWN OR RAW SUGAR. THE IMPERIAL MEASUREMENTS USED HERE ARE AN APPROXIMATION ONLY.

1 Preheat oven to 150°C/300°F. Grease and line base and side(s) of cake pan with baking paper, extending paper 5cm (2 inches) above side(s).

2 Combine chopped butter, broken chocolate, coffee, the water and sugar in saucepan; stir over low heat until smooth. Transfer mixture to bowl; cool 15 minutes.

3 Whisk in sifted flours, lightly beaten eggs and liqueur. Pour mixture into pan.

4 Bake cake for the time given in chart. Cover cake with foil halfway through baking if cake is over-browning, or lower the oven temperature by 10-20 degrees if cake is over 20cm.

5 Cake will develop a thick sugary crust during baking (cracks are normal); test for firmness by touching with fingers about 5 minutes before the end of baking time, then, test with a skewer. If cooked, skewer will be clean, if there is cake mixture on the skewer, bake a further 10 minutes before testing again.

6 Cool cake in pan.

tip The cake will keep well for 1 week in an airtight container, or can be frozen for 3 months.

Fruit Cake

INGREDIENTS	DEEP 10CM (4-INCH) ROUND	DEEP 12CM (5-INCH) ROUND	SHALLOW 15CM (6-INCH) ROUND	DEEP 15CM (6-INCH) ROUND	SHALLOW 18CM (7-INCH) ROUND	DEEP 18CM (7-INCH) ROUND	SHALLOW 20CM (8-INCH) ROUND
MIXED DRIED FRUIT	175g (5½oz)	250g (8oz)	250g (8oz)	350g (11oz)	350g (11oz)	650g (1¼lb)	650g (1¼lb)
MARMALADE	2 teaspoons	3 teaspoons	3 teaspoons	1 tablespoon	1 tablespoon	1½ tablespoons	1½ tablespoons
DARK RUM	1½ tablespoons	2 tablespoons	2 tablespoons	¼ cup	¼ cup	⅓ cup	⅓ cup
BUTTER	60g (2oz)	90g (3oz)	90g (3oz)	125g (4oz)	125g (4oz)	160g (5oz)	160g (5oz)
FINELY GRATED CITRUS RIND	½ teaspoon	¾ teaspoon	¾ teaspoon	1 teaspoon	1 teaspoon	1½ teaspoons	1½ teaspoons
DARK BROWN SUGAR	¼ cup	⅓ cup	⅓ cup	½ cup	½ cup	¾ cup	¾ cup
EGGS (60g/2oz)	1	1	1	2	2	3	3
PLAIN (ALL-PURPOSE) FLOUR	½ cup	¾ cup	¾ cup	1 cup	1 cup	1½ cups	1½ cups
MIXED SPICE	¼ teaspoon	¼ teaspoon	¼ teaspoon	½ teaspoon	½ teaspoon	¾ teaspoon	¾ teaspoon
BAKING TIME (approx)	1¼ hours	2 hours	1½ hours	2½ hours	1¾ hours	2½ hours	2¼ hours

INGREDIENTS	DEEP 20CM (8-INCH) ROUND	DEEP 22CM (9-INCH) ROUND	SHALLOW 25CM (10-INCH) ROUND	DEEP 25CM (10-INCH) ROUND	DEEP 30CM (12-INCH) ROUND	DEEP 35CM (14-INCH) ROUND
MIXED DRIED FRUIT	750g (1½lb)	1kg (2lb)	1kg (2lb)	1.5kg (3lb)	2.2kg (5lb)	3kg (6½lb)
MARMALADE	1½ tablespoons	2 tablespoons	2 tablespoons	¼ cup	5 tablespoons	½ cup
DARK RUM	⅓ cup	½ cup	½ cup	¾ cup	1¼ cups	1⅓ cups
BUTTER	200g (6½oz)	250g (8oz)	250g (8oz)	375g (12oz)	625g (1¼lb)	800g (1½lb)
FINELY GRATED CITRUS RIND	1½ teaspoons	2 teaspoons	2 teaspoons	2 teaspoons	1 tablespoon	½ tablespoon
DARK BROWN SUGAR	¾ cup	1 cup	1 cup	1½ cups	2½ cups	3 cups
EGGS (60g/2oz)	3	4	4	6	10	12
PLAIN (ALL-PURPOSE) FLOUR	1⅔ cups	2 cups	2 cups	3 cups	5 cups	6⅔ cups
MIXED SPICE	1 teaspoon	1 teaspoon	1 teaspoon	1½ teaspoons	2½ teaspoons	1 tablespoon
BAKING TIME (approx)	3 hours	3½ hours	3 hours	4 hours	6 hours	7 hours

INGREDIENTS	SHALLOW 10CM (4-INCH) SQUARE	DEEP 10CM (4-INCH) SQUARE	SHALLOW 15CM (6-INCH) SQUARE	DEEP 15CM (6-INCH) SQUARE	SHALLOW 18CM (7-INCH) SQUARE	DEEP 18CM (7-INCH) SQUARE	SHALLOW 20CM (8-INCH) SQUARE
MIXED DRIED FRUIT	175g (5½oz)	250g (8oz)	350g (11oz)	650g (1¼lb)	650g (1¼lb)	750g (1½lb)	1kg (2lb)
MARMALADE	2 teaspoons	3 teaspoons	1 tablespoon	1½ tablespoons	1½ tablespoons	1½ tablespoons	2 tablespoons
DARK RUM	1½ tablespoons	2 tablespoons	¼ cup	⅓ cup	⅓ cup	⅓ cup	½ cup
BUTTER	60g (2oz)	90g (3oz)	125g (4oz)	160g (5oz)	160g (5oz)	200g (6½oz)	250g (8oz)
FINELY GRATED CITRUS RIND	½ teaspoon	¾ teaspoon	1 teaspoon	1½ teaspoons	1½ teaspoons	1½ teaspoons	2 teaspoons
DARK BROWN SUGAR	¼ cup	⅓ cup	½ cup	¾ cup	¾ cup	¾ cup	1 cup
EGGS (60g/2oz)	1	1	2	3	3	3	4
PLAIN (ALL-PURPOSE) FLOUR	½ cup	¾ cup	1 cup	1½ cups	1½ cups	1⅔ cups	2 cups
MIXED SPICE	¼ teaspoon	¼ teaspoon	½ teaspoon	¾ teaspoon	¾ teaspoon	1 teaspoon	1 teaspoon
BAKING TIME (approx)	1 hour	2 hours	2¼ hours	2½ hours	2¼ hours	3 hours	3½ hours

INGREDIENTS	DEEP 20CM (8-INCH) SQUARE	SHALLOW 22CM (9-INCH) SQUARE	DEEP 22CM (9-INCH) SQUARE	SHALLOW 25CM (10-INCH) SQUARE	DEEP 25CM (10-INCH) SQUARE	DEEP 30CM (12-INCH) SQUARE
MIXED DRIED FRUIT	1kg (2lb)	1kg (2lb)	1.5kg (3lb)	1.5kg (3lb)	2.2kg (5lb)	3kg (6½lb)
MARMALADE	2 tablespoons	2 tablespoons	¼ cup	¼ cup	5 tablespoons	½ cup
DARK RUM	½ cup	½ cup	¾ cup	¾ cup	1¼ cups	1⅓ cups
BUTTER	250g (8oz)	250g (8oz)	375g (12oz)	375g (12oz)	625g (1¼lb)	800g (1½lb)
FINELY GRATED CITRUS RIND	2 teaspoons	2 teaspoons	2 teaspoons	2 teaspoons	1 tablespoon	½ tablespoon
DARK BROWN SUGAR	1 cup	1 cup	1½ cups	1½ cups	2½ cups	3 cups
EGGS (60g/2oz)	4	4	6	6	10	12
PLAIN (ALL-PURPOSE) FLOUR	2 cups	2 cups	3 cups	3 cups	5 cups	6⅔ cups
MIXED SPICE	1 teaspoon	1 teaspoon	1½ teaspoons	1½ teaspoons	2½ teaspoons	1 tablespoon
BAKING TIME (approx)	3½ hours	3 hours	4 hours	3¾ hours	5 hours	6½ hours

INGREDIENTS	DEEP 18CM (7-INCH) HEART SHAPED	DEEP 15CM (6-INCH) OCTAGONAL	DEEP 20CM (8-INCH) OCTAGONAL	12-HOLE MUFFIN PAN (⅓-CUP/80ML)
MIXED DRIED FRUIT	650g (1¼lb)	650g (1¼lb)	1kg (2lb)	750g (1½lb)
MARMALADE	1½ tablespoons	1½ tablespoons	2 tablespoons	1½ tablespoons
DARK RUM	⅓ cup	⅓ cup	½ cup	⅓ cup
BUTTER	160g (5oz)	160g (5oz)	250g (8oz)	200g (6½oz)
FINELY GRATED CITRUS RIND	1½ teaspoons	1½ teaspoons	2 teaspoons	1½ teaspoons
DARK BROWN SUGAR	¾ cup	¾ cup	1 cup	¾ cup
EGGS (60g/2oz)	3	3	4	3
PLAIN (ALL-PURPOSE) FLOUR	1½ cups	1½ cups	2 cups	1⅔ cups
MIXED SPICE	¾ teaspoon	¾ teaspoon	1 teaspoon	1 teaspoon
BAKING TIME (approx)	2½ hours	2½ hours	3½ hours	45 minutes

WE USED 7.5CM (3-INCH) DEEP CAKE PANS WITH STRAIGHT SIDES. BUTTER AND EGGS SHOULD BE AT ROOM TEMPERATURE FOR BEST RESULTS; BROWN SUGAR SHOULD BE FIRMLY PACKED INTO MEASURING CUP. USE EQUAL AMOUNTS OF LEMON AND ORANGE RIND TO MAKE CITRUS RIND.
THE IMPERIAL MEASUREMENTS USED HERE ARE AN APPROXIMATION ONLY.

1 Preheat oven to 150°C/325°F. Grease and line base and side(s) of pan (see pages 206-7).
2 Mix fruit, marmalade and rum in bowl. Beat butter, rind and sugar in another bowl with electric mixer until combined; beat in eggs, one at a time. Stir butter mixture into fruit mixture; stir in sifted flour and spice. Spread mixture into pan. Tap pan firmly on bench to settle mixture, level top of cake with wet spatula.
3 Bake cake for the time given in chart. Cover cake with foil halfway through baking if cake is over-browning, or lower the oven temperature by 10-20 degrees if cake is over 20cm.
4 Feel surface of cake; it should feel firm. Remove cake from oven, close oven door, gently push blade of a sharp-pointed vegetable knife straight through centre of cake, right to base of pan. Withdraw knife slowly, feel blade with your fingers; if you feel uncooked mixture, return cake to oven for another 15 minutes before testing again. If the blade is free from mixture, the cake is cooked through.
5 Immediately the cake is cooked, cut off paper around edge(s) of pan. Turn cake, in pan, top-side down onto foil; wrap cake and pan tightly with foil. Cover pan with a towel; cool completely upside down.

tips Cooling cakes upside down will make them sit flat and level for decorating. Fruit cakes will keep indefinitely; the biggest problem is insect infestation. Cake will keep well at room temperature if wrapped in plastic wrap and stored in an airtight container; or freeze, wrapped in plastic wrap in an airtight container.

CAKE PANS

Cut strips of baking paper to line the inside of the pan, overlapping slightly. Make a 2cm fold; snip paper, on an angle, up to the fold.

Lightly grease the pan to hold the lining paper in place. Position the paper around the side of the pan, with snipped fold at the bottom.

Trace the pan base onto baking paper. Cut paper out slightly inside the marked circle. Position in the pan, to cover snipped paper.

CHOICE OF CAKE PANS

Cake pans are often measured and referred to using imperial inches – we have done the same in this book. The conversions from metric to imperial are not exact; however, this will not affect your baking. The charts at the beginning of this chapter (pages 190-205) were tested using all the different-sized pans used in this book.

Cake pans come in all shapes and sizes. Square, rectangular and octagonal shaped pans etc, have sharp corners as opposed to rounded corners; these styles of cakes are better to work with when decorating, as they start off well-shaped. We used 7.5cm (3-inch) deep cake pans with straight sides.

Cake pans are made from various metals: our chosen pans are made from a good-quality heavy tin. Aluminium pans are also good as they conduct heat evenly. We avoid pans that have a non-stick surface or are made from flimsy metal, as cakes cooked in these tend to develop a thick crust, which can be quite tough to bite into – to counter this, reduce the oven temperature by 10 to 20 degrees.

Make sure you wash and dry cake pans thoroughly after use – drying them in a low or just-turned-off oven is a good idea. They can develop rust if they're not dried properly after use.

Before you buy a larger than normal cake pan, first measure and check that it will fit in your oven. Cakes do need a little space around them during the baking process to allow for even heat circulation. Many cake decorating shops will hire cake pans, and this is a good option if you're making a one-time-only cake.

PREPARING CAKE PANS

All cake pans must be either greased, greased and floured, or lined to make sure the cakes don't stick. If the recipe requires a long baking time, due to the type or the size of the cake, it's vital to line the pan correctly to insulate the cake, protect the top of the cake from over-browning and to retain the shape of the cake to minimise patching and trimming, especially if the cake is to be iced and decorated.

Large cakes, over 20cm (8-inch), round or square, usually need to be baked in lined pans. The larger the cake, the more lining paper required. For added insulation, use a layer of brown paper on the outside against the side(s) of the pan, and line with baking paper on the inside of the pan. As a guide, use one layer of baking paper for cakes that take less than 2 hours to bake, and three

Lining a square or rectangular pan is the same as for a round one. Trace the pan base onto baking paper; position over snipped paper.

For unusual-shaped pans, use melted butter and a pastry brush to lightly, but evenly, grease the pan. Place in the fridge to set the butter.

Sprinkle the cold, greased pan evenly with flour. Tap and turn the pan to coat it evenly. Tap inverted pan to remove excess flour.

layers of baking paper for cakes that take 2 to 4 hours to bake. Use a layer of brown paper and three layers of baking paper (or greaseproof paper) for cakes needing longer than 4 hours to bake.

Lining rectangular, square, octagonal, round or oval cake pans: Cut strips of baking paper, long enough to encircle the inside of the pan, overlapping the ends slightly, and wide enough to extend 5cm (2-inches) above the side(s) of the pan. Also, allow for a fold-over at the base of the pan. Fold 2cm (¾ inch) of the paper over, snip

the paper, on an angle, up to the fold, making cuts about 1½ cm (¾ inch) apart. Lightly grease the inside of the pan with cooking-oil spray or melted butter to hold the lining paper in place.

Position the snipped paper around the side of the pan with the snipped fold at the base of the pan. Using the base of the pan as a guide, trace around the base on baking paper. Cut out paper, cutting slightly inside the marked circle/square to allow for the thickness of the pan. Neatly position the paper in the pan, to cover the snipped paper.

Preparing unusual-shaped pans: Some of the unusual-shaped pans, such as the heart pan, can't be lined efficiently. In this case, grease the pan lightly, but evenly, with melted butter, then refrigerate or freeze the pan to set the butter. Sprinkle a little plain (all-purpose) flour all over the greased area, tap and turn the pan so that all the butter is lightly coated with flour. Turn the pan upside down over the sink or bin and knock out any excess flour. If you prefer, line the base of the greased pan with baking paper, then just grease and flour the side(s) of the pan.

CAKE BOARDS

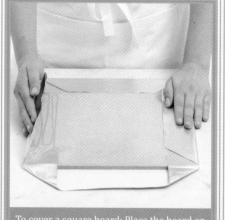

To cover a square board: Place the board on the back of the covering paper, fold sides of paper over neatly; secure with glue or tape.

Covering a round board (1): Place board on the back of the covering paper; using scissors, snip paper at a slight angle around the board.

Covering a round board (2): Secure snipped paper to board with glue; glue plain paper to the back of the board to cover snipped paper.

To cover a board with ready-made icing (1): Use a pastry brush to evenly coat a paper-covered board with sugar syrup (page 217).

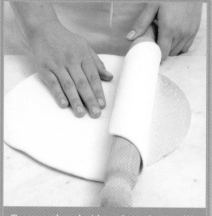

To cover a board with ready-made icing (2): Using rolling pin, cover board with rolled icing. Smooth with hands and smoothing tools.

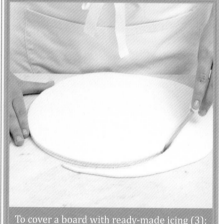

To cover a board with ready-made icing (3): Using a sharp knife, trim excess icing from edge of board; smooth edge(s) with fingertips.

We used wooden cake boards, as wood is strong enough to support the cakes, making them easy to handle and move. They also complement the cake, whether it's single or multi-tiered. They are available from cake decorating shops. If the cake is to be displayed on a stand, you may need to re-think the size of the base board; consider this before starting to decorate. We used imperial inches to measure the boards; the metric conversions are not exact. Covered boards can be bought from cake decorating shops. If you want to cover your own, choose a covering that is non-absorbent; cake decorating shops supply this type of paper. We used cardboard cake boards, available from cake decorating shops, for small individual cakes. Occasionally these must be trimmed to fit the base of the cake.

Covering rectangular or square boards: Cut the covering paper about 5cm (2-inches) larger than the board. Place the board, top-side down, on the back of the paper. Use tape or craft glue to stick the paper to the board. If the paper is thick, cut the corners of the paper as if covering a book. Glue a piece of paper to the back of the board to neaten the appearance.

Covering round boards: Cut the covering paper about 5cm larger than the board. Place the board, top-side down, on the back of the paper. Snip the paper border, on an angle, all the way around. Fold snipped pieces onto the board and tape or glue in place. Glue a piece of paper to the back of the board to neaten the appearance.

Covering boards with ready-made icing: To cover a 30cm (12-inch) board, knead 500g (1 pound) of icing on surface dusted with a little cornflour until icing loses its stickiness. Brush the surface and the side(s) of the board with sugar syrup (page 217). Roll the icing large enough to cover the board, about 3mm thick. Use the rolling pin to lift the icing onto the board; smooth icing using cornfloured hands. Use smoothing tools to gently smooth the icing, easing the icing over the edge(s) of the board. Use a sharp knife to trim the icing neatly around the bottom edge(s) of the board, then smooth the edge with your fingertip (dipped first into cornflour). Stand board for 3 hours or overnight, or until the icing is firm and dry.

PREPARING CAKES FOR COVERING WITH READY-MADE ICING

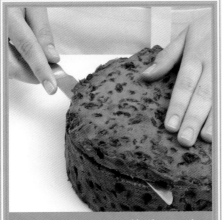

Use a large sharp serrated knife to cut the rounded top off the cake so that it will sit flat when turned upside-down.

Cakes need to be secured to the boards with either royal icing, softened ready-made icing or ganache – royal icing does the best job.

Turn the trimmed cake upside-down; position on the royal icing as soon as it's been applied to the board. Wriggle cake into position.

It's important cakes are properly prepared before icing. A poor covering means the cake won't stay fresh for long, and bacteria may contaminate the cake, degrading both the cake and the icing, not to mention affecting those who eat it. The cakes will keep for up to 2 weeks if covered correctly with an initial layer of ganache or almond paste, then finally covered with ready-made icing so it is airtight. Fruit and mud cakes, if covered and stored correctly, will keep for longer than other cakes. Cupcakes and smaller or cut cakes, will only keep a couple of days. The cakes must be stored in a dust-free area at a cool room temperature. If the weather is humid, it's best to make and keep the cakes in an air-conditioned room.

Trimming cakes: Cakes must first be trimmed before any covering is applied. Most cakes need some trimming to make them flat and a good shape for decorating. We found by cooling heavy cakes, such as mud and fruit cakes, upside-down, their own weight flattens them quite a lot, and this should minimise trimming. A cake needs to sit flat and level on its board, and is almost always turned top-side down to cover with icing. After the cake has cooled

and the lining paper removed, turn the cake top-side up and, using a large serrated knife, cut enough from the top of the cake so it sits flat when turned top-side down. Use a ruler and a small spirit level to get the cake as flat as possible; it's well worth the effort.

Securing cakes to boards: After trimming, cakes need to be secured to their boards so they can be carried safely. Royal icing anchors the cakes well, but if you're not using it to decorate the cakes, then a walnut-sized piece of ready-made icing works well, too. Knead a little cooled boiled water or sugar syrup (page 217) into the icing until it is soft and spreadable. Spread icing into the centre of the board then position the cake on the icing, move it around until it's where you want it. Leave to dry out and set – it will hold the cake securely within about 24 hours.

Patching cakes: Once secured to the board, patch the cake if there are any large holes in its surface – this mainly applies to fruit cakes. Use tiny balls of ready-made icing or almond paste to fill the holes (page 216); smooth level with the cake surface, using a metal-bladed spatula, before initially covering with either almond paste, ganache or ready-made icing.

Initial covering: We prefer either ganache or almond paste for the initial covering. Alternatively, you can use just one thick layer of ready-made icing, in which case, triple the quantities of ready-made icing used to cover the cake. After the cake is trimmed, secured and patched, it is then ready for the initial covering.

Initial covering with almond paste: If a cake is to be covered with almond paste, it first needs to be brushed with sugar syrup or warmed sieved jam (page 217). This helps the paste stick to the cake's surface. The almond paste needs to be brushed again with sugar syrup to make the ready-made icing (final covering) stick to the paste.

Initial covering with ready-made icing: You can use a thin layer of ready-made icing (about 2mm-thick) under another thin layer of ready-made icing; brush the cake with sugar syrup before applying the initial layer, then brush that layer with syrup before applying the second (final) layer.

Initial covering with ganache: Apply the initial covering of ganache very thinly, then, if covering with ready-made icing, brush the ganache with sugar syrup so the icing sticks.

GANACHE

Ganache is a mixture of melted chocolate and cream. It is wonderfully simple to make and versatile to use. It can be used while it's still warm as a glaze over a cake, or even as a sauce with cake. Or, let the ganache partly set, either at a cool room temperature or in the refrigerator, then beat it with a wooden spoon until it's spreadable – making it a perfect filling or frosting. Ganache can be refrigerated for around 30 minutes, or until it becomes thick and spreadable, then whipped with an electric mixer until it increases in volume and becomes fluffy, making it ideal for a frosting or filling.

Ganache will keep in the refrigerator, covered tightly, for about two weeks (stand at room temperature to soften before use), or frozen for 3 months; thaw overnight in the refrigerator, or thaw it in the microwave oven, using short bursts of power.

CHOCOLATE

We used dark- or milk-eating chocolate when testing the ganache recipe, use whichever type you'd be happy to eat and suits the cake. We prefer not to use cooking chocolate, but it will still work in the recipe (right). We don't use high-fat (over 70%) or low-fat chocolate. Couverture chocolate is expensive, but the results are wonderful. It can be bought at some delicatessens and specialty food stores.

White chocolate deserves a special mention as it can be a little tricky to work with – be very careful not to overheat it or it will "split" (turn grainy). We found that by adding more chocolate in proportion to the amount of cream (as compared to milk or dark chocolate) we got better results. Also, we found by chopping white chocolate finely, it melted faster and was less likely to split. We broke the chocolate into pieces straight into the bowl of a food processor, then processed it until finely chopped. If the ganache does split, cool it in the refrigerator, then beat the mixture with an electric mixer; this method hasn't failed us yet. See the finer points of melting chocolate on page 222.

Covering cakes with ganache: This method of using ganache as the initial covering under ready-made icing will result in a well-shaped cake that will taste good, too.

Make the ganache recipe (right). Level and trim the cake (page 209), and secure it to the board; patch the cake, if necessary (page 216), and brush lightly with sugar syrup (page 217). Spread a very, very thin coating of ganache all over the cake to hold the crumbs in place and to use as a base for the next layer of ganache (or ready-made icing or frosting). Think of this fine ganache layer as an undercoat. Stand ganache at a cool room temperature until firm to touch. (If the cake is firm, and has no crumbs, this undercoat is not necessary.)

If also using ganache as the second covering, once the undercoat is firm, lightly brush the cake again with sugar syrup, then use a metal spatula to spread a 1cm (½-inch) layer of ganache over the cake, as evenly as possible. Take your time to get the shape of the cake as perfect as possible; it's worth the effort. Use a straight-sided scraper to smooth the top and side(s) of the ganache covering. Stand the cake at a cool room temperature (an air-conditioned room is perfect) for about 24 hours, or the until ganache is firm and dry to touch. If no other covering is to be applied to the ganache-covered cake, it can be refrigerated, if the weather is hot, or stand at a cool room temperature, until needed (up to a week). Bring to room temperature before cutting and serving.

When covering a ganache undercoat with ready-made icing or frosting, brush the ganache lightly, but evenly, with sugar syrup so the next layer will stick. Trim and neaten any rough edges from the surface of the cake so you don't tear the ready-made icing when applying.

(Note: If covering cakes with ganache then ready-rolled icing, the cake should not be refrigerated as the ganache will absorb the moisture from the fridge, and transfer this to the ready-made icing, making it wet to the touch, sticky and it won't hold its shape.

WHITE CHOCOLATE GANACHE
360g (11½ ounces) white eating
   chocolate
½ cup (125ml) pouring cream

1   Break chocolate into food processor, process until chocolate is chopped finely.
2   Bring cream to the boil in a small saucepan; remove from heat.
3   Add chocolate to cream; stir until smooth.
4   Cool mixture to room temperature if not being used as a glaze (in which case use while warm and pourable) before beating or whipping to the desired consistency.

Makes enough to cover a deep 20cm (8-inch) round cake.

DARK OR MILK CHOCOLATE GANACHE
200g (6½ ounces) milk or dark
   eating chocolate
½ cup (125ml) pouring cream

1   Bring cream to the boil in a small saucepan; remove from heat.
2   Break chocolate into pan with hot cream; stir until smooth.
3   Cool mixture to room temperature if not being used as a glaze (in which case use while warm and pourable) before beating or whipping to the desired consistency.

Makes enough to cover a deep 20cm (8-inch) round cake.

Note: For a really impressive cake, cut it into layers, as we have done in the step shots, and top the layers with ganache, before covering the cake. You could also layer the cake with butter cream, curd, jam or any type of filling that suits the cake.

You can make the ganache by placing the chocolate and cream in a heatproof bowl over a saucepan of simmering water.

The heat from the water will melt the mixture, stir occasionally until smooth. The water should not touch the bottom of the bowl.

Cool ganache at room temperature or in the fridge, stirring occasionally. Beat ganache with an electric mixer until light and fluffy.

If ganache is the only icing being used on the cake, use a dollop to secure cake to board (or plate); spread ganache with a spatula.

Position cake, or a layer of a split cake, on the board (or plate). Gently push the cake layer to centre it or position it as desired.

When layering a cake, spread each layer with ganache. If the weather is hot, refrigerate the layered cake before completing it.

When covering a firm cake (with no crumbs) with ganache, it doesn't need an undercoat; just spread the ganache all over the cake.

Smooth the ganache covering all over with a scraping tool. Take your time to get the shape of the cake as perfect as possible.

Dip the blade of a long-bladed metal spatula into very hot water; dry. Smooth the top of the cake, reheating the blade as necessary.

STACKING AND SUPPORTING TIERS

Throughout this book we've used quite a lot of tall cakes to get the effect we wanted. Sometimes we needed to stack two deep cakes for a really impressive tall cake, other times one deep and one shallow cake stacked together gave us enough height. When stacking and joining same-sized cakes, always stack the shallow cake on top of the deep cake. The charts on pages 190 to 205, listing eight different cake choices, will give you the recipes for making the correct-sized cakes. You can buy the cakes, but make sure you buy deep cakes, or you might have to stack three shallow cakes to achieve the height.

Joining uniced cakes: Cakes can be joined using either jam or ganache. Use any jam you like to join the cakes, one that will complement the flavour of the chosen cake or cakes (page 217). Sometimes it's pleasantly surprising to mix and match two or three different-flavoured cakes. If joining different-flavoured cakes, attach each cake to its own board (page 209), so that the cakes are easy to separate at serving time using a long-bladed metal spatula.

Trim the tops of the cakes to be joined, so they will sit flat on each other (page 209). Join the cut surfaces of the cakes with jam or ganache to minimise any crumbs escaping. Secure the cake to the board (page 209). Once joined to the board(s), patch the cakes, if necessary (page 216); brush with sugar syrup and apply the initial covering of almond paste, ready-made icing or ganache and dry overnight or until dry to touch. Apply the second (final) layer to the cakes and leave overnight or until dry (this may take 2 days). You are now ready to support and stack the cakes.

Supporting tiers: Thick wooden skewers are used to support the weight of the upper tiers. Measure the diameter of the board under the next cake tier. Lightly mark this area in the centre of the tier below. (This is to ensure the next tier is centred on top of the bottom tier, otherwise the weight of the tiers will not be evenly distributed, which can cause heavy cakes to tilt and look unbalanced.) Insert the skewers, pointy end down, right through to the cake board about 1cm (½ inch) in from the marked area to make neat holes in the bottom cake. Remove the skewers, then push them into the same holes, blunt-side down, through to the board. Mark each skewer level with the surface of the cake tier (note which skewer came from which hole). These skewers will support the next tier, so it's important to have no gaps where the tiers join. Use a hacksaw, strong secateurs or a strong serrated knife to cut the skewers as straight as possible, so they are level with the top of the cake tier. Push the skewers into their correct position, cut-side down. (It's best to do this one skewer at a time, so that each skewer is returned to its original hole.) Repeat the skewering process with all the tiers, except the top tier. We use three skewers for each round cake and four skewers for each square cake between each tier. Skewers can be inserted into uniced cakes, if they are to be stacked then iced, as with the *Silhouette Spectacular, page 162* (cakes must be on boards if using skewers).

Stacking cakes: Once the skewers have been inserted into the cakes, the tiers can be stacked on top of each other. Stack and secure the next tier onto the centre of the cake below with royal icing or ready-made icing softened with some cooled boiled

water. Carefully sit the next tier of the cake on top of the skewers, pressing down gently to secure the bottom of the cake board to the iced cake below. Continue stacking all the tiers in the same way, being careful not to damage the covering when skewering and stacking. Fill any gaps between the tiers, where the cakes join the boards.

Filling any gaps: If a cake is to be covered with ganache or a similar frosting, gaps will be easy to cover. If the cakes are covered with ready-made icing, sometimes decorations or an edging around the tiers will cover any small gaps. To fill larger gaps, and keep the cake airtight, tint some royal icing the same colour as the icing covering the cake, and pipe a line of icing around the cake; use your finger to blend the icing around the cake. At serving time, remove the top tier of the cake by sliding a long metal-bladed spatula under the board to remove it from the tier below. Remove all the skewers when cutting and serving the cake.

note: Except for the bottom cake, which is positioned on a board that is 10cm-15cm (4-6 inches) larger than the cake (or, if being displayed on a cake stand or plate, should be positioned on a board of similar size), each tier is positioned on a wooden board that is the same size as the cake. This is to minimise any gaps between the tiers – these boards should not be visible at all.

Transporting cakes: Tiered cakes can be very heavy – especially if fruit or mud cakes are used. Often it takes two people to carry a stacked tiered cake (and one to direct where you're walking and positioning the cake). Transporting a tiered cake can be a problem – it's large, it's heavy and you'll need to anchor the cake for its journey in the car (do not transport it on the car seat).

A thin piece of sponge rubber is usually enough to hold the cake still. Allow plenty of headroom for the cake. The only other way of handling and transporting multi-tiered cakes is to assemble the tiers at the venue. This is often impractical to do.

The *Wedding Cake Wonder* (page 120), uses a wooden dowel to secure the cakes in position. Many cake professionals use this method if the cake is three or more tiers. You can use the same technique for any cake in this book over three tiers, if you like (we used a 12mm dowel, cut to below the height of the cake). You need to drill holes through the centres of all the cake boards.

You also need an undrilled wooden cake board about 5-10cm smaller than your largest board; this is glued onto the bottom of the largest board, and is used to give height beneath the board, so you can get your fingers under it and lift it off the bench (and out of the car). Glue the dowel into the hole in the largest board and allow to dry. The cakes (attached to their drilled boards) are pushed down over the dowel. These cakes still need to be joined with icing, stacked and supported in the usual way with skewers.

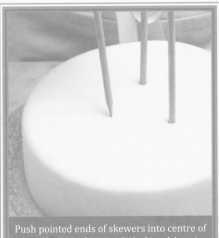

Push pointed ends of skewers into centre of cake right through to touch the board, keeping them straight. This makes a neat hole.

Remove the skewers, one at a time, then push back into the cake, blunt-side down. Mark the skewers close to the cake surface.

Use a serrated knife to cut the skewer at the mark; discard pointed end. Replace skewer into cake. It's best to do one skewer at a time.

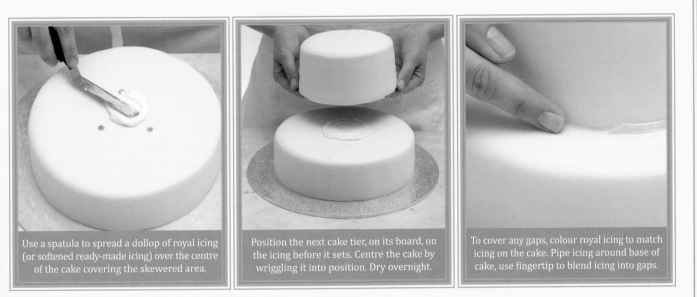

Use a spatula to spread a dollop of royal icing (or softened ready-made icing) over the centre of the cake covering the skewered area.

Position the next cake tier, on its board, on the icing before it sets. Centre the cake by wriggling it into position. Dry overnight.

To cover any gaps, colour royal icing to match icing on the cake. Pipe icing around base of cake, use fingertip to blend icing into gaps.

READY-MADE ICING

This is a great product and very forgiving for the amateur cake decorator. As with anything, you will get better at handling the icing with practise. It's available in 500g (1 pound) packets from supermarkets (usually found amongst the baking goods), and some health-food shops and delicatessens and is found in much larger quantities from cake decorating shops. We have specified the amount of this icing you will need for each recipe. We have presumed you have initially covered the cake with either almond paste, ganache or a thin layer of ready-made icing (page 209), so we have specified only enough ready-made icing to make a thin layer over the initial covering. Should you want to use ready-made icing as the only covering on a cake, you will have to triple the quantity called for in each recipe. In most cases, cakes covered with this icing need to be left to dry for about 2 days – the time depends on the weather. If the weather is humid or wet and the icing is not drying out, put the cake in a small room, such as a bathroom or laundry, with a fan heater. Don't have the fan too hot or blowing directly onto the cake, just in case there is dust in the heater. The hot air will soon dry out the

icing. If possible, work in air-conditioning when cake decorating, as it makes the processes so much easier. Some cakes in this book need to be decorated with the ready-made icing unset so patterns can be imprinted on it; others require it to be firm or completely set. Follow individual recipe instructions.

Colouring ready-made icing: Use good quality food colourings for best results (not the liquid dyes found in supermarkets). Always start with a tiny dab of the colouring (use a skewer or toothpick), work it through a small ball of the icing with your fingers until it is evenly coloured. Determine the depth and strength of the colouring before adding any more and kneading it through the rest of the icing. Some cake decorating suppliers stock ready-made icings already coloured – this saves a lot of time and effort.

To cover a cake with ready-made icing: Brush the initial covering on the cake well, and evenly, with sugar syrup before you roll out the icing. Cut off as much icing as you need; re-wrap the remaining icing to exclude air or a crust will develop, which will spoil the smooth texture of the icing. Knead icing,

working colouring in, on a surface dusted lightly with a little cornflour until icing is smooth and loses its stickiness. Then use a little cornflour on both the work surface and your hands, to handle the icing when rolling it out. It's important you don't use too much cornflour, as it will dry out the icing, which will cause cracks to occur in the icing when you cover the cakes. Cover any rolled icing with plastic wrap or a vinyl mat while not working with it to prevent it from drying out. Roughly measure up the side of the cake, across the top and down the other side so you have an idea of how large to roll the icing (the icing will stretch once you pick it up and while you're placing it over the cake). Use your hand to press the icing out first to a manageable thickness in the shape of the cake (circle, square), then start rolling from the centre of the icing outwards; don't roll over the edge of the icing. Use a rolling pin to roll the icing to the correct size and thickness (about 3-4mm/⅛-inch, for the final cover). The icing can be rolled between sheets of baking paper, or use a non-stick mat that's suitable for rolling out icing. The mats can be bought from cake decorating shops. When rolling,

Use a toothpick to dab a little colouring onto the icing. Knead on a lightly cornfloured surface to work the colouring through evenly.

Roll out the icing on a lightly cornfloured surface. Roll from centre to the outside edge turning and easing the icing to fit the cake.

Gently roll icing around rolling pin. Hold the pin with one hand while supporting the icing with the other. Lift icing over cake.

try to keep the icing the shape you need, to match the shape of the cake, and the same thickness all over; do this by gently stretching and rotating the icing around as you roll. Never turn the icing over when rolling it out. Roll the icing around the rolling pin, then lift the icing over the cake. Dust your hands lightly with cornflour, and mould and smooth the icing around the shape of the cake, gently easing out any folds in the icing. Make sure the icing feels as if it is clinging to the cake and there are no air pockets under the icing. Using the plastic smoothing tools, smooth the edges and corners of the cakes neatly. Use a small sharp pointed knife to carefully trim away excess icing from around the base of the cake. Scraps of icing will keep well for months if they're wrapped tightly in plastic wrap to exclude the air. If you're making a tiered cake, incorporate the scraps into the next batch of icing. If air bubbles develop in the icing during kneading, use a fine pin or fine needle to burst the bubbles, then gently smooth the icing with your fingers, the bubble and the hole from the pin will soon disappear.

HOME-MADE ICING

If you really want to make your own icing (often referred to as fondant), it's easy to make, but not as easy as buying it.

3 teaspoons powdered gelatine
2 tablespoons water
2 tablespoons glucose syrup
2 teaspoons glycerine
500g (1pound) pure icing (confectioners') sugar

1 Combine gelatine, the water, glucose and glycerine in a small saucepan. Stir over medium heat, without boiling, until gelatine is dissolved. Remove from the heat; cool until liquid is barely warm.
2 Meanwhile, finely sift icing sugar into a medium bowl. Add warm liquid; stir until mixture becomes too stiff to stir.
3 Use your hand to work ingredients into a ball, then turn the icing onto a surface dusted with more sifted icing sugar. Knead icing until smooth. Enclose icing in plastic wrap to keep airtight.

Makes 500g (1 pound)

tips Keep icing at a cool room temperature for 2 days, or in the fridge for 1 week. It can also be frozen for 3 months; thaw overnight in the fridge. Knead icing on a surface dusted lightly with cornflour to return it to its correct consistency.

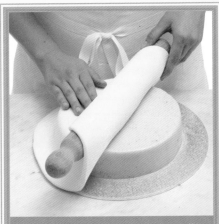

Lower the icing onto cake surface, unrolling it from the rolling pin at the same time. The icing will stretch a little at this stage.

Lightly cornflour your hands. Quickly smooth top of the cake, then smooth side(s) of cake, easing the icing around the shape of the cake.

Trim excess icing from base of the cake. Burst any air bubbles with a fine pin. Use smoothing tools to smooth icing. Neaten the cake base.

ALMOND PASTE

Almond paste, often referred to as marzipan or marzipan paste, is the traditional undercoat for rich fruit cakes, which are then usually covered with ready-made icing. Almond paste is easy to make, however, it can be bought ready-made from cake decorating suppliers, some health-food shops, delicatessens, supermarkets and specialty food shops; price is a good guide to quality.

Ideally, almond-paste covered cakes need to stand for at least one day (depending on the weather – longer if the weather is humid) at room temperature to set (dry) before they are covered with ready-made icing. This gives a firm, manageable surface for the final layer. Roll out the paste on a surface lightly dusted with sifted pure icing sugar.

Covering cakes with almond paste:
Trim and level the top of the cake, so it will sit flat on the board (pages 209). Secure the cake to the board, top-side down. Use tiny balls of almond paste to patch any large holes in the surface of the cake; smooth the paste with a small metal-bladed spatula. Roll thin ropes of almond paste, thick enough to fill any gaps where the cake joins the board; gently push the paste around and under the base of the cake to fill any gaps, then smooth the paste with a spatula.

There are two methods for covering cakes with almond paste. Cakes 20cm (8-inches) or less are easily covered with one large piece of almond paste. Larger cakes are better covered using strips of almond paste for the side(s), and a square, rectangular or round shape cut-to-size, to cover the top of the cake. Brush sugar syrup over cake before covering.

To cover a large cake: To cover the sides of the cake, measure up the side of the cake to determine its height then around the cake. Brush the cake all over with sugar syrup. Roll a piece of paste into a long strip, trim to fit around the side(s) of the cake; do this in about four batches, depending on the size of the cake. Position the strips of paste around the side(s) of the cake. If you like slightly rounded corners on a square or rectangular cake, wrap strips of paste around the corners, joining strips somewhere along the side of the cake. If you prefer sharper corners, take the strips to the corner edge, use your fingers to mould the joins together at each corner.

To cover the top of the cake, use the base of the cake pan as a guide, and roll out a piece of paste large enough to cover the top of the cake. Use your hands or a rolling pin to lift the paste into position on the cake. Use your fingers to mould the joins together. Smooth the paste with cornfloured hands, then use the smoothing tools to smooth the paste. Using a small sharp knife, trim around the base of the cake to neaten.

Use small pieces of almond paste to fill and patch any holes in the cake's surface; smooth level with the cake, using a metal spatula.

Roll long thin pieces of almond paste thick enough to cover gap around the base where it sits on the board. Smooth with a spatula.

Roll paste on lightly cornfloured surface until large enough to cover cake; lift paste onto cake, smooth icing over cake with hands.

ALMOND PASTE

2⅓ cups (375g) pure icing
 (confectioners') sugar
1 cup (125g) almond meal
2 tablespoons brandy
1 egg yolk
1 teaspoon strained lemon juice

1 Sift icing sugar and almond meal into
a large bowl; discard any lumps. Stir in
remaining combined ingredients.
2 When mixture becomes too stiff to stir,
use your fingers to press the ingredients
together. Turn paste onto surface dusted
with extra sifted icing sugar; knead gently
until paste becomes smooth and pliable.
3 Wrap paste in plastic wrap to keep
airtight until required.
Makes 500g (1 pound)

tips Almond paste will keep well in the
refrigerator for 2 weeks or frozen for
several months. Thaw the frozen paste
in the refrigerator overnight. If you're
covering cakes with almond paste before
ready-made icing, you will need the same
quantity of almond paste as the ready-made
icing specified in the recipes.

SUGAR SYRUP

*This can be bought from cake decorating
shops, but it is quick, easy and inexpensive
to make at home. This is used to brush onto
the cake's surface before initially covering
with almond paste, ready-made icing or
ganache (to make them stick). The syrup is
then brushed over the initial covering before
the final layer of ready-made icing, or
ganache, is applied.*

1 cup (220g) caster (superfine) sugar
1 cup (125ml) water

1 Combine sugar and the water in a small
saucepan; stir over high heat, without
boiling, until sugar is dissolved.
2 Bring syrup to the boil; boil, uncovered,
for 5 minutes without stirring. Cool.
3 Pour syrup into a screw-top jar, store in
the fridge for up to 4 weeks.

JAM

Rather than brushing or joining the cakes
with sugar syrup, you can use jams, conserves
or jellies combined with complementary
liqueurs or spirits instead. As a guide, for
a deep 20cm (8-inch) cake you will need
¼ cup jam and 1 tablespoon liqueur. Warm
jam in a small bowl over a small saucepan
of simmering water; strain the jam while it's
warm into another small bowl, then stir in
the liqueur. Alternatively, warm the jam in
a microwave safe bowl, strain it, then add
the liqueur. Make sure the combinations of
flavours marry well with the cake itself.

Here are some ideas:
Apricot jam and Grand Marnier or
 Cointreau or limoncello
Orange marmalade and whisky
Raspberry or strawberry jam and Framboise
Plum jam and brandy
Fig jam and rum or brandy
Redcurrant jelly and brandy

When the cake feels smooth and even, trim
around the base. Use smoothing tools to
make the paste as even and flat as possible.

To cover a large cake, 22cm or more (round,
square or rectangular), cut manageable
strips of paste large enough to cover side(s).

Mould the joins together with cornfloured
fingers. Use the cake pan as a guide to cut
out a piece of paste to cover top of the cake.

BUTTER CREAM

Butter cream, also known as vienna cream, is a popular, easy-to-make frosting to use on cakes. We've left our recipe unflavoured, but if you want, you can use any extract, essence or grated citrus rind you like to flavour it. You can use either regular icing sugar (also known as icing sugar mixture or soft icing sugar – this has cornflour added to soften it) or pure icing sugar (with no added cornflour).

It's important to have the butter at room temperature, not melted or too soft. Use a small narrow mixing bowl, so that the beaters of the electric mixer can get well-down into the mixture.

The best way to cover a cake with butter cream is to spread a thin layer all over the cake, then refrigerate the cake to set the butter cream; this, in turn, will capture any loose crumbs. Apply the remaining butter cream to the cake, spreading it as evenly as possible.

Colouring the butter cream: Butter cream will always have a slightly yellow tinge to it from the butter content. This is quite tricky to counteract, especially if you want to colour the butter cream pink, as it is inclined to end up turning an apricot/salmon colour. You can buy a whitening agent from cake decorating suppliers, which will fix the problem. Beat this in before adding any colouring.

Use a skewer or toothpick to dab a tiny amount of colouring onto the butter cream. Use a wooden spoon to mix the colouring through the butter cream evenly before adding any more. Cakes covered with butter cream can be stored in the fridge for up to 24 hours. Return cake to room temperature before serving.

tips Coloured butter cream will usually change colour within a few hours. It's a good idea to colour a small amount and let it stand overnight to see what happens. Some colours darken, others become lighter. Butter cream will keep for about a week in the fridge. Allow it to come to room temperature before beating it again either with a mixer or a spoon. If it's beaten when it's too cold, it will separate. If this happens, let the mixture come to room temperature, then drain off and reserve the liquid. Beat the remaining butter mixture with an electric mixer until it becomes smooth, then beat in the reserved liquid.

BUTTER CREAM
125g (4 ounces) softened butter
1½ cups (240g) icing (confectioners') sugar
2 tablespoons milk

1 Beat the butter (and any flavouring, if using) in a small narrow bowl with an electric mixer until the butter is as white as possible. (This will result in a whiter butter cream, which will give you better results when colouring it.)
2 Gradually beat in half the sifted icing sugar, then the milk, then the remaining sifted icing sugar.
3 Beat until the butter cream is smooth and spreadable. Keep scraping down the side of the bowl during beating.

To make a chocolate butter cream:
Sift ⅓ cup (35g) cocoa powder in with the icing sugar.

Makes enough to cover a deep 20cm (8-inch) cake.

Beat the butter in a small narrow bowl with an electric mixer until butter is as white as possible before adding sifted icing sugar.

Gradually beat in half the sifted icing sugar, then the milk, then remaining icing sugar. Beat until the butter cream is spreadable.

Use a skewer or toothpick to dab a tiny amount of colouring onto butter cream. Use a wooden spoon to beat in the colouring.

FLUFFY FROSTING

We love this frosting, it looks and tastes wonderful. It can be flavoured with any extract or essence and, because it's so white, it will happily take on any colour. We always stick to pastel colours when we use this frosting. If you want a strong-coloured frosting, however, such as red, this recipe won't work, as you need to add so much colouring that it softens the frosting, and it won't set.

Once all the syrup has been added, start beating in the colouring, a tiny dab at a time to control the colour. Scrape down the side of the bowl and the beaters to ensure the colouring is evenly distributed throughout the frosting.

We used a candy thermometer in the recipe below, but it's not essential, just boil the sugar syrup until it's thick with heavy bubbles; it should not be coloured. Remove from the heat and let the bubbles subside, then test the thickness of the syrup by dropping 1 teaspoon of it into a cup of cold water. The syrup should form a ball of soft sticky toffee.

Have the cake ready to be frosted as the frosting will begin to set quite quickly as it cools down. The frosting will be glossy for a few hours, then it will become dull and meringue-like in appearance and taste.

FLUFFY FROSTING
1 cup (220g) caster (superfine) sugar
⅓ cup (80ml) water
2 egg whites

1 Stir sugar and the water in a small saucepan over high heat, without boiling, until sugar is dissolved. Boil, uncovered, without stirring, about 5 minutes or until syrup reaches 114°C/240°F on a candy thermometer. Remove from heat, allow the bubbles to subside.
2 Begin to beat the egg whites in a small bowl with an electric mixer on a medium speed towards the end of the syrup's cooking time. Keep beating the egg whites while the sugar syrup reaches the correct temperature, or the egg whites will deflate.
3 With the mixer on medium speed, slowly pour in the hot syrup in a thin, steady stream; if the syrup is added too quickly, the frosting will not thicken. Once all the syrup is added, continue beating on medium to high speed for about 10 minutes or until the mixture is thick and stands in stiff peaks; the frosting should be barely warm at this stage. Use the frosting immediately.

Makes enough to cover a deep 20cm (8-inch) cake.

Using a candy thermometer: Candy thermometers must be heated to boiling point before placing into boiling syrup, otherwise the thermometer can break. Put the thermometer into a small saucepan of cold water, bring it to the boil. When the syrup begins to boil, put the thermometer into the syrup. Leave it in the syrup until the temperature required is reached, then return it to the pan of boiling water; turn the heat off and cool the thermometer before cleaning and drying it. Digital thermometers are easier to use; they are simply placed into the boiling syrup.

When making syrup: Stir sugar and the water over heat until the sugar dissolves; any grains of sugar on the side of the pan should be brushed down into the liquid using a wet pastry brush. When the sugar is dissolved, bring the syrup to the boil; once the syrup is boiling, stop stirring. Any stirring at this point will cause the sugar to recrystallise and turn grainy, and you will have to start all over again.

Stir the sugar and the water in a pan over high heat until the sugar dissolves. Boil until the temperature reaches 114°C/240°F.

Begin to beat the egg whites in a small bowl with an electric mixer towards the end of the cooking time of the syrup.

With the mixer on medium speed, gradually pour the hot syrup into the egg whites in a thin steady stream. Beat until frosting is thick.

ROYAL ICING

All cake decorators mainly use royal icing for piping. It's easy to make, but a little harder to achieve the right consistency for whatever you're using it for. Using royal icing for piped flowers requires the stiffest consistency; while piping dots and lines etc, requires the softest consistency; piping shells, stars, basket weave and leaves etc, needs a medium consistency. The amount of icing sugar to use is determined by the size of the egg white and the consistency required. Getting the icing just right is a matter of experience.

We use an electric mixer for the quantity given in our recipe. Smaller quantities can be mixed in a cup using a teaspoon. A teaspoon, or even less, of egg white is good to work with, especially for finer piping. A lot of cake decorators make royal icing by hand, not using an electric mixer, as this gives good results and minimises the development of air bubbles.

It's most important to keep this icing away from the air, as it soon develops a crust, making it unusable for piping – tiny bits of crust will block the piping tubes. Cover the surface of the icing closely with plastic wrap, then a damp cloth, just to be sure.

ROYAL ICING

1½ cups (240g) pure icing (confectioners') sugar, approximately
1 egg white
¼ teaspoon strained lemon juice

1 Sift the icing sugar through a fine sieve.
2 Lightly beat the egg white in a small bowl with an electric mixer until mixture is just broken up – do not whip into peaks. Beat in the icing sugar, a tablespoon at a time, to get the required consistency.
3 When icing reaches the right consistency, mix in the juice using a wooden spoon.

tips Beat the egg whites slowly, just to break them up. You don't want to turn them into meringue, or add air bubbles – air bubbles are hard to get rid of and will affect the look of your icing and the way in which it comes out of the piping tube. An air bubble can cause a piped line of icing to break.
Sifting pure icing sugar through a very fine sieve is important, as any tiny lumps will block fine piping tubes.
If properly covered and sealed, royal icing will keep at a cool room temperature or in the fridge for several days. Beat it with a

wooden spoon to bring it back to the correct consistency before using it again. Keep a wooden spoon aside just for beating royal icing. Regularly-used wooden spoons absorb fat from sweet and savoury foods, and the last thing you need in royal icing is any trace of fat.
You can buy a royal icing mix from cake decorating suppliers; this works well and is very convenient to use.

Colouring royal icing: Because the icing is white it will take on any colouring. Good quality colourings are expensive, but they are concentrated, so a little goes a long way. They are also quite stable – in other words, the colour usually doesn't change much on standing. Use a toothpick or a skewer to dab a little colouring onto the icing. Mix the colouring through with a wooden spoon, scraping down the side of the bowl often.

Beat the egg white on low speed in a small bowl; gradually add sifted icing sugar. Beat until combined; do not whisk into peaks.

When icing reaches the desired consistency, use a wooden spoon to stir in the juice and to break up any large air bubbles.

Cover surface of icing closely with plastic wrap, then a damp cloth, to exclude air and to prevent a crust from forming on the icing.

PIPING BAGS AND TUBES

Paper piping bags: You will find paper piping bags incredibly useful, especially if you're working with different coloured icings in small quantities. They can be used for piping ganache and butter cream as well as royal icing. You can make your own using baking paper, or greaseproof paper, though baking paper is the stronger of the two. You can also buy large paper triangles suitable for making larger piping bags; these are available from cake decorating shops, shops that stock craft equipment and shops that supply chefs and cooks.

Basic piping used for dots, lines, loops, snail trails and so on (page 224), don't really require the use of a piping tube. Half- or three-quarters fill a paper piping bag with royal icing – whichever feels comfortable in your hand. Gently squeeze the icing down to the tip of the bag; fold the top of the bag over to enclose the icing. Use a pair of sharp scissors to snip the tiniest tip from the base of the bag, then do a test run to see if enough icing comes out of the hole to suit whatever it is you want to pipe. If not, snip another tiny piece from the bag until you get the opening just right. You can use piping tubes in these bags too; the tubes do give you more control over piped icing. If you're using piping tubes, use two thicknesses of baking paper to make the bags stronger when piping. Follow the steps below to making paper bags: with practise you will become quick at making them in no time. .

Disposable plastic piping bags: These can be bought from supermarkets in a useful medium size. You need to use piping tubes with these bags, unless you're doing some simple piped work like dots or writing (in which case, put the icing in the bag and snip the tip from the bag until the opening is of the correct size). Some boxes of bags may include a kit of a few plastic piping tubes; these are good for some piping, but not for any fine work.

Fabric piping bags: These come in a wide range of sizes, from quite small to very large. The small ones are usually used for cake decorating, either with a piping tube inserted in the opening, or fitted with a piping screw (also known as a 'coupler'), which secures the piping tube to the outside of the piping bag, making it a simple process to change tubes (to pipe a different decoration) or to use the tube with a different coloured icing. Larger piping bags are usually fitted with large tubes; these are suitable for piping whipped cream, meringue and butter-based frostings. After use, wash the bags in warm water and leave to dry over a bottle.

Piping tubes: These are available in many sizes, either made from plastic or metal. We prefer metal tubes, they're more expensive than plastic but will last a lifetime. Wash in warm water, using a small paint brush around the tip to clean them thoroughly. Whatever you do, don't clean out leftover mixture by poking your finger through the end of the tube, as it can get stuck, which is particularly painful if it's a sharp fluted tube. Smaller diameter tubes and fluted tubes are delicate and can, with rough handling, easily become distorted, which will affect the outcome of your piping. So treat your tubes with care and store them properly.

Cut a perfect square from baking paper, fold it in half diagonally. Use a sharp knife to cut paper along the fold to make two triangles.

Hold apex of triangle towards you, wrap one point of triangle around to form a cone. Wrap remaining point around to make bag.

Wriggle the points of the triangle together until they line up perfectly. Staple the bag to secure the three points in place.

CHOCOLATE

There are several ways to melt chocolate, regardless of the colour. We prefer to use a glass, china or ceramic bowl when melting chocolate over a pan of simmering water as these bowls heat slowly, and melt the chocolate gently. Stainless steel bowls also work, but be aware that metal conducts heat rapidly, which can cause the chocolate to overheat if it's not watched carefully.

Seizing: This occurs when water comes in contact with the chocolate, it causes it to turn hard and grainy, making it impossible to work with. You will have to start again with another batch of chocolate. It only needs the tiniest amount of water to seize.

Melting in a medium saucepan: Place a medium heatproof bowl over a pan of simmering water; don't let the water touch the base of the bowl as this can overheat the chocolate. Stir occasionally. Remove the bowl from the pan as soon as the chocolate is smooth, to prevent it from overheating.

Melting in the sink: Another method that is easy and mess-free is to put the chocolate into a bowl – we use a stainless steel bowl for this method. Stand the bowl in a sink of hot tap water, or a larger bowl of hot water. Stir occasionally until the chocolate is smooth. This method takes a little longer, but it's fail-proof. The water should come about half-way up the side of the bowl.

Melting in a microwave oven: This works a treat if you don't overheat the chocolate. Check your instruction manual for the best way. Mostly 50% or 75% power is right for melting chocolate. Place chocolate in a microwave-safe bowl, then microwave it using short bursts of power. Check every 20 seconds by pressing it with a spatula – it

Melt in a sink: Place chocolate in a stainless steel bowl in a sink (or a larger bowl) half-filled with hot tap water; stir occasionally.

Melt over a saucepan: Place chocolate in a glass bowl over a pan of simmering water; don't let water touch bowl; stir occasionally.

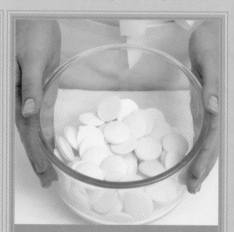

Melt in the microwave: Place chocolate in a microwave-safe bowl; heat on medium heat. Stir often, as it holds its shape when melted.

Stir chocolate away from the heat until smooth. Microwaved chocolate will hold its shape, so test by pressing with a spoon.

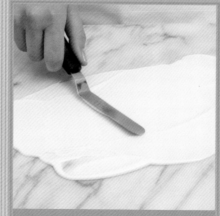

To make curls: Spread melted chocolate thinly, but evenly, onto a cold surface such as marble or stainless steel; stand until almost set.

For long curls, use a sharp long-bladed knife, holding the blade at a 45° angle on surface, drag the knife over chocolate to make curls.

could be melted even though it has retained its shape. Don't let the tiniest drop of water near the chocolate or it will seize. Never cover or partially cover chocolate – or the bowl it is in – while it's melting, as condensation will form under the lid or covering, and drops of moisture will fall into the chocolate – and it will seize and be useless.

Making chocolate curls: There are quite a few ways to make curls, all of which will make different-sized and shaped curls. The classic way is to spread melted chocolate evenly over a cold surface, such as marble, a stainless steel bench top or a flat oven tray; leave it at room temperature until it is almost set; this shouldn't take long – up to 10 minutes. Drag the blade of a large sharp knife, held at about a 45 degree angle, across the chocolate to make curls. It is important the chocolate is at the right stage. If the chocolate is not set enough, it will not curl and if the chocolate is set too much, the curls will break.

Another way to make simple small chocolate curls is to scrape a vegetable peeler along the side of a block of chocolate. A cheese slicer is good if you want larger curls. Make the curls from the back of a whole block of chocolate. Place the chocolate block, flat-side up, on a board and place your hand on the surface to warm it very slightly. Drag the slicer over the chocolate block. You may have to re-warm the chocolate with your hand several times during the process.

If you want large chunky curls, spread melted chocolate onto a cold surface and drag an ice-cream scoop across the surface of the almost-set chocolate.

Piping chocolate: A small paper piping bag (page 221) is the best to use when piping chocolate. Cut a small snip off the end and you can pipe messages or shapes directly onto a cake, or onto baking paper – the chocolate dries quickly and can be lifted straight onto the cake. You almost always have to pipe more than you need as breakages will occur.

For short chunky curls (1): Allow the melted chocolate to almost set then hold the tip of an ice-cream scoop on the surface.

For short chunky curls (2): Firmly drag the ice-cream scoop over the surface of the chocolate using an even pressure.

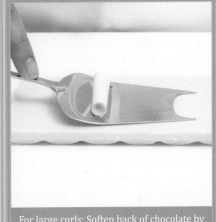

For large curls: Soften back of chocolate by holding your hand on the surface for about a minute. Drag cheese slicer across chocolate.

For smaller chocolate curls: Slightly warm the chocolate block; drag the blade of a sharp vegetable peeler evenly down the side.

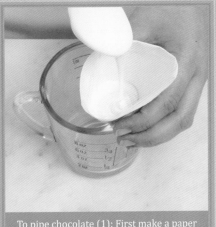

To pipe chocolate (1): First make a paper piping bag (page 221), then half-fill the bag with melted chocolate; fold over top of bag.

To pipe chocolate (2): Snip a tiny tip from the piping bag. Pipe chocolate, holding bag at a 45° angle. Pipe freehand or use a pattern.

PIPING TECHNIQUES

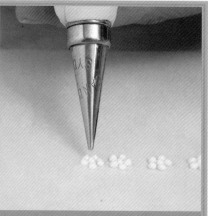

To pipe dots: Touch the tip of the tube on the surface while holding bag upright. Squeeze to make dot, stop squeezing, pull tube straight up.

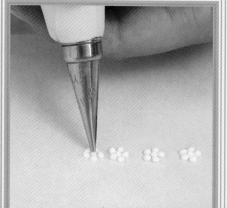

To make forget-me-nots using a plain tube: Pipe five dots in a circle, then finish with one dot in the centre of each circle.

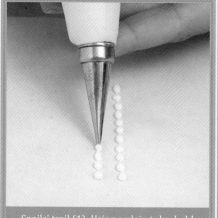

Snails' trail (1): Using a plain tube, hold bag at a 45° angle, touch down with tube squeezing bag to make a teardrop of icing.

Snails' trail (2): Gradually reduce pressure on bag, lifting tube slightly. Touch tube on surface, stop squeezing, making a tiny trail.

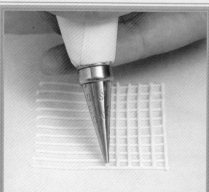

Straight lines (1): Using a plain tube, hold bag at a 45° angle, touch tube down, squeeze bag to make and anchor a dot of icing.

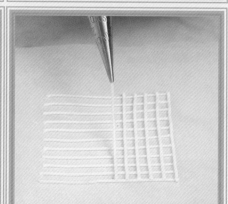

Straight lines (2): Keep pressure on bag by squeezing gently. Lift tube up from anchor point, piping evenly, towards where it ends.

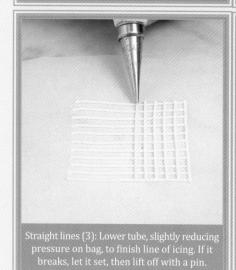

Straight lines (3): Lower tube, slightly reducing pressure on bag, to finish line of icing. If it breaks, let it set, then lift off with a pin.

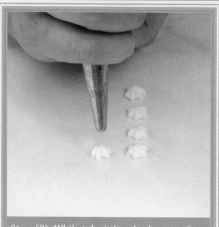

Stars (1): Using a fluted tube, hold the bag upright, squeeze the bag, keeping tip of tube barely above surface; pipe a star shape.

Stars (2): While tube is barely above surface, gradually reduce, then stop squeezing the bag. Pull tube up without leaving a point.

We used royal icing and a number 2 plain (writing), number 8 fluted (shell) and number 22 (basket weave) tube on these two pages. Piping is not difficult, it just takes practise.

Shell edging (1): Hold bag at a slight angle. Touch tip of fluted tube on surface, squeeze bag, lifting tube slightly to make a shell shape.

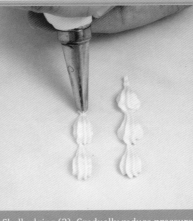

Shell edging (2): Gradually reduce pressure on the bag to make a short tail on the shell. Start a new shell shape at the end of this tail.

To pipe a rope: Using fluted tube, touch tube on surface, squeeze bag and lift tube at same time, moving clockwise in a small tight circle.

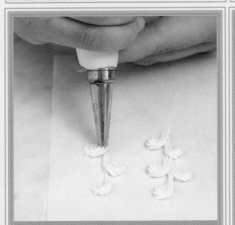

Feather and fan (1): Hold bag almost upright, touch fluted tube down on surface, squeeze bag, and twist tube to pipe a question mark.

Feather and fan (2): Reduce pressure on bag as you pipe to make the tail of the question mark. Repeat on other side to make pattern.

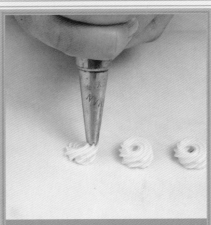

Candle holders: Touch tip of a fluted tube on surface squeezing the bag at the same time, and moving the tube in a circular pattern.

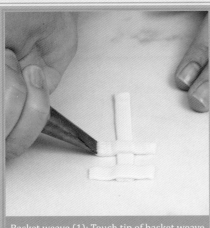

Basket weave (1): Touch tip of basket weave tube on surface, pipe a vertical line towards you. Pipe horizontal lines a tube's width apart.

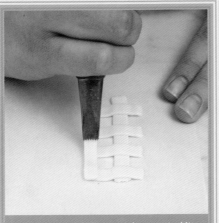

Basket weave (2): Pipe another vertical line, parallel with the first – a tube's width apart, barely covering ends of the horizontal lines.

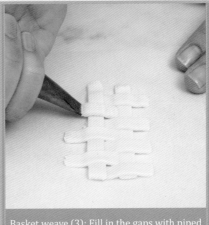

Basket weave (3): Fill in the gaps with piped short horizontal lines. Keep an even pressure on the bag of icing during the piping.

MAKING BOWS

We've used bows to decorate and neaten some of the ribbons on the cakes in this book. Here's how to make them.

Sewing a tailored bow (1): Fold a length of ribbon to make four loops. Stitch in the centre of bow to hold loops together.

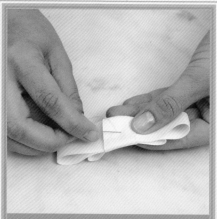

Sewing a tailored bow (2): Sew a small strip of ribbon into position in the centre of the bow to cover and neaten the looped ribbon.

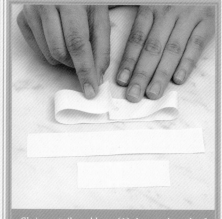

Gluing a tailored bow (1): Loop a length of ribbon bringing ends into the centre. Glue into position using a glue gun or craft glue.

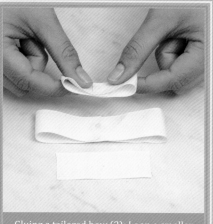

Gluing a tailored bow (2): Loop a smaller length of ribbon, secure ends in centre with glue. Glue smaller loop onto larger loop.

Gluing a tailored bow (3): Glue a small strip of ribbon over the centre of the double bow to cover and neaten the middle of the bow.

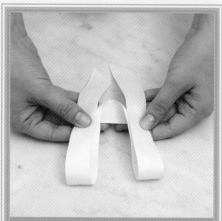

Tying a simple bow (1): Make two loops from a length of ribbon. Leave enough ribbon for tails – make these as long as you want them.

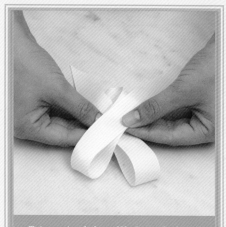

Tying a simple bow (2): Cross the loops over; bring the top loop under bottom loop then through the hole under the bottom loop.

Tying a simple bow (3): Pull the tops of the loops at the same time to make the bow even and roughly the size you want it to be.

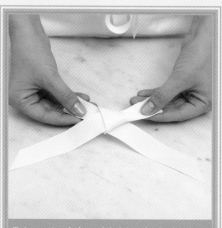

Tying a simple bow (4): Wriggle the loops of the bow until they are the same length, and the bow and its centre are as you want them.

MODELLING PASTE

Many different shapes can be made using this paste. It's easy to make, and keeps for several days at room temperature, wrapped in plastic wrap to keep airtight. It can be bought in cake decorators' shops, however, we found the home-made paste best to work with, as the shapes dried and stayed firmer longer than those made with bought paste. Modelling paste, also called flower, petal or gum paste, can be moulded into cute 3D shapes, etc – such as animals, people, toys, which can then be wired to stand up on the cake.

The paste can also be rolled out thinly, and cutters used to cut out petals and other shapes. Petals are often dried separately, then assembled into buds and flowers by using royal icing to secure petals together, or by wiring the petals together with floral wire.

Work with small amounts of paste only, as once it's exposed to air it dries out quickly. Plastic wrap is perfect for enclosing pieces of paste to keep it airtight. Most cut-out shapes need further shaping, so keep unshaped cut-outs under plastic wrap, or a piece of vinyl, until you're ready to use them. Everything made using modelling paste needs to be dried. This takes varying amounts of time depending on the weather and the thickness of the paste. As a guide, thin petals will dry in a few hours; more solid shapes, say letters 1cm (½-inch) thick, may take two days to dry out completely.

Many shapes are wired and positioned in the cake. Because of health reasons, don't insert the wired shapes into the cake until the day of the function as, once pierced, the cake's seal is no longer intact and bacteria may enter. A more hygienic way to insert decorations is to use flower spikes: these hollow, inert plastic spikes are pushed into the cake and used to hold the decoration in place. Fresh flowers can also be positioned in spikes; add a couple of drops of water to keep the flowers fresh during the celebration.

MODELLING PASTE

2 teaspoons powdered gelatine
1½ tablespoons water
2 teaspoons glucose syrup
1½ cups (240g) pure icing (confectioners') sugar

1 Sprinkle gelatine over the water in a heatproof cup; stand cup in small saucepan of simmering water, stir until gelatine is dissolved. Stir in glucose.
2 Sift icing sugar into medium bowl; stir in gelatine mixture then, when mixture becomes too stiff to stir, use your hand to combine the ingredients.
3 Knead on surface dusted with extra sifted icing sugar until smooth and elastic. Wrap tightly in plastic wrap to keep airtight.

Makes 250g (8 ounces)

Colouring modelling paste: Since the paste is white it colours easily. Start with a small dab of colouring, applied to a small ball of paste, to determine the strength of the colouring. Once you're happy with the colour, tint the amount of paste you need. Shapes made from modelling paste can be painted once they're dried out, use food colouring for this.
Wiring shapes made from modelling paste: This must be done as soon as the shape is established. Wire is usually dipped in flower glue and pushed into the shape, then allowed to dry.

FLOWER GLUE

1 tablespoon tylose powder
2 tablespoons water

1 Combine ingredients in a screw-topped jar; shake well, stand overnight (lumps will dissolve overnight).
2 Stir in a little more water to bring the glue to the consistency of unbeaten egg white; shake well.

tips This glue must be made at least 12 hours before using. It keeps indefinitely at room temperature, but will thicken on standing. Return it to the consistency of unbeaten egg white by stirring in a little more water each time you use it.

Sift icing sugar into a medium bowl; pour in combined liquids. Stir with a wooden spoon until mixture becomes difficult to stir.

Work the ingredients together. Turn paste onto surface dusted with sifted icing sugar; knead until smooth. Enclose in plastic wrap.

Keep paste covered with plastic wrap or a piece of vinyl to stop it from drying out. Only work with small quantities at a time.

CAKE
Patterns

LATTE LACE CAKE (PAGE 132)

TOP (LARGER)

MIDDLE (SMALLER)

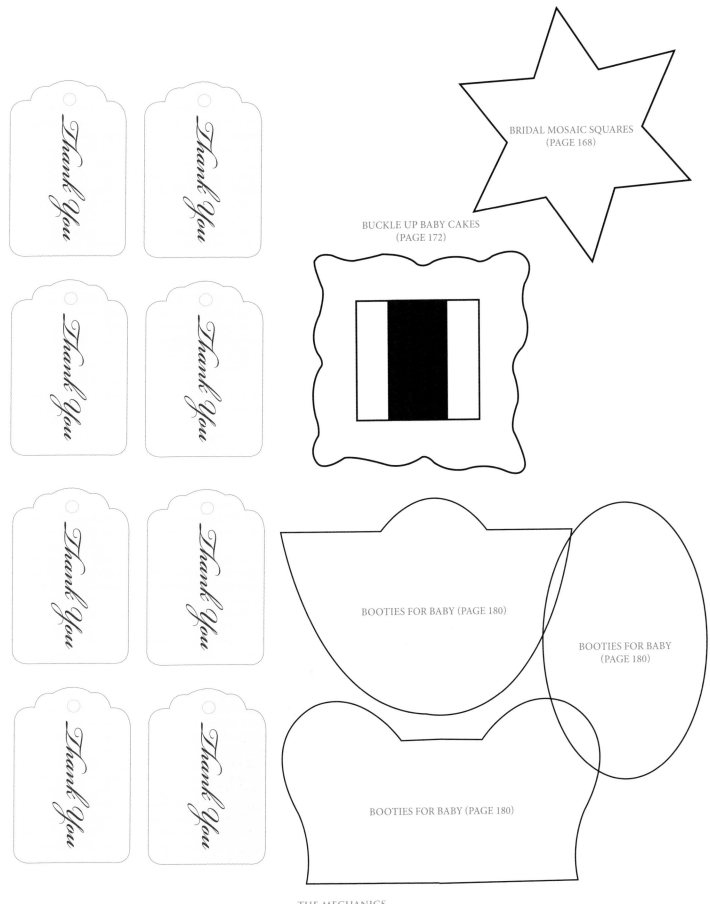

Thank You

Thank You

Thank You

Thank You

Thank You

Thank You

Thank You

Thank You

BRIDAL MOSAIC SQUARES
(PAGE 168)

BUCKLE UP BABY CAKES
(PAGE 172)

BOOTIES FOR BABY (PAGE 180)

BOOTIES FOR BABY
(PAGE 180)

BOOTIES FOR BABY (PAGE 180)

EQUIPMENT

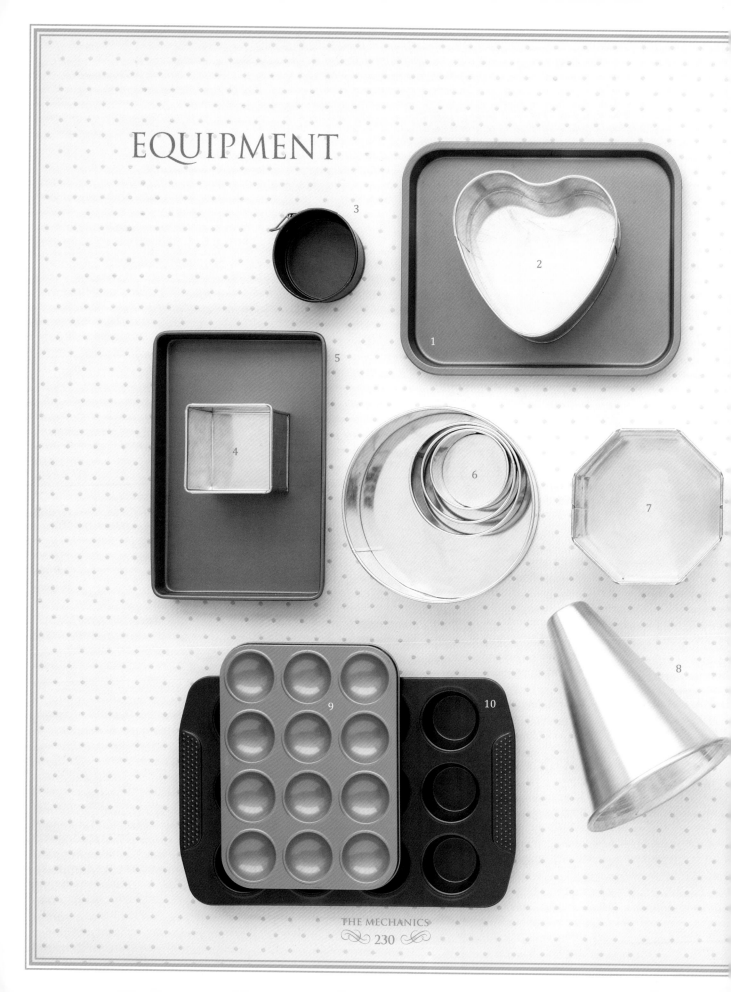

3

2

1

5

4

6

7

8

9

10

1 swiss roll pan
2 heart-shaped cake pan
3 springform pan (small 10cm)
4 square cake pan
5 lamington pan
6 round cake pans
7 octagon cake pan
8 croquembouche mould
9 shallow round-based patty pan
10 muffin pan
11 large wooden rolling pin
12 ice-cream scoop
13 serrated knife
14 spirit level
15 digital thermometer
16 large metal scraper
17 small metal scraper
18 square wooden board, uncovered
19 drill bit
20 pliers
21 pasta machine
22 secateurs
23 metal spatulas (palette knives: small, medium large)
24 lazy susan (rotating stand)
25 wire balloon whisk (ends removed)
26 rubber spatula
27 round wooden cake board, covered
28 wooden spoon
29 pizza cutter
30 round styrofoam block
31 stanley knife
32 cheese slicer
33 craft glue
34 hot glue gun
35 glue sticks
36 hacksaw
37 shaker (for lightly dusting surface)

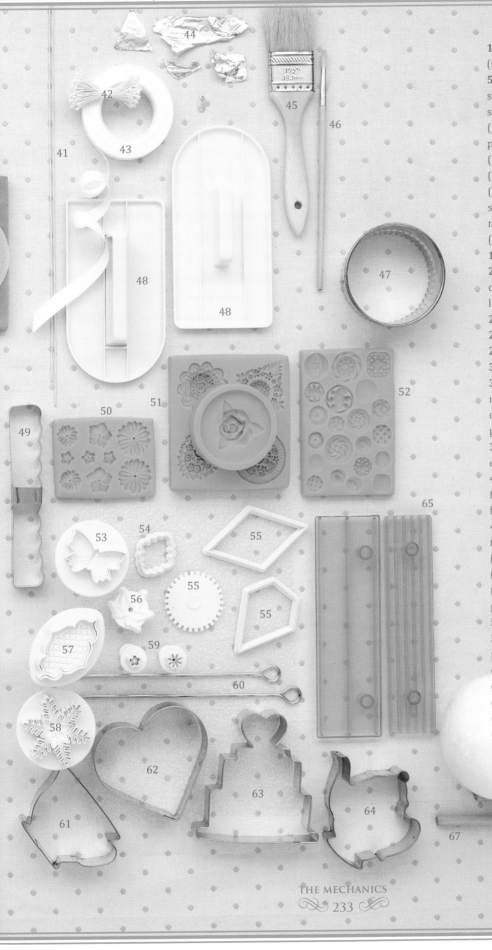

1 fondant cutter/embosser 2 ball tool (small) 3 frill tools 4 ball tool (large) 5 alencon lace stencil 6 blue modelling sponge (flower mat) 7 filigree damask stencil 8 textured acrylic rolling pin (patchwork) 9 small non-stick rolling pin 10 textured acrylic rolling pin (swirl) 11 textured acrylic rolling pin (filigree) 12 lollypop candy sticks (cake pop sticks) 13 large wooden skewers 14 toothpicks 15 perspex measures (various sizes) 16 stencil (coffee) 17 petal veiner 18 plastic ruler 19 number cutters 20 eyelet cutters 21 lustre dust 22 petal dust 23 food colouring (concentrated paste not liquid) 24 metal blossom cutters 25 magnolia cutters 26 peony cutter 27 round cutter 28 rose petal cutter 29 plain metal piping nozzles 30 plastic star nozzle 31 piping bags 32 tweezers 33 square cutter 34 vinyl mat 35 pearl-headed pins 36 patchwork cutter trellis 37 diamond-sided patchwork cutter 38 small scissors 39 cupcake wrappers (decorative cupcake wrappers) 40 tape measure 41 floral wire 42 stamens 43 white florist's tape 44 gold leaf 45 pastry brush 46 artist's fine paint brush 47 round fluted cutter 48 smoothing tools 49 frill cutter 50 silicone mould (small flower) 51 silicone moulds (floral pendant) 52 silicone mould (beads & buttons) 53 veined butterfly plunger cutter 54 scalloped cutter 55 patchwork set 56 leaf cutter 57 plaque plunger cutter 58 snowflake plunger cutter 59 blossom cutter plunger 60 metal skewers 61 teacup cutter 62 heart-shaped cutter 63 wedding cake cutter 64 teapot cutter 65 strip cutter 66 sytrofoam ball 67 wooden dowels

GLOSSARY

almond meal also known as ground almonds; nuts are powdered to a coarse flour-like texture.

almond paste similar to marzipan, but is less granular and contains less sugar (see also marzipan).

baking paper (parchment paper or baking parchment) a silicone-coated paper primarily used for lining baking pans and trays so cakes and biscuits won't stick, making removal easy.

baking powder a raising agent consisting of two parts cream of tartar to one part bicarbonate of soda.

ball tool a plastic stick with a ball of different sizes at either end. Is used to thin ready-made icing when making flower petals, and to smooth curves and rounded ends. There are a number of sizes available.

bicarbonate of soda also known as baking or carb soda; is used as a leavening agent in baking.

blossom cutters tiny cutters used to make small flowers; come as 3, 4 or 5 petals.

brushes artist's paint brushes and make-up brushes are excellent when brushing cakes, models, flowers and myriad other decorations with glitter, powder or dusts, or painting colours, water or sugar syrup onto cakes. Larger-sized brushes are also useful for brushing crumbs off cakes or dried icing from boards.

butter use salted or unsalted (sweet) butter; 125g is equal to one stick (4oz) of butter.

cachous also known as dragées; these minuscule (3mm to 5mm) metallic-looking-but-edible confectionery balls are available in silver, gold or various colours.

cake boards often made from masonite and covered in a thick non-absorbable paper, silver or gold coloured. Come in myriad sizes, usually round or square, occasionally octagonal. If displaying on a cake board, rather than a plate, the base board is often 10-15cm larger than the cake, so it can be lifted and transported without fingers poking holes in the icing. The remaining cakes are placed on cake boards of the same size. If displaying on a cake plate, the base board should be the same size as the cake.

chocolate
dark eating also known as semi-sweet or luxury chocolate; made of a high percentage of cocoa liquor, cocoa butter, and a little added sugar.
milk mild and very sweet; similar in make-up to dark with the difference being the addition of milk solids.
white contains no cocoa solids but derives its sweet flavour from cocoa butter. Very sensitive to heat so watch carefully when melting.

cocoa powder also known as cocoa; dried, unsweetened, roasted and ground cocoa beans (cacao seeds).
dutch cocoa is treated with an alkali to neutralise its acids. It has a reddish-brown colour, a mild flavour and is easy to dissolve in liquids.

coconut
desiccated dried, unsweetened, finely shredded coconut.
essence produced from coconut flavouring, oil and alcohol.
flaked dried, flaked coconut flesh.
shredded strips of dried coconut.

cornflour (cornstarch) often used as a thickener, here we use it to roll out ready-made icing and modelling paste.

coupler this device lets you quickly change piping tubes without changing the bag. It has two parts; the base sits on the inside of the bag with the end poking out; the piping tube is then placed over the part poking out and the ring is twisted or screwed over the tube to lock it in place.

cream we use fresh cream, also known as pouring, single and pure cream, unless otherwise stated. It has no additives, unlike commercially thickened cream, and has a minimum fat content of 35%.

sour a thick cultured soured cream. Minimum fat content 35%.

cream cheese commonly known as Philadelphia or Philly, a soft cow's-milk cheese.

cream of tartar an acid ingredient in baking powder; keeps frostings creamy and improves volume when beating egg whites. Helps prevent sugar from crystallising when added to confectionery mixtures.

cutters come in many sizes, shapes, styles, plunging etc. Used to cut ready-made icing and modelling paste into different shapes.

edible dust, glitter, powders are available from cake decorating suppliers. Used to add details and highlights to cakes.

embossing tools are pressed or rolled onto soft ready-made icing leaving a print of the design. Textured mats are also a type of embossing tool.

filigree an intricate type of lace work done using royal icing. Is very delicate and breaks easily.

floral wire also known as florist's or craft wire. A covered flexible wire that comes in different thicknesses. The higher the number of the gauge (eg 33-gauge) the finer the wire and the finer the wire the more delicate and flexible it is (used for smaller pieces); the lower the number of the gauge (eg 18-gauge) the thicker the wire (used for making large sugar flowers). Also used to bind petals when making flowers, or to position shapes or flowers into cakes. The wire itself may be uncovered or wrapped in white or green florist's tape. Available from craft and cake decorating suppliers in cut lengths (36cm/14½ inches) and on spools. When we ask for a length of wire, we mean 36cm lengths.

florist's tape from craft and cake decorating suppliers. Wrapped around flower stems to provide a seal when placing fresh flowers on cakes. Also used to cover wooden dowels, or to cover floral wire when making flowers from modelling paste, etc, to hold the petals in place.

flour

plain a general all-purpose flour made from wheat.

rice very fine, almost powdery, gluten-free flour; made from ground white rice.

self-raising (rising) plain flour sifted with baking powder in the proportion of 1 cup flour to 2 teaspoons baking powder. Also called self-rising flour.

flower cutters used to cut small flower shapes (see blossom cutters).

flower mat also known as foam pad and celpad. Provides a soft surface when working with ready-made icing and modelling paste to make flower petals, etc. Also provides a soft base when pushing cutouts out of plunger cutters.

flower spikes are hollow plastic spikes that are pushed through the icing into the cake. Used to position wired flowers and other decorations, thus keeping the floral wire out of the cake. This is a safe, hygienic way to add embellishments to the cake. Fresh flowers can also be positioned in spikes; add a couple of drops of water into the spike to keep the flowers fresh during the celebration.

food colouring dyes used to change the colour of foods.

concentrated pastes, which is what we used throughout this book, are the easiest to use, though are a little more expensive.

liquid dyes the strength varies depending on the quality. Useful for pastel colours only, as adding large amounts of liquid colouring will break down most icings. Also useful for painting icing sculptures.

powdered colourings are best for primary colours or black.

frilling tool usually comes as part of a 'modelling' kit. Used to frill the edges of ready-made icing.

gelatine a thickening agent. Available in sheet form, known as leaf gelatine, or as a powder. Three teaspoons of powdered gelatine (7g or one sachet) is roughly equivalent to four gelatine leaves. We used powdered gelatine throughout this book.

glucose syrup also known as liquid glucose; a clear, thick liquid often made from wheat or corn starch.

glycerine a sweet, colourless liquid that retains moisture and adds sweetness to cakes. It also softens ready-made and royal icings.

golden syrup a by-product of refined sugarcane; pure maple syrup or honey can be substituted.

hazelnuts also known as filberts; a plump, grape-sized, rich, sweet nut.

meal known as ground hazelnuts.

jam also known as preserve or conserve; most often made from fruit. When heated and mixed with a little water, it can be used as a glaze to cover cakes, this acts as a glue helping the initial covering of the cake stick to the cake's surface. Strain the jam mixture before spreading over the cake to remove any solid pieces of fruit.

marzipan an almond and sugar paste used to cover cakes, as a filling in Danish pastries or sculpted into a variety of shapes to be eaten as candy or used as cake decorations. After kneading, it has the consistency of dough and can be rolled, shaped, cut or moulded (see also almond paste).

metal spatula also known as a palette knife. Come in small, medium and large. The larger ones have flexible steel blades. There are two types, straight-bladed, and offset or crank, which is used for getting into tight areas the flat straight blade can't.

mixed fruit consists of a mixture of sultanas, raisins, currants, mixed peel and sometimes glacé cherries.

mixed spice a blend of ground spices usually consisting of cinnamon, allspice and nutmeg.

modelling paste also known as BAS relief paste, gum paste, flower modelling paste and pastillage. Sets very hard, and is used to make all types of decorations for cakes.

modelling tools are used to draw, frill, shape, imprint, stencil, hollow or cut soft icing when making decorations for cakes. Can be found singly, but are also available in kits.

muslin a loosely-woven cotton fabric. Tie cornflour in a square of muslin and use to lightly dust the bench when kneading and rolling ready-made icing.

nougat a confectionery made from honey, nuts and egg whites. The nougat we are most familiar with is the chewy white confectionery studded with nuts, however, it can be either soft and chewy or crunchy.

nutmeg dried nut of an evergreen tree native to Indonesia; it is available in ground form or you can grate your own with a fine grater.

perspex measures clear rulers that come in different widths; used to cut icing ribbons to specified widths for cakes. Often come in a set of 5 widths.

petal cutters various metal or plastic cutters in the shape of flower petals. Available as a kit for specific flowers, which also include the veining tool.

piping bags

disposable bags are made of clear plastic. Discard after each use. Only available in one size and come in packs; available from supermarkets.

paper piping bags are made from baking paper (silicone or parchment paper) and discarded after each use. Used for small amounts of icing, writing, flooding (runouts), etc. See page 221 for directions on how to make them.

polyester bags are lightweight, flexible and reusable. Wash in hot soapy water after each use and dry, standing over a soft drink bottle. Are available in many different sizes.

piping tubes small metal or plastic cone shapes with various openings used to produce many different designs when icing or frosting is pressed through them. Smaller ones are quite fragile and must be treated carefully, otherwise they can be bent or squashed out of shape.
basket weave tubes are used for woven designs. They have both a smooth and a ribbed side, which pipe wide stripes.
drop flower tubes are the easiest to use and produce small flower shapes, either plain or swirled.
leaf tubes have a 'V' opening and are used to pipe leaves with pointy ends.
ruffle tubes have a teardrop tip, and are used to pipe bows, ribbons scallops and ruffles.
rose tubes have an opening that is wide at one end and narrow at the other. It's not only used for piping roses – daisies, carnations, pansies, etc, may also be piped with this tube.
round tubes are used for outlining details, filling and writing. Also piping dots, balls, beads and filigree, etc.
star tubes are used to pipe shells, stars, rosettes and flowers.
pizza cutter used to cut through ready-made icing. The blade presses down vertically, rather than dragging, through the icing, which gives a clean, sharp cut.
plunger cutters have a plunger on top: push to cut the shape, then push to release the cut shape. Doesn't damage the shape as it pushes it out.
powders and dusts are also known as petal, pearl, sparkles, blossom tints and lustres.
quilting tools also known as tailor's or stitching wheels. Used to create 'stitches' on ready-made icing. Wheels are removable so the stitching can be of different lengths.
raisins dried sweet grapes.
raspberries known as the 'king of the berries'; cylinder-shaped, about 1.5cm-2cm long, with a deep red colour and a sweet flavour. Also available black or yellow in colour. Are fragile and spoil rapidly, so check for mildew when buying. Also available frozen.

ready-made icing also known as ready-to-roll icing (RTR), fondant icing, sugar paste, plastic icing and soft icing. Is sweet tasting, and has a dough-like consistency when kneaded. Is used to cover cakes and make decorations. Roll on a surface dusted lightly with cornflour; don't use too much cornflour, as the icing will dry and crack when lifted over the cake.
rolling pins come in a variety of sizes; use large ones to roll out the icing, use medium and smaller ones to thin out icing for decorations. They can be made of wood, granite, non-stick plastic, etc.
royal icing is a mixture of egg white and pure icing sugar. Pure icing sugar has no softener (cornflour) so it sets very hard. Do not use icing sugar mixture or soft icing sugar for this. Is the best to use when securing cakes to their boards. Instant mixes (just add water) are available from cake decorating suppliers.
scrapers can be either plastic or metal (stainless steel). Used to scrape excess ganache off the side of a cake, or to remove excess royal icing off stencils. Plastic scrapers are useful when cleaning up, to scrape any leftover icing stuck to the bench top.
skewers are used in cake decorating to support the cake tiers, they are not the same as the skewers used in kebabs, etc. They are much thicker so they are able to support the weight of the cakes stacked above. They are pointed at one end to push all the way through the cake before cutting down to size.
smoothers these plastic paddles with handles are used to smooth ready-made icing, and remove air bubbles after the icing has been positioned on the cake. When smoothing the icing you need to use the two plastic paddles together; they give the cake a smooth, shiny, appearance.
stamens (the reproductive part of the flower, usually found in the centre). Most often sold double-ended, which are either cut in half before using, or are pulled through a hooked wire and folded up in a bunch. May also be found single-ended. Used to make flower centres.

styrofoam is a tightly-packed polystyrene foam that resists moisture. It is available in different-shaped blocks from cake decorating and craft supply stores.
sultanas dried grapes, also known as golden raisins.
sugar
brown a very soft, fine sugar retaining molasses for its flavour.
caster also known as superfine or finely granulated table sugar.
icing also known as confectioners' sugar or powdered sugar; granulated sugar crushed together with a small amount of added cornflour.
pure icing this sugar is also known as confectioners' sugar or powdered sugar, but it has no cornflour added; this means it is very lumpy and it has to be sifted well before use.
white a coarse, granulated table sugar, also known as crystal sugar.
sugar syrup is brushed all over the surface of a cake before applying the initial covering of ganache, almond paste or ready-made icing. It sticks the initial covering layer to the cake and sticks the final layer to the initial layer. It also stops the cake from drying out. It may be flavoured with alcohol, if you like.
textured mats see embossing tools.
tylose powder when mixed into royal icing, almond paste, ready-made icing or modelling paste, tylose powder creates a strong paste that dries very hard. Used when something is required to set in a certain position.
vanilla
bean the tiny black seeds impart a luscious vanilla flavour.
extract made by extracting the flavour from the vanilla bean pods.
veining tool also known as a leaf veiner. Plastic moulds that leave an imprint of a leaf when pressed on ready-made icing. Available in kits along with matching flower petal cutters.
wooden dowels or dowel rods, are used to support cakes over three tiers so they can be carried and transported safely. Cut with a small hacksaw to the size required (just below the height of the cake).

CONVERSION CHART

MEASURES

One Australian metric measuring cup holds approximately 250ml; one Australian metric tablespoon holds 20ml; one Australian metric teaspoon holds 5ml.

The difference between one country's measuring cups and another's is within a two- or three-teaspoon variance, and will not affect your cooking results. North America, New Zealand and the United Kingdom use a 15ml tablespoon.

All cup and spoon measurements are level. The most accurate way of measuring dry ingredients is to weigh them. When measuring liquids, use a clear glass or plastic jug with metric markings.

We use large eggs with an average weight of 60g.

DRY MEASURES

METRIC	IMPERIAL
15g	½oz
30g	1oz
60g	2oz
90g	3oz
125g	4oz (¼lb)
155g	5oz
185g	6oz
220g	7oz
250g	8oz (½lb)
280g	9oz
315g	10oz
345g	11oz
375g	12oz (¾lb)
410g	13oz
440g	14oz
470g	15oz
500g	16oz (1lb)
750g	24oz (1½lb)
1kg	32oz (2lb)

LIQUID MEASURES

METRIC	IMPERIAL
30ml	1 fluid oz
60ml	2 fluid oz
100ml	3 fluid oz
125ml	4 fluid oz
150ml	5 fluid oz
190ml	6 fluid oz
250ml	8 fluid oz
300ml	10 fluid oz
500ml	16 fluid oz
600ml	20 fluid oz
1000ml (1 litre)	32 fluid oz

LENGTH MEASURES

METRIC	IMPERIAL
3mm	$^1/_8$in
6mm	¼in
1cm	½in
2cm	¾in
2.5cm	1in
5cm	2in
6cm	2½in
8cm	3in
10cm	4in
13cm	5in
15cm	6in
18cm	7in
20cm	8in
23cm	9in
25cm	10in
28cm	11in
30cm	12in (1ft)

OVEN TEMPERATURES

The oven temperatures in this book are for conventional ovens; if you have a fan-forced oven, decrease the temperature by 10-20 degrees.

	°C (CELSIUS)	°F (FAHRENHEIT)
Very slow	120	250
Slow	150	300
Moderately slow	160	325
Moderate	180	350
Moderately hot	200	400
Hot	220	425
Very hot	240	475

The imperial measurements used in this book are approximate only. Metric/imperial conversions are approximate only. Measurements for cake pans are approximate only; using same-shaped cake pans of a similar size should not affect the outcome of your baking. We measure the inside top of the cake pan to determine sizes.

INDEX

First published in 2012. Reprinted in 2013.
Published by Bauer Media Books, a division of Bauer Media Ltd,
54 Park St, Sydney; GPO Box 4088, Sydney, NSW 2001.
phone (02) 9282 8618; fax (02) 9126 3702
www.awwcookbooks.com.au

MEDIA GROUP
BAUER MEDIA BOOKS
Publishing director Gerry Reynolds
Publisher Sally Wright
Editorial & food director Pamela Clark
Director of sales, marketing & rights Brian Cearnes
Creative director Hieu Chi Nguyen
Art director & designer Hannah Blackmore
Food concept director Sophia Young

Published and Distributed in the United Kingdom by Octopus Publishing Group
Endeavour House
189 Shaftesbury Avenue
London WC2H 8JY
United Kingdom
phone (+44)(0)207 632 5400; fax (+44)(0)207 632 5405

info@octopus-publishing.co.uk;
www.octopusbooks.co.uk

Printed by C&C Offset Printing, China.

International foreign language rights, Brian Cearnes, Bauer Media Books
bcearnes@bauer-media.com.au

A catalogue record for this book is available from the British Library.
ISBN: 978 1 74245 285 2 (hbk.)